"Atwood knows that guns are not just weapons, but symbols, and not only symbols, but idols that demand enormous sacrifice in American lives. This book gets at both the depth and meaning of this on-going tragedy. As a gifted organizer and thinker, Atwood then unveils the inspiring theological bases of an awakening to gun violence [prevention] that has already begun in some cities and congregations."

—**Christian Iosso**

Coordinator of Advisory Committee on Social Witness Policy for The Presbyterian Church, USA

"When it comes to tackling the plague of gun violence in the U.S., no one 'walks the walk' with more integrity than Atwood. He has devoted his life to saving lives from gun violence by increasing awareness and challenging popular myths about guns. He now gives us a much needed theological undergirding for our work to end the violence."

—**John W. Wimberly Jr.**

Pastor of Western Presbyterian Church, Washington, DC

"Atwood's fervent account of the multiple costs of gun violence and the need to restrain it is of urgent and timely importance. This book is a challenge to Christians to lead the way in unmasking the peculiar American obsession with guns. It illuminates the origins of that obsession and recounts a distressing record of statistics and broken laws, all in a compelling theological framework."

—**David Little**

Harvard Divinity School

"Atwood writes with righteous purpose and theological wisdom. All people of faith should read and embrace his admonition to the American faith community to heed God's call to save the lives of our sisters, brothers, and children by renouncing the idolatry of guns and joining together in a faith-based movement to end the uniquely and devastatingly American regime of gun violence."

—**Bryan Miller**

Executive Director of Heeding God's Call

AMERICA AND ITS GUNS

America and Its Guns:
A Theological Exposé

James E. Atwood

 CASCADE *Books* · Eugene, Oregon

AMERICA AND ITS GUNS
A Theological Exposé

Cascade Books
An Imprint of Wipf and Stock Publishers
199 W. 8th Ave., Suite 3
Eugene, OR 97401

www.wipfandstock.com

ISBN 13: 978-1-61097-825-5

Cataloging-in-Publication data:

Atwood, James E.

America and its guns : a theological exposé / James E. Atwood.

xx + 228 p. ; 23 cm. — Includes bibliographical references.

ISBN 13: 978-1-61097-825-5

1. Religion and politics—United States. 2. Gun Control—United States.
3. Firearms—Law and legislation—United States. I. Title.

BR526 .A56 2012

Manufactured in the U.S.A.

To Roxana Mebane Atwood with gratitude
for our years together.

To Mebane and Harry David,
and to Alan and Robin who bring us joy.

To Woody, Roxana, Oliver, and Ellen
who bless us with hope.

Contents

ILLUSTRATIONS AND TABLES

ABBREVIATIONS

ASSC	American Shooting Sports Council
ATF-BATF	Bureau of Alcohol, Tobacco, and Firearms
CCWP	Concealed Carry Weapons Permit
CDC	Centers for Disease Control and Prevention
CEO	Chief Executive Officer
CSGV	Coalition to Stop Gun Violence
DNA	Deoxyribonucleic Acid
DOJ	Department of Justice
FBI	Federal Bureau of Investigation
HGC	Heeding God's Call
NCCUSA	National Council of Churches of Christ in USA
NICS	National Instant Criminal Background Check System
NRA	National Rifle Association
NSSF	National Shooting Sports Foundation
NTC	National Tracing Center
PCUSA	Presbyterian Church, USA
PTSD	Post Traumatic Stress Syndrome
SALW	Small Arms and Light Weapons
VPC	Violence Policy Center

Foreword

The report says that on Black Friday, November 25, 2011, more hand-guns were sold in the United States than on any previous single day in U.S. history. That datum might produce staggering dismay, for it indicates a level of fear and anxiety, posturing power, and readiness for violence that defies reason. Sadly, however, that dismaying report does not in fact even evoke surprise among us, so inured are we to guns and to the culture that sustains their legitimacy and popularity. Jim Atwood has written a compelling and summoning response to that gun culture that now so much dominates the life and discourse of our society. His book is important because it serves to expose our social reality and to penetrate the "psychic numbing" that has come to treat that gun culture as though it were a normal, acceptable, and defining dimension of our common life.

There can hardly be any doubt that the popular epidemic of guns, supported by many people who do not subscribe to its implied violence, is more than a sale of guns. Rather it is a consuming culture with its own universe of discourse (often, as Atwood chronicles, expressed in code or euphemism) with its network of information, disinformation, and influence. It is a culture with its regular rituals of gun shows and fly-overs and a deliberately aggressive lobby under the guise of "constitutionalism."

Atwood makes a compelling case, in the words of its own advocates, that this culture falls only slightly short of a religious claim. It amounts to nothing less than an idolatry, a false authority that requires uncompromising allegiance and that makes promises of well-being that it cannot keep.

Atwood delineates the several supports that sustain this culture, that both contribute to the idolatry and are fed by it:

- At bottom is a militant notion of US exceptionalism, that the U.S. is peculiarly the land of freedom and bravery that must be defended at all costs. It calls forth raw exhibits of power, sometimes in the service of colonial expansionism, but short of that, simply the strutting claim of strength, control, and superiority.

- Such U.S. exceptionalism, in turn, requires not only a strong military force, but a military ideology that gives privilege to military adventurism and military personnel, and that assures limitless funding for such adventurism that is deeply engrained in machismo posture. The presence of the military ideology in advertising and sports means that military posturing is pervasive, so that the national anthem must be sung everywhere always, a kind of pervasiveness that shocks us when we see it performed in "lesser" societies of an authoritarian ilk. Thus military exhibits of flags, anthems, marching, and saluting of the kind that endorsed National Socialism in Germany become commonplace among us.

- The mix of church and state adds religious fervor to aggressive nationalism, so that the rhetoric of militarism falls only short of evangelical crusade. The irony of such a linkage, of course, is that those who commit to a "strong military" are often the ones who otherwise resist "government control," all the while signing a blank check for aggressive government that serves corporate interest.

- The National Rifle Association is the frontal lobby that sustains influence and passion for the cause. The Association requires and receives the tacit support from many of its members who are in fact hunters who do not subscribe to its idolatrous ideology or its political aggressiveness, but who join in the posturing that puts democratic governance at risk.

- Appeal to the Second Amendment, given the courts' ludicrous reading of it, gives cover to the most outrageous claims.

- The myth of the Old West, endlessly reperformed, gives sanction for the redress of social wrong not by the rule of law but by the force of guns.

The sum of all of this is an elemental commitment to violence, a commitment that is voiced in terms of self-righteous faith, but that eventuates in a society of extreme vulnerability that is, according to the ideology, the "cost of freedom."

Atwood's book is a careful, detailed reflection on that culture. Beyond that, Atwood summons the reader, in his passion and indignation, to action that may break the hegemony of this ideology. He has read everything, but is especially informed by Walter Wink, who has taught us that the "powers and principalities" are a spiritual force that requires a counter-act by the spiritual forces of peacemaking and justice. The dominance of the gun culture is the same old narrative of the way in which a small cadre of resolved, smart, calculating people can impose its will on the body politic. Atwood, in his passion and indignation, knows very well that it need not be so. I commend this book as a challenge to resist the "business as usual" acceptance of this toxic ideology that undermines our capacity for well-being. It is without doubt the case that the gun culture pertains not only to guns but to a vision of our society that excludes large segments of our population—Muslims, gays, immigrants—who do not conform to an anxious, self-serving image of what it means to be "American." Atwood's book is insistent; it is also hopeful that an alternative way of ordering our society is possible. That alternative requires self-critical folk to take up the important tasks of patriotism that pertain to the common good.

Walter Brueggemann
Columbia Theological Seminary
December 13, 2011

Preface

After I buried Herb Hunter, who was killed by a teenager who picked up a Saturday night special at the local bowling alley so he could get some money, I've been anxiously waiting for someone to write a book that would motivate the church to reduce the gun violence that is destroying the social fabric of our communities.

I've been waiting for thirty-six years and reading books and articles on every aspect of our gun culture: the gun industry, the gun control movement, the Second Amendment, militias and insurrection, the inner workings of the National Rifle Association, and the myths—like "guns don't kill" and "more guns equal less crime"—that perpetuate the violence. I've read about the slippery slope, the Million Mom March, tracing crime guns, the economic costs of gun violence, the Bureau of Alcohol, Tobacco, and Firearms, concealed carry, and, of course, the trauma associated with mass shootings at Columbine, Virginia Tech, Ft. Hood, Tucson, and thirty-six other places in the last ten or so years.

That's a lot of reading, but I've not come across even one book written for the faith community that puts the 30,000 gun deaths we experience each year in biblical and theological perspective and calls on the church to speak up and speak out. I wondered why *someone* didn't step up to the plate.

Then, rather unexpectedly, in the spring of 2008, I was invited by the Presbyterian Peacemaking Program and the Presbyterian Peace Fellowship to give some theological reflections on gun violence and gospel values at a conference by that name, at the Stony Point Center in New York. I began my remarks by quoting the warning the Presbyterian Church, USA, gave its members in 1990: "The religious community must also take seriously the *risk of idolatry* that could result from an unwarranted fascination with guns that overlooks or ignores the social consequences of their misuse."

By the fall of that year when the conference began, an additional 600,000 American civilians had been killed and guns injured a million more. This led me to say, "The warning issued by the church eighteen years ago about the risk of idolatry was no longer a risk; it was our reality." My speech was titled, "The Idols of Power and the Tools of Violence."

The nucleus of those theological reflections on idols appear in the following pages and were a clear indication that I could no longer wait for someone more qualified to write a book that would light a fire under the church to name and unmask the idols. I would have to write it myself. I hope this book can light some fires.

America and its Guns: A Theological Exposé has been a long time in coming. My involvement with the work of the Coalition to Stop Gun Violence for thirty-six years has given me a broad understanding of the issue, helped me focus on what the faith community can do about it, and provided me many opportunities to preach and teach about America's unique gun problem, which makes us the most dangerous country in the industrialized world.

The three-year hiatus after the Stony Point Conference was also providential. I was appointed to serve on a denominational writing team that was charged to "prepare a comprehensive study on gun violence which articulated a Reformed Theology of proactive, constructive, nonviolent way of life . . . [and] assess the social and economic costs of gun violence; explore how it fits into a larger national culture of violence, and identify ways that the church can effectively address gun violence issues both domestically and internationally, and to report these findings along with proposed action items to the 2010 General Assembly." Our report, *Gun Violence, Gospel Values: Mobilizing in Response to God's Call*, was unanimously adopted by the 2010 General Assembly. If one has ever been to an assembly it is difficult to believe that a bunch of *Presbyterians* could adopt any measure *unanimously*, let alone on a controversial subject like guns.

Serving on this writing team was an epiphany. What I learned from my colleagues solidified a growing conviction that mobilizing the church to reduce gun violence requires the leadership of an educated, spiritually aware, and committed community. Heretofore, the church as a whole has not been educated or spiritually aware of the issues and has had no clue about the stranglehold the Gun Empire has on America. Perhaps this explains in part why the church has been so reluctant, even afraid, to address the subject. Gun violence has been the elephant in the living room.

If our nation finally decides to save thousands of lives every year by reducing gun violence, it will be because a sleeping spiritual giant is waking up and realizes God is calling it to name and unmask the idols of power and deadly force that are perpetuating murder and violence in our communities. These idols are the principalities and powers, which are nourished by death. The good news is it does not have to be this way. There *are* things we can do. It is not the will of God that between eighty-two and eighty-four people die every day by guns. Many of these lives will be saved the moment the faith community wakes up, learns about the Gun Empire, and decides to do something about the violence that is all too routine in America.

C. S. Lewis wrote, "Christianity is a statement which, if false, is of no importance, and if it is true, of infinite importance. The one thing it cannot be is moderately important."[1] When violence and guns destroy the character and moral fiber of our nation, it is of infinite importance that the faith community boldly refutes the non-sensical messages of the Gun Empire, which proclaim, "guns do not kill" and "the answer to gun violence is more guns."

This book is primarily addressed to those who take their faith in God seriously and believe in the ultimate power of love and truth. Gun violence is not so much a political or social problem as it is a *spiritual* problem, and God's people must be in the lead of the moral and ethical struggle for the soul of America.

I confess that in my earliest years in this movement I focused my energies and hopes not on the moral and ethical power of my faith in God nor on the moral authority God gives to people of faith, but on the power of national and state legislatures that could but would not write balanced laws to respect two basic American constitutional rights: the right to bear arms and the right for people to live in safety.

My efforts and hopes for a saner and safer America were misplaced. While I worked along with others to convince legislators to protect the American people and prevent more violence, the Gun Empire was busy writing laws on behalf of the legislators that protected guns instead of people. It is no secret the NRA distributes a

1. Lewis, *God in the Dock*, 101.

lot of campaign checks to those who do their bidding. I should have listened more carefully to Upton Sinclair. "It is difficult," he said, "to get a man to understand something, when his salary (or his power) depends upon his not understanding it!"

I always knew that gun violence was a profound spiritual matter and as a pastor I prayed every week with my congregation: "Thy Kingdom come, Thy will be done, on earth as it is in heaven." Nevertheless, I bypassed or virtually ignored the people of faith as I struggled with this issue. I will do so no longer. Because the United States is a country governed by law, eventually our legislators will write the necessary laws; but not before they are morally and ethically challenged to do so. I believe that will happen when the church and people of faith understand how grievously we have been deceived by the Gun Empire to trust that violence will bring us peace and security.

On the moral high ground, with confidence in the rightness of our cause, with indisputable facts at our disposal, and with strong biblical and spiritual resources, people of faith will be able to convince those in Congress and in statehouses to vote for fair and balanced laws that they know in their hearts is the right thing to do.

In the first round of drafts for this book I tried diligently to write with an ecumenical spirit and appeal to all faith traditions. However, my writing grew stilted and forced. Reluctantly, I shifted my approach and addressed the Christian church, which is my spiritual home. I knew its language and I was able to express myself with greater freedom. I trust there will be readers from other faith traditions, and I'm confident they will be able to transcend my focus on the Christian church and apply the same spiritual principles and concepts to their own.

Some of my friends call me "the gun man" because confronting gun violence has been my passion and calling for these many years. What kept my feet to the fire, however, was a bundle of personal friends and colleagues. I'm so grateful to all of them who understood where I was coming from and let me speak so frequently about guns and gun violence; special thanks to those whose concerns and enthusiasms matched my own. Thanks to all who showed up at meetings and study sessions, who came to demonstrations and made time to speak to legislators, and gave generously of their finances to support the Coalition to Stop Gun Violence and Heeding God's Call and other organizations. I will not start naming dear friends who have been my inspiration through the years because I'm bound to leave some one out who, as St. Paul said of Barnabas, "oft refreshed me."

I must however express a personal word of thanks to those who gave me special help, guidance, and encouragement in this effort: Chris Iosso, Katy Day, Bryan Miller, Catherine Snyder, David Little, John Wimberly, Reuben Brigety, Dan Giosta, Andy Goddard, Colin Goddard, Mike Beard, Joshua Horwitz, Ladd Everett, Christian Heyne, Josh Sugarman, Kristen Rand, Garen Wintemute, David Hemenway, Tom Diaz, Rick Ufford-Chase, Jim Sollo, Lori Haas, Mark Koenig, Dennis Henigan, Becca Knox, Dacya Abrahamyon, Joe Vince, Walter Owensby, Gary and Chess Campbell, Jim Drinkard, Sara Lisherness, David Barnhart, Scott Ippolito, Donna Dees-Thomases, Mary Leigh Blek, Michele Duell, Yvonne Grandaux Miller, Omar Samaha, Pauline Endo, Kim Reed, Sarah Hench, Tim Johnson, and the members of Paul Fiddick's Church School Class, the Men's Group and Mission Committee of Western Presbyterian Church in Washington DC. I feel most blessed that Dr. Walter Brueggemann, esteemed Professor Emeritus of Old Testament at Columbia Theological Seminary, wrote the foreword.

I give particular thanks to two individuals whose editorial expertise have made the book in my opinion more readable and believable. First, I'm grateful to my copyeditor, Heather Wilson, whose calm spirit, competence in her craft, and encouragement kept me on track. If these pages hold the reader's interest, she deserves the most credit. Rodney Clapp of Wipf and Stock then took over to make the book more believable. With persistent attention to detail, he insisted that all quotes, footnotes and bibliographical material be accurate, fully accessible and fully documented. Thank you both!

I could not have worked all these years in this field if I had not received the unqualified support of my entire family. Thanks to Mebane and Harry David and to my sister Harriet and their families who have not only given me constant encouragement, but their physical presence at countless events and their financial gifts to support the organizations with which I was affiliated. Most of all, I'm grateful for my wife, Roxana, who shares her life so unselfishly with all in our family and always steps up to read my stumbling attempts at the first few drafts. Thankfully, we share the same passion not only for this issue, but for sports. Writing this book has been a long haul. It's been fun, but a virtual taskmaster. Every free moment I was at the computer, instead of watching ball games with Roxana. Now that this book is finished, I look forward to joining her in rooting for the Redskins, the Capitals, and the Nationals.

Jim Atwood
December 2011, Springfield, Virginia

1

A Tale of Two Guns

MY FIRST GUN

My first gun was a Remington twelve-gauge shotgun, which I ordered in 1958 from a Sears Roebuck Company catalog. It never crossed my mind that most countries would consider buying a gun through the mail a dangerous practice. I used my Sportsman 58, with its patented poly-choke, to hunt quail, dove, rabbit, and deer in southeastern North Carolina, when I was pastor of the Wallace Presbyterian Church.

In August 1965, my wife, our two young children, and I boarded the *USS President Wilson* for Japan, where we served for nine years as missionaries with the United Church of Christ. With our passage we shipped two large crates of household goods to our new home in Kobe, where we studied Japanese for two years. I packed my shotgun in one of the crates because I learned Japan had good duck and pheasant hunting.

Passing through customs in Yokohama, I discovered quickly that my host country did not have America's laissez-faire attitude about guns. When I presented the customs declaration form to the official he was troubled and informed me the police were required to take my gun because no unlicensed guns were allowed in the country. He assured me the Yokohama Police would send the gun to the Kobe Police Department, which would tell me how it could be returned.

The Yokohama police helped me open my crate, and I turned the gun over to them. Several weeks later, I received a telephone call from the Kobe Police asking if some officers could come to my home and bring the gun. Two officers arrived and after we had tea, they took the gun from its case and asked me to identify it. After taking measurements and recording serial numbers, the lieutenant asked me to open and close the firing mechanism. They wanted to see if I knew how to use the gun and if it was in good working order. Passing muster, the officers told me I had three more things to do to reclaim my shotgun.

I had to bring the following documents to the Kobe Police Station:

1. A written statement from a physician declaring I was mentally and physically able to operate the firearm.

2. A certificate showing I attended and passed a course on gun safety and hunting regulations in Japan.

3. A receipt from the prefecture showing I paid the license fees.

Soon thereafter, I presented these documents to the Kobe Police, who returned my shotgun. I was somewhat irritated that I had to jump through all these bureaucratic hoops and spend so much time simply to get a license for an ordinary shotgun. I had no criminal intent; I just wanted to hunt some birds. Why all the fuss?

All the same, I changed my mind about these bureaucratic hoops. When I read the papers back home in North Carolina, there were always articles on gun deaths, which I accepted without much thought. They were simply part of American life, like automobile accidents. The Japanese newspapers, however, didn't have recurring stories about gun deaths because they didn't have many. In the fall of 1965, I read a short report on gun deaths in Japan for the previous year. I don't remember the exact numbers, but I do recall it was only a handful.

Slowly, I saw the wisdom of regulating firearms and was somewhat embarrassed I considered those few hours spent securing the three documents to be such a burden on my busy life. Japan's commonsense gun policies made the streets of Kobe and Tokyo, where we lived for nine years, some of the safest in the world. No child in Japan was afraid to go to school for fear of being shot, and no gunshots were heard in their inner cities. Suicides, while prevalent, were not committed with guns. America should have been so blessed.

I returned home in 1974. That year, Tokyo, which was then the largest city in the world, had one death by firearms and the nation's death toll from guns was infinitesimal. In contrast, America had 35,000 deaths by guns and some cities were virtual shooting galleries.

THE GUN THAT CHANGED MY LIFE

Even so, the unique American tragedy of gun violence was still an abstraction for me. I paid little attention to it until one autumn day in 1975, when I received a telephone call from the Intensive Care Unit of Alexandria (Virginia) Hospital. I rushed to the bedside of Herb Hunter, a charter member of my church who was dying from a lacerated liver, having been shot by a teenager who picked up a gun from a friend at the local bowling alley. The youngster complained he had no money, so his friend reached into his jacket and pulled out a Saturday night special. "Here, go get yourself some money," he said, "and when you get some, give me twenty bucks and you can keep the gun."

The boy entered the Hunter Motel in Springfield and pointed the gun at Herb, demanding money. Herb opened the cash register and, holding his hands in the air, backed away from the youth, who took the cash. Unfortunately, Herb tripped on a rug, which startled the boy. He turned around and shot Herb three times. Two days later we prepared for Herb's funeral.

I remembered Japan's commonsense laws and was both sad and angry as I realized that back home it was as easy to get a Saturday night special as a Big Mac. There were more gun dealers in the country than McDonalds restaurants, more gun dealers than gas stations. A dealer's license cost only ten dollars per year and most of them did their business from the trunks of their cars. They drove to Virginia and other states with lax or nonexistent gun laws, loaded up their trunks with high-powered guns, and returned to metropolitan areas to sell their merchandise at huge profits. No questions were asked. What buyers did with their purchases was none of their business. Guns were everywhere and I learned *one* indisputable fact: where the most guns are, society records the most gun deaths. It was no coincidence that in the seventies most gun deaths were in the South; the same is true today.

The day after I buried Herb, I drove to the offices of the National Coalition to Ban Handguns in Washington, D.C. (After the introduction of assault rifles to civilian markets and the attempted manufacture of plastic handguns, which we called "hijacker specials," the name was changed to the Coalition to Stop Gun Violence (CSGV).) I met Mike Beard and the Rev. Jack Corbett of the Methodist Church, its co-founders, and shared my grief over Herb's murder. I spoke of the gun laws under which I lived in Japan and volunteered to help in any way I could. I have now worked with the coalition for the past thirty-seven years, serving as chairman of their national board, writing letters, making speeches, preaching, drafting resolutions, lobbying Congress, raising money, marching in demonstrations, and putting my arms around those whose family and friends were shot and killed. In 2000, I was the Interfaith Chair of the Million Mom March, as one million Americans gathered on the Mall in Washington, D.C., to demand sensible gun laws. I'm presently serving as Chair of Heeding God's Call in Greater Washington, an ecumenical movement that organizes faith communities to put public and spiritual pressure on gun stores that sell inordinate numbers of guns found at crime scenes. The retailer code we ask them to sign would virtually eliminate straw purchasing.

I'm not a gun hater or a gun grabber as many pro-gun people describe those of us who work for balanced laws. I go deer hunting every fall, a fact that has led some to call me a hypocrite because I hunt and kill "those beautiful, defenseless creatures."

I don't apologize for hunting or eating venison. I look forward each November to being with my close friend Will Johnston on his beautiful tree farm in Gore, Virginia and also enjoy the camaraderie of Will's nephew, Mike, who depends on getting several deer each year to help feed his family.

There is a profound difference between shooting a wild animal and shooting a human being created in God's image. The Bible says God made people just a little lower than the angels and crowned us with glory and honor. God has put all creation under our feet, and he has given us dominion over all the works of his hands, including all sheep and oxen and the beasts of the fields and the birds of the air (Gen 1:26). God did not, however, place other human beings "under our feet" (Ps 8:5–8). No human being is created to have dominion over other people. No human being is made to be hunted or killed. No human being should be in the crosshairs of another's rifle or the target of an assault pistol. We are all brothers and sisters in God's family.

Though I own guns, I do not believe they should be exempt from safety requirements, wise regulation, and restrictions. Guns *are* made to kill. America has an abominable record of balancing an individual's right to have a gun with the public's inalienable right to life, liberty, and the pursuit of happiness. Public safety in the company of three hundred million guns should not be a wish or the pipe dream it is today. Children in the United States are twelve times more likely to die from firearms injury than children in twenty-five other industrialized nations *combined*. Gun murder rates in the United States per one-hundred thousand people are more than seventeen times higher than those in Australia; thirty-five times higher than in Germany; thirty-seven times higher than in Spain; and 355 times higher than in Japan.[1] If the United States respected both the constitutional right to keep and bear arms and the right of its citizens to live on safe streets, these figures would drop precipitously. We should be embarrassed to be first in the developed world for gun deaths.

WHY PEOPLE JOIN THIS MOVEMENT

My anguish over Herb Hunter's death was a call from God to try and stop so many senseless deaths. How was a kid in a bowling alley able to pick up a gun so easily and nonchalantly snuff out the life of such a good and generous man? I was angry that our country was so indifferent to 30,000 gun deaths every year. I joined the movement in anger, but I stay in the movement because I believe the wrong will fail and the right will prevail. Trusting in God's power and love have kept me working these thirty-six years to try and save precious lives. I can't be casual before thousands of preventable deaths. Although these years have been stressful, and I've known only a few large victories, I've had the privilege of working with some of the kindest and

1. Krug et al., "Firearm-related Deaths," 214–21.

IN ONE YEAR, GUNS MURDERED

17 PEOPLE IN FINLAND

35 IN AUSTRALIA

39 IN ENGLAND AND WALES

60 IN SPAIN

194 IN GERMANY

200 IN CANADA

AND 9,484 IN THE UNITED STATES

GOD BLESS AMERICA.

Brady Campaign

To Prevent Gun Violence

SENSIBLE GUN LAWS SAVE LIVES

Statistics supplied by individual countries.

Used with permission of the Brady Campaign to Prevent Gun Violence.

International Murders by Guns (2008)

most courageous people I have ever known. I've grown stronger in the presence of these people, who have suffered their own virtual hells, yet have managed to keep a loving spirit while dedicating their lives to preventing the same heartbreak in others. The survivors I know are not sentimental people filled with bubbly feelings; theirs is a love that is tough, bold, and demanding, and they work largely for the safety of those they will never know personally.

Naturally, their anger burns hot because a loved one or friend was cruelly snatched away. Their grief and anger often resurface and will for as long as they live. Nonetheless, they struggle to cobble together common-sense, balanced legislation, which, had it been in place, would have prevented at least *some* of their tragedies, not all, but at least *some*.

I consider it a miracle that I can count on one hand the times I have heard these survivors say, "All guns should be banned." Their responses to their misfortunes have been restrained, and this should compel every zealous gun owner to support the balanced laws they propose.

A BRIEF SAMPLING OF THE VICTIMS AND SURVIVORS I HAVE WORKED WITH

- A young mother, who after hearing gunshot and broken glass, rushed to her infant daughter's crib, only to find her lifeless, killed by a stray bullet in the inner city.

- Brenda Jaskolka, who took her son, Joe, to a Philadelphia hospital on New Year's Eve. He had been hit on the head by a bullet fired into the air in celebration. The bullet struck Joe on the head, almost taking his life. He was in a coma for weeks, then spent six months in rehabilitation. He will forever carry the physical and emotional scars.

- Carol Price told her twelve year old son, John, he could go see his buddy at a neighbor's house, but he never came back. His friend's father had a gun in the dresser drawer to protect the family. Think too of John's friend who killed his playmate.

- A senior in high school received an academic scholarship to college. She was gunned down while celebrating, in a drive-by shooting. It was a case of mistaken identity.

- Parents of a medical student told us of their son who dreamed of working with Doctors Without Borders, but was shot and killed by a jealous friend.

- Bryan Miller, co-founder of Heeding God's Call, had a brother who was an FBI agent and was killed at his desk in Washington, DC, by a mentally sick man who wanted to kill police.

- At the Million Mom March in 2000, a weeping mother told of her twin sons who got into a spat the morning of their high school graduation. One shot and killed the other and, in utter despair, took his own life.

- A young governmental analyst, soon to be married, took her dog for a walk and met a man who "heard voices to kill."

These are only a few of the heart-rending stories that haunt me and keep my feet on the path. Collectively they say, "Wake up, America. It doesn't have to be this way."

There are stories also that haunt me in a different way because the deaths are so unbelievably ridiculous.

- On July 18, 1996, a man who lost an early morning Bible quoting contest killed the man who beat him. Gabriel Taylor, 38, was shot once in the face outside of his apartment. Taylor, a preacher's brother, and the suspect were comparing their Bible knowledge outside an apartment complex, each quoting different versions of the same passage. The suspect retrieved his Bible and realized he was wrong. He said that Taylor did know more and that made him mad. He threatened to kill Taylor before the night was out. He left with two other people who witnessed the exchange.[2]

- A fifty-seven-year-old man shot and killed his wife because she would not have sex with him.

- A son of a personal friend of mine shot and killed his college roommate because he put the dishes on the wrong shelf.

- A Woodbine, New Jersey, man was charged with aggravated manslaughter after a practical joke turned deadly. Anthony Sadluk, Jr., and his roommate, Wesley Geisinger, 31, were hosting a party at their home early Sunday morning when Sadluk loaded a muzzleloader rifle with cigarette butts and paper towel wadding, police said. Sadluk aimed and fired the rifle at Geisinger, who was standing nearby. and he was hit in the chest. Geisinger collapsed and was later pronounced dead at the scene. An autopsy determined that three cigarette butts

2. Chuck Shepherd, "Bible-Quoting Contest: Loser Shoots, Kills Winner." *Montgomery Advertiser*, Associated Press, July 18, 1996.

penetrated Geisinger's rib cage directly above his heart, causing his death.[3]

- A ten-year-old boy was grazed in the right cheek by a bullet when an off-duty police officer conducting a demonstration at a Philadelphia school dropped her gun. The officer, whose child was among the twenty-three students in the class, had shown the magazine clip and had just put it back in the gun when she dropped the weapon.[4]

- A Texas man is facing up to twenty years in prison for shooting his girlfriend because he thought she was about to say, "New Jersey." Although he did not claim insanity in his defense, relatives testified that Thomas Ray Mitchell, 54, gets angry, curses, and bangs on walls when he hears certain words or phrases, including "New Jersey," "Snickers," "Mars," and "Wisconsin."[5]

WHAT MOTIVATES US?

It's not a requirement that volunteers who work in the movement experience the death of a family member or friend. What motivates them to give their time, energy, and resources to this uphill struggle? Why work on an often-thankless task when gun zealots can be vicious to their opponents? Why would one of my friends endure middle of the night death threats because she tried to stop terrorists from getting guns? Why try to reason with the paranoid who believe our government is scheming to confiscate their guns, padlock their hunting lands, and deny all citizens the right to have a gun?

I asked several of my colleagues why they are involved, and I wish I had the space to convey all their replies. Abby Spangler, the founder of Protest Easy Guns, acknowledged a common thread for all of us. She said, "It is a mixture of heartbreak and empathy for those who have known devastating loss, mixed with a profound

3. "Man Shot Dead with Cigarette Butts." February 13, 2001. http://abcnewsgo.com/US/story?id=94079&page=.

4. *Los Angeles Times*, February 7, 2002.

5. Associated Press, "Man Shoots Woman over 'New Jersey,'" February 14, 2002. *Gun Policy News*. www.gunpolicy.org.

sense of outrage that our country permits these killings to occur again and again."

Presbyterian minister David R. Taylor developed a liturgical innovation that he uses each Sunday just before the benediction. To remind the congregation that life is totally unpredictable and each day is a precious gift from God, he asks the congregation to say: "Across our paths this week may walk more challenge, more sorrow, more fulfillment than any other week in our lives or the next seven days may be a routine repeat of a hundred unspectacular weeks we have known before." David wrote these words because of what happened to his sister-in-law, Lisa Kiser, whose life, in the twinkling of an eye, was radically changed.

In 2002, she was taking a test in the School of Nursing at the University of Arizona and seated in the front row, center seat. A fellow student walked into the classroom, came to the front, shot the professor straight on, and turned and shot the assistant professor in the back of the room. He then calmly walked out, went down the hall and shot another professor, killing all three before he killed himself. Lisa struggles with post-traumatic stress disorder, and each time a school shooting occurs, she is dragged back to October 28, 2002, to repeat her nightmares all over again. Between 1997 and Virginia Tech in 2007, there were forty-one separate school shootings where children, youth, and faculty were murdered.

Let no one say, "There is nothing we can do." It is not so. Your efforts and mine make a difference. I'd quit this work in a heartbeat if I were not convinced in God's long run, "justice will roll down like waters and righteousness like an ever-flowing stream" (Amos 5:24). We have God's promise that our work makes a difference. "My beloved, be steadfast, immovable, always excelling in the work of the Lord, because you know that in the Lord your labor is not in vain" (1 Cor 15:58). Martin Luther King reminded the nation of that promise when he said, "The arc of the moral universe is long, but it bends toward justice."

2

Closing the Door on Discussion

IS GUN VIOLENCE A POLITICAL OR SPIRITUAL PROBLEM?

Frequently, when the subject of gun violence is mentioned in the church, the PTA, or a public service organization that is held together by the unified spirit of its members, gun zealots are quick to complain, "This is a political issue; we are a church or a civic organization. It is inappropriate for us to be talking about this." Calling a concern for thousands of needless deaths a political issue can stop cold an honest attempt to talk about the matter in church. Three personal vignettes illustrate the dilemma.

On a summer Sunday I was a guest minister at an interdenominational church near Washington, D.C. My sermon was on how the church could be instrumental in saving lives if we would insist on reasonable measures to keep guns out of the hands of dangerous individuals. I was about halfway through my sermon when I noticed a man nervously fidgeting with his bulletin. After worship when I greeted him at the door he was irate. He scolded me severely: "You should be ashamed of yourself to turn the pulpit of a church into an opportunity to speak about your own *political views.*"

I knew my sermon would not be received well by all who were there. I realize people have vastly different understandings of guns. Some regard them as fearful instruments that maim and kill; others see them as prized family heirlooms that evoke memories of hunting trips and family gatherings; still others consider them the difference between life and death. Maybe the man felt that raising the subject, about which there is wide difference of opinion, *could* destroy the "sweet, sweet spirit" of the church, but I doubt it.

There *are* political dimensions whenever guns are discussed, but what happens in society *because of guns* makes them a profound spiritual concern that must be dealt with by people of faith. In spite of the metaphysical rhetoric to the contrary, guns actually *do* kill. That is their purpose. Although one cannot dismiss the political implications of guns, the spiritual implications, in my mind, far outweigh the purely political.

For the man mentioned here and tens of thousands like him, gun violence is not a subject a Christian minister should consider from the pulpit. They contend all conversation about guns should be held in the political arena because the church is where we focus on spiritual matters.

The millions of Americans who have died at the barrel of a gun demand that the subject be examined in God's house. Human beings made in the image of God are slaughtered while every denomination in the country affirms that people are "the crown of creation." Nothing is more sacred than a human being. Each human body is the "temple of the living God" (1 Cor 3:16–17). Nothing is more spiritual than that.

The same barrier was raised by a local Baptist Pastor when I asked for his help to close the gun show loophole in Virginia. I offered several reasons why he and his church should work with us. Namely, I explained that the Bureau of Alcohol, Tobacco, Firearms, and Explosives (ATF) regard gun shows as the second leading source of crime guns in the country behind corrupt gun dealers. There are more than 5,000 annual gun shows nationwide and almost every week in Virginia, a gun and knife show is promoted. Felons, domestic abusers, terrorists, youth, and persons with adjudicated mental illness can go to a gun show and buy a gun from unlicensed sellers with no questions asked. Guns killed 800 Virginians in the past year and more than 30,000 nationwide. By getting involved his church could help change this.

The reverend asked many questions, which signaled an interest, but at the end of our talk he said: "I'm thankful for this conversation. I've learned a lot. I appreciate your work and I will pray for you, but I am unable to help. Our deacons have said, 'Our church is not to engage in any political activity whatsoever.'"

Then came the tragedy at Virginia Tech, which I did not consider a political matter. Even in the aftermath of tragedies brought on by gun violence there are obstacles to open and honest discussions. Less than two weeks after the mass shooting, I was asked to serve on a two-person presbytery team to visit a church located in a geographical area that suffered three of those thirty-three deaths. All three were recent graduates of the local high school, which was but a stone's throw away from the church. Our visit was administrative and pastoral in nature: discuss the church's ministry, assess its strengths and weaknesses, and learn of its future goals. My colleague and I were impressed by their sense of call to minister to the nearby high school students.

I was surprised that in our two- hour meeting, the incident at Blacksburg, Virginia, which was national news and fresh on everyone's mind, merited only a cursory reference. Before the meeting closed I asked, "Since three of those killed at Virginia Tech were from this community, are those of you on the Session doing anything about gun violence?" Two or three volunteered they had opened the sanctuary for students who wanted to pray and made the pastoral staff available to any youth who sought counseling. I pressed further: "Are you doing anything to stop the proliferation of guns in our state? Are you, for example, doing anything to close the gun show loophole in Virginia?"

When I asked *this* question, one elder's face grew red and he said in a loud, angry voice: "We ought not to be talking about this. This is *a political problem* and we are a church. This is not an appropriate conversation for us to be having." I replied, "Don't you think there is *something* the church should be doing about gun violence?" "Yes," he said, "we should be praying for those who are thinking about doing such horrible things. We should pray that they have a change of heart."

No one else said a word and it was getting late so we all joined hands as a symbol of our unity, bowed our heads, and the pastor led us in a closing prayer. The lives of three youth from their own community had been snuffed out by a mentally ill young man with powerful guns, and while these spiritual leaders were able to pray for the families of those who had been murdered and ask God's strength for the youth who were emotionally distraught, they could not discuss what the church might do to prevent a similar tragedy from happening.

If the city council announced an adult book and video store had applied for a business license close to the church and high school, would the elder gather the congregation for a prayer meeting? Would the elder merely pray that the owner of the porn shop would have a change of heart? Would the proposed store be a political or a spiritual problem?

Gun violence is nonpartisan. Guns kill Republicans, Democrats, and Independents every day. The victims are Jews, Christians, Muslims, Sikhs, Buddhists, atheists, agnostics, whites, blacks, Latino, Asian, men, women, boys, girls, young, old, gay, straight, rich, poor, rural, and urban. No category of person escapes. Gun violence is no more a political issue than drunken driving, selling crack cocaine, or arson.

When a human being is killed, the family does not call their congresswoman, senator, or civil magistrate. They call their pastor, rabbi, or imam. Dealing with death and its aftermath is *not* a political activity. Why would working to prevent violent deaths be a political matter?

God's people are called collectively to address such societal problems. Deuteronomy 21:1–9 concerns a stranger who was murdered out in the countryside far away from the city limits of any of the area's villages. Even so, the death could not be ignored. A human being made in the image of God had been murdered and the very ground cried out for cleansing. Community leaders from all the surrounding villages rushed to the scene of the crime and literally stepped off the distance from the body to their respective town limits to see which village would be responsible for burying the corpse and leading worship to purify the land and wash away the collective sins of all. Although a representative priest was determined by proximity to the remains, every Hebrew for miles around was accountable because their lands had been defiled. Can we moderns excuse ourselves and bear any less social responsibility when our cities and towns are defiled by innumerable murders? Can anyone who believes in God read about our mass shootings and say, "It's not *my* responsibility?" If God, as Jesus told us, cares about a sparrow's death, preventing the death of any of God's children is an urgent matter.

SPIRITUAL THINGS

Then again, I've seen dedicated gun activists and others who insist the church has no business in societal or secular matters derail sincere conversations about life on Main Street by pejoratively using the word "spiritual." They are ready to divide the whole world into things secular and sacred. Marilee Zdenek and Marge Champion in their book, *God Is a Verb*, expose such heresy in simple verse:

> I've been told that some things are sacred
> and some things are secular —
> but those are confusing terms.
> So I looked up the word "secular"
> and the dictionary said:
> "things connected with the world;
> things not religious or sacred."

> But, what is more sacred than life?
> Isn't work sacred, Jesus? And laughter—
> Isn't all that touches your brothers touching you?

> You must have been doing your Father's will
> when you worked as a carpenter in Joseph's shop.
> You were about your Father's business
> talking with rabbis in the temple
> dining with whores and tax collectors
> playing with children
> sailing with fishermen
> forgiving sins and healing lepers.

Tell me, Jesus—
which part of your life was sacred;
which part was concerned with the world?
And in my life—
speak to me of today
and tell me,
what part of it
does not concern you?[1]

Church folk should be aware that those who resent any organized restraints on their personal power, wealth, or control, however they are expressed, are skilled in introducing both of the concepts inherent in the words "political" and "spiritual" to defend their ideology and keep certain subjects like guns, profits, and sharing the wealth out of the realm of moral and ethical discourse. Both words can be used with great effectiveness.

Gun zealots are well aware when they label gun violence a political matter, whether in the faith community, the PTA, or gatherings of citizens that the charge will make enough members nervous over losing unity or togetherness or their 501-c-3 status, that they will drop or table the subject. If someone is determined to keep a particular concern from being raised in the church, the most effective tactic is to label it "political" and remind the body we are "spiritual," not community leaders.

The ploy has been used before. In the early nineteenth century when slavery was questioned by some of Jesus' followers, not only slave owners, but those in every section of the nation who benefited from slave labor, said, "slavery is a political and economic matter; it is not a spiritual concern and the church should stay out of it." They quoted Paul's counsel: "Slaves, obey your earthly masters with fear and trembling, in singleness of heart, as you obey Christ" (Eph 6:5).

In 1861, when the Presbyterian Church split over the issue of slavery, Southern apologists who defended slavery as beneficial to both races were on the defensive morally and called upon theologians for new understandings of the church's role in society. They created a very popular doctrine called "the spirituality of the church." Proponents argued that the church could not go beyond scripture,

1. Zdenek and Champion, *God Is a Verb*.

that slavery was not condemned by the Bible, and that Jesus and the apostles accepted slavery. They believed, therefore, that the church could not condemn it. The doctrine did not stop the church from speaking out on other social ills such as "Sabbath observance, intemperance, and the worldly amusements of dancing, theatre going and card playing."[2] The heretical doctrine of "the spirituality of the church" continues to assault Jesus' church to this day.

THE FOLLY OF LOOKING FOR SOLUTIONS IN THE POLITICAL PROCESS

From the 1960s onward the Presbyterian Church made dozens of statements about America's epidemic of gun violence. I've personally written three of them, which became denominational policy. I was proud of my work, but looking back with 20/20 hindsight, I realize now two of the three statements were doomed to failure. Why? They were totally naïve and included an unwarranted hope in the political process. We asked that letters be sent to every member of Congress, asking them to find a remedy for the violence that was ripping apart our cities. A few faithful Congresspersons took the letters seriously but the majority threw them in their wastebaskets.

We asked Congress *to take the lead* in stopping gun violence, instead of taking the moral and ethical lead *ourselves* with our sermons, Bible studies, conferences, and trips to the nation's inner cities to see first-hand the inescapable links between violence and poverty. We did not even notice at those very moments, NRA lobbyists were busy drafting laws to protect the buying and selling of guns, instead of the people who were being killed by them. It never occurred to many of us that the gun legislation Congress was passing actually made it easier for criminals and the mentally ill to buy guns.

I am not by nature a cynic, but I confess that in later years, a touch of cynicism crept into my life. I should have paid closer attention to the Bible and John Calvin as they described the human condition. For decades I was the eternal optimist, convinced that reason would prevail under the Capitol's dome. I believed in my depths that

2. Thompson, *Through the Ages: A History of the Christian Church*, 383–84.

once our public servants knew that America was the most dangerous nation in the industrialized world, they would change their minds and write laws that simultaneously protected gun rights and provided safe streets.

I was blind to the truth that Upton Sinclair shared with the world years before: "It is very difficult to get someone to understand something when his salary, *or his power* (italics mine) is dependent on not understanding it." For the church to ask Congress to confront America's idolatry of guns was asking the fox to guard the chickens.

What our nation needs is balanced legislation that respects two fundamental constitutional rights: the right to keep and bear arms and the right to enjoy domestic tranquility as one pursues life, liberty, and happiness. Because we are a country governed by laws, *eventually*, Congress will write balanced laws. But, first, there must be a spiritual awakening from God's people for those laws to find the necessary traction in our highest legislative bodies.

Being responsible for spiritual awakenings is not in Congress' job description. It *is*, however, in the job description of the church. As our situation is initially addressed biblically and theologically by the church, as we rediscover the moral authority God gives us and speak out for commonsense laws, and as we internalize the fact that the ecumenical faith community is the most powerful instrument for change in the nation, we will rejoice in our clout and pressure legislators to do what they know is right. When God's people become convinced too many people are dying, balanced legislation will become the law of the land.

In the meantime, faith in God's eventual victory compels us to work for that day foreseen by the prophet, when, "Old men and old women shall again sit in the streets each with staff in hand, and the streets of the city shall be full of boys and girls playing in the streets. And none shall make them afraid" (Zech 8:4–5).

3

Guns as Idols—A Risk or a Reality?

In the mid-sixties the Presbyterian Church began calling the nation's attention to the gun violence that was tearing apart our inner cities. In 1990, they issued a warning: "The religious community must take seriously *the risk of idolatry* that could result from an unwarranted fascination with guns that overlooks or ignores the social consequences of their misuse."[1]

Twenty years after the warning, 600,000 more American civilians have been killed and a million more injured.[2] These numbers convince me that the warning has become reality.

DEFINING OUR TERMS

Not for one minute do I believe *all* guns are idols, but I do believe *some* guns are idols. I'd never say *all* gun owners are idolatrous, but I insist *some* gun owners are. I don't use the words "idol" and "idolatry" to be melodramatic, only accurate. Former NRA executive, Warren Cassidy, was serious when he exclaimed, "You would get a far better understanding of the NRA if you were approaching us as one of the

1. The Presbyterian Church, USA, 202nd General Assembly Minutes, 604.

2. According to U.S. National Center for Health statistics, since 1979 the nation's gun deaths have never dipped below 30,000 annually. In 1989 the figure was 34,471; in 1990, there were 36,866 gun deaths; in 1991, 38,077 were killed by guns. Gun violence prevention organizations nevertheless use the conservative average of 30,000 gun deaths per year. Twenty years multiplied by 30,000 equals 600,000.

great religions of the world."[3] This belief helps explain why the fight over any gun control measure immediately takes on the quality of a crusade for those whose guns have become idols.

For most Americans who believe all NRA members think alike, it will surprise them to know the majority of their membership, albeit a silent one, are very concerned about the nation's gun violence. In December 2009 Republican pollster Frank Luntz, whose most recent assignment was providing talking points against the Democratic Party's healthcare bills, conducted a poll of America's gun owners. The poll, sponsored by Mayors Against Illegal Guns, surveyed 832 gun owners, including 401 NRA members who agreed with Luntz's core idea that gun regulations and gun rights complement each other. Luntz began the survey claiming: "We can do more to stop criminals from getting guns while also protecting the rights of citizens to freely own them." Eighty-six percent of all respondents agreed. Clearly, *their* guns are not idols.[4]

Conversely, the Gun Empire, which includes manufacturers, distributors, dealers, and the vocal extremists and elitists who control the NRA, have deep emotional, even religious attachments to their guns and make no pretensions otherwise. They resonate with one of their activists who said, "If it goes boom, I like it."

Their lifestyle choices indicate idolatry as they:

1. Nurture deep emotional attachments to instruments that are made to kill.

2. Grow threatened and angry when gun values are questioned and refuse honest dialogue about the place of guns in society.

3. Support no preventive measures to stop gun violence, only punishment.

4. Show little or no grief for society's gun victims.

5. Vigorously oppose any law to restrict sales of guns to the most dangerous members of society.

---

3. Davidson, *Under Fire*, 44.

4. E. J. Dionne, "Beyond the NRA's Absolutism," *Washington Post,* December 10, 2009.

6. Claim an absolute, unrestricted, unregulated constitutional right to use their guns against our government if *they* consider it tyrannical.

7. Claim the blessing of a loving God on weapons that kill.

8. Believe the solution to gun violence is to have more guns.

In short, I believe a gun becomes an idol when the following conditions prevail:

1. An owner believes there are no circumstances when a regulation or restriction for public safety should be placed upon it.

2. An owner believes that guns don't kill; they only save lives.

3. An owner has no doubt that guns preserve America's most cherished values.

IDOLATRY IN ACTION

Each Martin Luther King Jr. Day both sides of this debate lobby Virginia's legislators. In 2008, those who support balanced gun laws conducted a vigil at the bell tower at the state capitol in Richmond to commemorate the deaths of 800 Virginians who had been killed the previous year. As a young mother stood weeping at the microphone, and between sobs, told of rushing to her infant daughter's crib where a stray bullet killed her, gun rights people pushed their way into our vigil and drowned out this woman's trembling voice as they angrily shouted, "Guns Save Lives. Guns Save Lives."

These individuals came to Richmond to protect their idols. Their intense anger proved forces beyond their control manipulated them. Often in church or social gatherings when the subject of gun violence is broached, some storm angrily out of the room rather than engage in reasoned dialogue. Gun rights, for them, are sacrosanct and non-negotiable. While one can never prove what is in another's heart, a red face or neck, agitated shifting in a chair, a voice out of control, irregular deep breathing, and an angry spirit are signs that should not be missed. Psychologists or counselors would not overlook such behavior and would ask their clients, "Why are you so upset?" Such signals prove the validity of the Presbyterian Church's warning in

1990 that some people "have an unwarranted fascination with guns that overlooks or ignores the social consequences of their misuse."

THE PRESENCE OF IDOLS

One of the most popular TV shows today is *American Idol.* The word "idol" is usually reserved for one whose musical or athletic talent deserves admiration. Role models become our idols and their exploits add spice and excitement to our lives, but to use the word in reference to a false god sounds old-fashioned, as if false gods belonged only to primitive societies or to those nomads who fashioned the golden calf in the Sinai Desert. In truth, idols never go out of style; they are as up to date as the latest tweet. Those who create modern idols insist their creations be state-of-the-art and relevant to human needs and values in order to tempt admirers to give them respect, allegiance, and money.

I define America's idolatry with guns as a confrontational belief system based on acquiring power over others. The system is buttressed by a fascination for and devotion to the violence guns provide. Those who *believe* need guns to prove to themselves and others they are in control, to protect them from harm, and to give them a sense of security. This belief system is committed to the expansion of gun ownership that encourages owners to take their guns literally everywhere to stop crime and save lives. Claiming divine blessing and the highest of national values, they depend on deception and distortion of the truth to gain influence in the world, but take no responsibility when thousands of Americans die by guns each year.

The first entry in Martin Luther's *Larger Catechism* deals with idolatry. To the question: What does it mean to have a god, Luther replies:

> A god means that from which we are to expect all good and
> to which we are to take refuge in all distress, so that to have
> a God is nothing else than to trust and believe Him from the
> [whole] heart; as I have often said that the confidence and
> faith of the heart alone make both God and an idol. If your
> faith and trust be right, then is your god also true; and, on

the other hand, if your trust be false and wrong, then you have not the true God; for these two belong together faith and God. That now, I say, upon which you set your heart and put your trust is properly your god. God says to us "See to it that you let Me alone be your God, and never seek another," i.e.: Whatever you lack of good things, expect it of Me, and look to Me for it, and whenever you suffer misfortune and distress, creep and cling to Me. I, yes, I, will give you enough and help you out of every need; only let not your heart cleave to or rest in any other."[5]

H. E. Mertens expands on the idea: each of us believes in, wagers on, and trusts in a god or a deity, meaning to say an all-orientating and all-dominating prime value, something or someone whereby all else ultimately matters, and to which or to whom all the rest is related. "Tell me which prime value dominates your thoughts, your actions, your life in fact (perhaps unconsciously), and I will tell you what is the concrete name of your god and what is the color of your real religion, even if sociologically you belong to another."[6]

The American essayist and poet, Ralph Waldo Emerson, realized in his own time that human personality conforms to that which it worships or considers of inestimable worth: "That which dominates our imaginations and our thoughts will determine our life and our character. Therefore, it behooves us to be careful what we worship, for what we are worshipping we are becoming."

Idols are always with us and are nourished over long periods of time within one's culture in symbiotic relationships. They gain no power by drawing lines in the sand and forcing people to choose between them and the God/god usually worshiped in that culture. It is self-defeating for an idol or its devotees to distinguish itself as a separate entity apart from the religious and cultural norms of a society. Idols insist on being part of an established order, never conspicuous from it. They gain power as they appropriate the culture's personality and character, its value systems, and particularly its religious texts and cherished images. They claim everything within a culture that would enhance their believability and trustworthiness.

5. Janzon, *Getting Into Luther's Large Catechism*, 29.

6. Burggraeve et al., *Desirable God*, 38.

Humanity is never limited in its choice of idols. In every generation people have bowed down and worshiped everything on earth,
including themselves, stones, flowers, trees, streams, wells, oceans, and
animals. Yet, they have never really worshiped anything that did not
represent what they both cherished and feared the most . . . *power.*

Many biblical scholars agree when the Israelites fashioned the
golden calf they had no intention of rejecting the God who saved
them from bondage in Egypt. They planned to use the calf only as
a tangible symbol of their redeeming God. They could not see their
God, nor could they see Moses who was up on the mountain with
God, but they *could* see and touch the calf, which served as a vivid
reminder of God's power and presence. They believed this symbol
enabled them to tap into God's power as they struggled in the desert.
This young, virile bull also confirmed their own dreams of being virile and powerful, just like their God.

As the golden calf gave the ancients a false sense of security,
many twenty-first-century Americans look for security in weapons.
When our leaders are absent or fail us; when our God is invisible and
from all appearances is absent from our lives; when we don't know
how we can keep going; when we are consumed by our fears and
feel threatened by those who are not like us, those are the moments
when new idols are imagined and fashioned and desperate people
give them their ultimate concerns, devotion, and focused attention.

Our national trust in our weapons has grown exponentially
since the Second World War and has led us to purchase more and
more of them. Part of America's national creed is that the tools of
violence, be they large, as in war materiel, or small, as in handguns
and assault weapons, will keep us safe, secure, and "free."

America's military, for example, possesses 3,200 tactical combat
aircraft of all kinds. We lead the world in spending more for military
preparedness at $698 billion a year, compared to the expenditures of
the next nineteen countries *combined.*[7] The U.S. Navy is larger than
the next thirteen navies of the world *combined,* eleven of which belong to our closest allies and partners.[8] Domestically, we possess more

7. Perlo-Freeman, et al., chapter 4: "Military Expenditure," *Stockholm International Peace Research Institute Yearbook.*

8. Zakaria, "Be More Like Ike," *Newsweek,* August 16, 2010, 70.

than 300 million guns, almost enough for every man, woman, and child, and an additional three million come off assembly lines each year. Has all this firepower made us more secure? Have these weapons removed or reduced our fear? Suppose we only spent more than the next ten nations combined or if our navy was only larger than the next *seven* navies of the world combined, would we be any *less* secure? Are we safer today than we were four years ago when America had twelve million fewer handguns and assault weapons?

4

Commandments: More Than Rules—Relationships

The Ten Commandments are much more than a set of rules. Although rules are important, the commandments are about something much more significant: they keep us in relationship with God and neighbors. The first two commandments themselves alert us to the dangers idols create when they are introduced into a community that has made a covenant to be faithful to God and one another.

Even before the commandments are given, the Jews are reminded of God's initiative to connect with them. "I am the Lord your God, who brought you out of the land of Egypt, out of the house of slavery; you shall have no other gods before me" (Exod 20:2). All that follows is about living in a loving and faithful bond with a redeeming God and the others whom God has chosen. God says, in effect, "I have loved and redeemed you. Should you decide to be my people and take pleasure in my presence, *you shall have no other gods before me.*"

Old Testament scholar Patrick Miller writes that the phrase "before me" can also be rendered: "in front of me"; "alongside me"; "in my place," or "instead of me"; "over against me"; "in hostile confrontation with me"; "against my face." Other scholars add: "at my expense."[1]

Idols existed long before the commandments. People knew about the false gods both in the physical and metaphorical sense, and they are alluded to in the text. The fundamental question, therefore, in Moses' day, as well as in our own, is not whether one believes in God, but in *which* God/god one believes. An understanding of the nature of one's God/god is the most fundamental aspect of faith.

1. Miller, *The Ten Commandments*, 20.

The God/god one attaches one's heart to determines the direction one's life will take, where ultimate meaning and hope are found, and determines lifestyle choices. "For where your God/god is there your heart will be also."[2]

The people of Israel understood that their relationship with God required faithfulness to their redeemer and should they seek ultimate meaning in any other god, person, thing, or idea their covenant would be nullified. Only Yahweh was worthy of their trust and devotion because it was Yahweh who led them out of bondage in Egypt and gave them their identity.

Those who have been redeemed were not to be enticed by what Miller calls "other centers of meaning." He cites Deuteronomy 13:4 as one of the strongest positive formulations of the meaning of the First Commandment: "The Lord your God you shall follow, him alone you shall fear, his commandments you shall keep, his voice you shall obey, him you shall serve, and to him you shall hold fast."

The most fundamental theological principle in the Reformed Tradition is the sovereignty of God. If God is indeed sovereign, then nothing imagined by the human mind or made by the human hand is worthy of human awe. The word "idol" comes from the old French and Latin languages and means, "something visible but without substance." An idol is not *authentic*. It masquerades as something real, but it is incapable of giving life. It can bring death but it cannot breathe life into another and consequently it is unworthy of human devotion. It is a false god.

If one loves the Redeemer with *all* one's heart and soul and with *all* one's might, there is no room left for any other. When one promises in the marriage covenant to be a loving and faithful spouse, there is no room left for another lover or relationship. To make room in one's heart for another lover is adultery; to make room for another "center of meaning" is idolatry. The First Commandment does not require us to deny the existence of other gods, but it insists that we give them no ultimate credibility. Only God is sovereign, only God is ultimate, and only God can be an absolute.

The Second Commandment continues the theme of total allegiance to the God who redeems. It reads: "You shall not make for

2. Burggraeve et. al., *Desirable God*, 38.

yourself an idol, (graven image) whether in the form of anything that is in the heaven above, or that is in the earth beneath, or that is in the water under the earth. You shall not bow down to them or worship them" (Exod 20:4–5). Both commandments free us from being bound to any principle, institution, or ideology that originates in the human mind.

COMPETITION AMONG THE ULTIMATES

Idolatry, on the other hand, consists of claiming that something made or imagined by human beings is like God and worthy of our commitment and devotion. As this object of additional commitment evolves to the status of a god, more and more qualities of the divine are assumed and it becomes unassailable and essential, just like the Creator God. This new false god poses as another absolute that competes with the Almighty for our passions and allegiance. The masquerading new absolute makes demands of the follower and plays upon his or her desire to be powerful like the idol itself. As the bond is strengthened, the personality of the idol becomes more essential. One will go to extremes on an idol's behalf and surrender to the perceived source of well being. One develops an absolute attachment to the idol, which has come to mean not only comfort, but also omnipotence and security.[3]

The people of Israel understood that *every* image possessed an indwelling spirit that had the power to capture and demand obedience from those who considered it worthy. When one submitted to that spirit, it claimed one's own identity and who one wanted to become. A mutual bond was established between the image or the thing and the one who valued it. The idol was also dependent on the whims, beliefs, and/or superstitions of its followers. Those who revered an idol could seek deliverance and cry out, "Deliver me for you are my god" (Isa 44:17), but they could also transport the idol from place to place and make it vulnerable to be captured by enemies, discarded or lost, or thrown into the fire and/or totally desecrated.

3. Ibid., 31.

Traveling in the developing world one witnesses the power images can hold over individuals. Many turn away or hide their faces as tourists approach them with camera in hand. They are not unfriendly or anti-social; they are afraid of the camera. They believe if their image is captured, one can also capture their spirit and control them. A likeness or image in their world is perceived as power, just as it was in Moses' time in the Sinai. An image is *something more than a likeness.* It is the *essence or nature* of a person, thing, an idea or an ideology itself. Hence the Commandment: You shall not make any graven images of anything, real or abstract. You shall give ultimate trust only to God. Yes, an idol is only a thing, *but it is a thing with a spirit.*

Ancient Israel abhorred idols and idolatry because they destroyed relationships between individuals and a redeeming God, relationships between peoples within their own community, and relationships between communities. Those individuals who perceived there was ultimate value in other gods were stoned (Deut 17:2–7). Entire villages that worshipped other gods faced total annihilation. Every living thing, including the livestock, was killed and the entire village was burned to the ground (Deut 13:12–16).

COMPETING ABSOLUTES

Acknowledging another god within one's value system sets up an irreconcilable situation of competing absolutes, which is an oxymoron in itself. For an absolute means one and one only. It has been said there is more essential difference between one and two than between two and a thousand. By definition an absolute is considered "perfect in quality or nature; complete; not mixed; pure; unadulterated; not limited by restrictions or exceptions; unconditional; unqualified in extent or degree; total; not limited by constitutional provisions or other restraints; Unrelated to and independent of anything else; not to be doubted or questioned; positive; In philosophy, something seen as the ultimate basis of all thought and being."[4]

As guns become another absolute, we meet the ultimate irony. Gun enthusiasts not only insist on *as much* deference for their guns as God, they insist on *more.* In the Bible God's faithful people are

4. *American Heritage Dictionary of the English Language.*

great complainers. They do not like the way God governs the world. That one third of the book of Psalms are voices of complaint makes the point. God's people take God so seriously they fuss and complain directly to their redeemer. They also engage in periodic self-examination and confess their sins. Pro-gun people, on the other hand, entertain no public doubt or complaint about guns whatsoever, whether it be their gun or another's. When guns become absolutes questioning their ultimate value is forbidden.

These absolutists are fully committed people, but their commitment is to a *single issue: their guns.* Other matters are of small consequence, unless it is war. Personally, I can't come close to single-minded devotion. I have at least a dozen other causes that capture my attention and concern and I wrestle constantly with many shades of gray.

In the repercussions of the Virginia Tech disaster, Governor Tim Kaine appointed the Virginia Tech Review Panel to study the tragedy and make recommendations to the Virginia Assembly so another similar incident would not happen. The panel was composed of survivors of the attack, student representatives, parents of students who were killed, public officials, psychiatrists, law enforcement officers, and others.

The panel's findings caused some soul searching among public officials, one of whom was Captain Gerald Massengill, the former Police Superintendent of Virginia, who devoted his life to law enforcement. In January 2008, he testified at an open hearing before the Virginia Legislature's Justice and Courts Committee and reminded the body he had always been and continues to be a strong supporter of Second Amendment rights, but the tragedy at Blacksburg had opened his eyes to the dangers of unrestricted gun sales and had shown him the wisdom of closing the gun show loophole.

I attended that hearing and sat behind a middle-aged woman with a badge on her breast that read: "Guns Save Lives." As Capt. Massengill told the committee how Virginia Tech changed his mind on Virginia's unfettered access to guns, she gave an agonizing, audible sigh and in a stage whisper sneered, "Oh, you traitor!" When guns become absolutes, their owners entertain no grays, for their guns have supplanted God.

TRYING TO BRIDGE THE GAP

There was a moment in the 1970s when there was a flicker of hope that the chasm between the ideologies of inalienable gun rights and gun control could be bridged and some common ground discovered. The first Director of ATF, Rex Davis, convened a series of closed-door conversations between representatives from the NRA, the National Shooting Sports Foundation, Handgun Control, Inc. (later to become the Brady Campaign to Prevent Gun Violence), the National Coalition to Ban Handguns, (later to become the CSGV), law enforcement, and members of the Department of Justice. Their aim was to overcome the "rigidity" of their respective positions in order to discover some concrete ways to reduce gun violence.

Mike Beard, the President of CSGV, told me of their several meetings which were "civil, productive and hopeful." The participants reached consensus on a plan to draft a simple message about gun safety that would accompany each new gun sold. To agree on the exact wording of the message was the purpose of their final meeting. Unfortunately, the NRA representatives, with whom there had previously been openness and a good spirit of cooperation, announced their leadership had decided, "to tell anyone how to care for their own personal property was not a proper role of government." They informed everyone present there would be no further participation by the NRA in any meetings. They then walked out.

Between 1975 and 1980, the introduction of soft-body armor for law enforcement was credited with saving the lives of more than 400 officers. But, more powerful, armor-piercing bullets were introduced by the gun industry. They became known as "cop-killer bullets." Beard, ever the optimist, reached out again to the NRA to try and find common ground. In a letter to their President, Harlan Carter, he inquired if the two groups could work together on a bill banning the armor-piercing rounds that were killing so many police. The young Wayne La Pierre wrote back telling Beard to forget about any cooperation on the issue, as "A ban on those bullets found to penetrate soft body armor would undoubtedly impact on bullets used by sportsmen."[5]

---

5. Davidson, *Under Fire*, 88.

On March 14, 2011, the Obama Administration announced that the president was starting a conversation with leaders on both sides of the gun issue to try and reach a compromise on legislation to reduce gun violence. The next day, the NRA, through its familiar and now "well-seasoned" spokesperson, La Pierre, replied, "Why should we meet with those who want to take away our gun rights?"[6]

I have had only a few fleeting exchanges with those who believe "guns save lives." My sporadic attempts have been awkward and led to no substantive discussions. The most formidable barrier to honest communication has been the perception on both sides that we were standing behind ten-foot walls of suspicion. Moreover, at such times we were standing in open fields or on city sidewalks instead of sitting down together in a comfortable place and getting to know one another over a cup of coffee or a slice of pizza.

Can the church bring gun rights and public safety zealots together into the same space to start honest conversation? Can we find common ground on what has been an impasse for decades? It would not be an easy conversation and we can't find values to unite us in an hour and a half. It would require concerted efforts and a lot of good will on both sides over a long period of time. Perhaps a common faith in God could be the catalyst for an authentic conversation. Perhaps we could ask one another "what kind of society does God want for America?" The latest polls reveal the majority of gun owners and most members of the NRA would be open to such discussions. Too many people are dying unnecessarily. We must get together and talk. May God give the church the courage to take the risks and begin the conversation.

6. Jackie Calmes, "NRA Declines to Meet with Obama on Gun Policy," *New York Times*, March 14, 2011.

5

Violence Lite and Its Insatiable Observers

Those who love their guns often mockingly say: "Instead of trying to take our guns away, why don't you gun grabbers stop the violence and killing on television and in the movies. Why don't you do something about the violence that is in the music our young people listen to? That's what's wrong with America. That's where killings start. Guns don't kill; people kill." They have a point. Their criticism, at the very least, pushes us to think about our fascination with violence. Why are we so absorbed when we view violence on the athletic field, in the arena, or on our TV screens? Why are children drawn to violent toys and why do adults glorify war?

The front page of any major newspaper is full of violence or threats of future violence. Ben Bradlee, editor of the *Washington Post* is reputed to have said, "We don't cover safe landings at Dulles Airport." What then makes it into our papers? In spite of peacemaker's rhetoric and denunciations of violence, we gravitate to articles about violence in every part of the world. Some actually like it. We are used to it. It is as much a part of the American scene as McDonald's and Coca-Cola. To be candid, our lives would be rather boring without it. What kind of people would Americans become without our fascination with aggression and violence?

The Croatian theologian Miroslav Volf, in an article on "Christianity and Violence" said, "Religion is more associated with violence than with peace in the public imagination partly because the public is fascinated with violence. We, the peace loving citizens of nations whose tranquility is secured by effective policing, are *insatiable*

33

observers of violence. And as voyeurs, we show ourselves to be vicarious participants in the very violence we outwardly abhor.[1]

I recently led a series of studies on Gun Violence and Gospel Values in adult education classes at five different churches in the Greater Washington area. I often began the sessions by asking, "Do you like violence?" In each instance, there was a provocative, even embarrassing, silence until some honest soul replied, "It depends," or "sometimes." After a few reminders of today's most popular TV programs, movies and videos, and what we do for recreation, with some reluctance, virtually all of us in four of these groups agreed: in varying degrees, we *liked* violence. One class, however, refused to say they *liked it,* though they did confess, "Violence *engages* us." We then listed ways violence fascinates or engages us, and how it has become a valued, or at least, an accepted part of our daily lives. Our lists included the following subjects; the additional notes are mine.

MOVIES AND TELEVISION

Parents take their children to G- or family-rated movies but before the featured presentation, everyone watches at least ten minutes of previews that are "approved for all audiences." In spite of the G rating of the main feature, viewing these previews could give sensitive children nightmares.

In Europe, such movies are rated X because of violence. In the United States, an X-rated movie contains profanity or implicit or explicit sex. We are disturbed if our youngsters are exposed prematurely to sexuality on the screen, but we virtually ignore the effects of disproportionate violence that dominates almost every set of previews of coming attractions.

As our children mature they grow to be as fascinated by the violence in the media as adults. The head of programming at a major network was asked to describe the thinking process that influenced the network's selection of television programs. He replied: "There was no thinking process whatsoever. Television and movie producers provide whatever the ratings and box offices tell them will generate the

---

1. Volf, "Christianity and Violence," 16–17.

most immediate profit." All of which means that kids will get what interests and entertains them the most.[2]

Whether in movie theaters or on television screens, children and youth watch countless fistfights, gun fights, murders, explosions, gun battles in Afghanistan, airplane and automobile crashes, etc. Many consider them family entertainment. The American Psychological Association has warned parents that viewing these images have an adverse effect on each of us, particularly our younger set. Current scholarship verifies the link between the consumption of violent media and the development of aggressive, sadistic behavior among all age groups.

VIDEO GAMES

As much as we liked or were engaged by violence, the adult classes unanimously condemned video games such as *007 Goldeneye* and *Grand Theft Auto*, which are best defined as pathological. One scene in the latter, pictures a dad pleading for his life, saying he is the father of young children, nevertheless, he is mercilessly killed. Kids who have been bullied resort to games like this to vent their anger and hostility. As they do so they lose touch with what is real and what is not.

An array of psychologists contend some of these violent video games, which have been used as recruiting tools for the army, go way beyond youthful entertainment to simulation and teach operators to shoot and kill without a moment's hesitation. Users are taught to react when a hostile image appears, first on the screen and then on the streets of Iraq or in the mountains of Afghanistan.

Since 2006, *Call of Duty* has become a cultural institution. There are eight video games in this series, three of which are among the top sellers of all time. In 2009, the game "Modern Warfare 2" took in $310 million on its first day of sale, making it not only the biggest ever launch of a video game but the biggest launch in entertainment history. The games are described as a "visceral depiction of the immediate physical realities of war." Up through February 2011, gamers

2. Nagler, *America Without Violence*, 27.

had logged more than 2 billion hours playing *Call of Duty* online. That works out to about 229,000 years.[3]

For many, to watch the violence is not a problem. I know two young men who were in a game store when an irate grandmother tried to return a copy of *Grand Theft Auto: San Andreas,* which she purchased for her ten-year-old grandson. When she discovered it contained sexual content, she was outraged and shouted at the clerk. The murder of police, mugging of civilians, and killing of prostitutes with a baseball bat was of small importance to her, but having her ten year old exposed to sexual scenes was a scandal.

Such violence is not only captivating for youth. I once stopped at an Arlington, Virginia, 7-11 and watched a man in his late thirties or early forties play a video game set in a war zone. He used every muscle in his body as he bobbed and weaved, avoiding bullets and grenades and attacks from tanks and jets. He too was armed with a powerful weapon and was able to kill hundreds, perhaps thousands of enemies, and destroy dozens of tanks and planes before they killed him (or before the video machine got hungry for more quarters). Even though his soldier was killed in the end, he played very well. When the game was over and *literally* thousands of shots had been fired and his score was prominently recorded, he flashed a confident smile, then with a flourish, hitched up his pants. As he passed me on the way to the door, our eyes met. He remarked, "It makes you feel better, doesn't it?"

WESTERN MOVIES, COMIC BOOKS, AND CARTOON FIGURES

Some of the themes in today's comics, western movies and cartoons have changed, but many are not that much different from those of my childhood when every evening during the week, I sat mesmerized by the family radio and listened to *The Lone Ranger, The Green Hornet, Terry and the Pirates, Captain Marvel, Batman and Robin* and *Superman.*

---

3. Grossman and Narcisse, "Conflict of Interest Video Games Based on America's Real Wars are Big Business," 70–75.

The latter are still around fighting evil and appealing to an even wider audience through feature length movies.

Saturdays, I couldn't wait to get to the local theatre to see the latest exploits of Roy Rogers, Johnny Mack Brown, Hopalong Cassidy, and Tom Mix in their ongoing battles between good and evil. I could count on these honest, squeaky-clean moral champions to put the bad guys in their place. Today other new comic book heroes are introduced to our children and youth in age-appropriate books as well as videos and movies. *Spiderman, Ironman, The Flash, The X Men Series,* and *The Punisher* present what can only be called a paranoid view of reality. Bad people are out to get us and the message is crystal clear: violence is the *only* way to defeat the bad guys and right the wrongs of a sinful, dangerous world.

There are a handful of positive creations such as Art Spiegelman's Pulitzer-Prize winning *Maus,* which interprets the holocaust, and *Persepolis,* which is an autobiographical sketch of an Iranian immigrant, but they are the exceptions and not the rule.

People do not seem to tire of the same plots, where bad guys appear to be winning, placing the heroes in grave danger with no avenue of escape, but, the good guy *always* escapes, and, with superior weapons and cunning, beats the bad guys and/or blows them to smithereens. All this is not unlike Popeye who was often in dire straits before he gulped down his spinach, watched his muscles bulge, and then pulverized Bluto, who had offended Olive Oyl. The sophisticated may ridicule Popeye and his contemporary hero, but we do not disparage the good old American belief that the good guys are always going to win and their violence is expected and justified. As Tom Mix told us years ago, "Straight shooters always win."

TOYS

I recall a cartoon of an inventor who took his new creation to the CEO of a toy company. He demonstrated a little dove on wheels that carried an olive branch in its beak. The CEO said to the hopeful inventor, "You've got rocks in your head." Poor fellow. Wouldn't he have been more warmly welcomed had he demonstrated a toy tank

spewing sparks from its turret? The CEO could take *that* toy straight
to the bank.

According to the leading consumer and retail information company, The National Purchase Diary Group, U.S. retail sales of toys
generated more than $22 billion in sales in 2006 and 2007, despite
difficult economic conditions.[4] In former years big city department
stores devoted one floor for toys. Today, the toy industry has mush-
roomed so that toy stores or toy sections of larger department stores
are literally warehouses full of toys from floor to ceiling.

Some toys are creative, educational, and character building.
Others teach aggressiveness, violence, and hate. As children play with
toys, they imitate a slice of life that will become a life pattern. Through
toys, they determine who they are; how they will relate to the world;
how they will deal with conflict; and how they will solve their problems. Parents and families need to choose carefully which toys they
buy their children because what gets their attention gets them.

Two years ago, I visited the Toy Museum at the scenic Natural
Bridge, Virginia. The museum touts toys through the centuries. Their
best attraction was a section on antique toys. Most of the display
featured toys of battle scenes arranged chronologically and proved
Will Roger's observation that "Civilizations advance. In every war,
they learn to kill you a new way." Through these toys, I saw the
march of civilizations right before my eyes as the toys mirrored the
instruments grown men have used in the real world to destroy their
enemies. As I walked through history, the toys evolved from spears
to bows and arrows, toy catapults and battering rams, to knights
on horseback, to cowboys and Indians, to Civil War soldiers, to toy
tanks, flamethrowers, prop planes and then jets, submarines, and
aircraft carriers. The exhibit wound its way to the exit where Star
Wars figures and space-age, intergalactic fighters were displayed.
Needless to say, there were lots and lots of toy guns along the route,
although they did not show the new, fully automatic Nerf machine
gun that could never hurt a child, or so they say.

4. NPD Group Market Research, February 12, 2008.

LITTLE BOYS AND THEIR THUMBS
AND INDEX FINGERS

Little boys in particular are fascinated when they discover their thumb and forefinger make an instant gun. No definitive research exists as to why little girls are less driven to use their instant guns. With a simple hand movement, a little boy can go about shooting everyone and everything saying, "Bang, bang. You're dead." When you think about what is happening in that little mind, it's not so cute.

Recently, one of my friends responded to a financial appeal from CSGV. She enclosed a note with her check saying she was happy to support our efforts and told us she still thinks about the tragedy that took place in her neighborhood several years before. She hasn't been able to get Robby out of her mind. He was a precious little neighbor boy who liked to play "bang-bang, you're dead" with his daddy when he came home from work. His father, with dramatic flare, would always fall to the floor, pretending to be shot. It was such fun for both of them and it gave occasion for many laughs and hugs. Because it was such fun, before his daddy came home from work one afternoon, the boy got a chair and climbed up into his parent's closet to get his daddy's pistol that he kept there to protect the family from harm. When the father walked through the door he was greeted by his son who said, "bang-bang, you're dead" and pulled a real trigger. This time his daddy didn't get back up and laugh and give him a hug. The mother was initially charged with negligence, but was later exonerated. My friend remarked, "Robby almost lost two parents."

SPORTS

Anyone who cannot see a growing violence in our contact sports is not paying attention. I heard of one college football coach who was insulted when someone described football as a "contact sport." Said he, "Dancing is a contact sport; football is a collision sport." Most of us love it, don't we? I once heard Joe Gibbs, the Hall of Fame Football Coach of the Washington Redskins remark, "Anyone who doesn't like football or NASCAR is brain dead." Those who like the game are exhilarated when there is a jarring block or tackle on an opponent.

The home team players "chest bump" and the spectators exchange "high fives." Can we admit that at times we are pleased when the opponent's quarterback is carried off the field because our team's chances of winning increase?

I played high school football in the 1950s and was one of the larger players at one hundred and ninety pounds. Today's players are much bigger, faster, and stronger than they were sixty years ago. It is not unusual for many colleges to field teams whose linemen all weigh over three hundred pounds and can run like the wind. Doctors today are paying closer attention to physics in this "collision sport." So is Roger Goodell, Commissioner of the National Football League, who is asking retired football players to will their brains to Boston University for a study on concussions, which are increasing each year at all levels of the game.[5]

I love to watch football and ice hockey. I'm a conflicted Washington Capitals fan, because there are so many fights on the ice. I've never liked boxing because the purpose of the sport is to hurt one's opponent. But, at hockey games I'm perfectly comfortable watching that which I dislike.

In spite of the violence in sports in which aggression is praised and required, I find it both ironic and amusing to hear Christian football players say the Lord Jesus would have been all pro on the gridiron. One college lineman, who loved his Redeemer, observed, "Jesus would have been a great football player. He would have put people on their butts."

I don't think Jesus would have been aggressive enough to be a good football player, and I reject the idea my Lord would get joy out of "putting people on their butts." In 1963, my two-year-old daughter, Mebane, knew something wasn't quite right about people putting others on their butts. When she caught a glimpse of a football game on our black and white TV, she said in disbelief, "Daddy, that man knocked that other man down!" All of this, notwithstanding, don't think for a minute that I will miss the next Redskin's football game. Violence lite is exciting; it engages me, and I like it. I just wish some Christians would simply enjoy the game without trying to baptize the violence.

5. "NFL Partnering with BU Study," New York Times, December 20, 2009.

MIXED MARTIAL ARTS

It is popularly called, "Ultimate Fighting," a mixture of boxing, kick-boxing and wrestling, as men fight like gladiators in an octagon, or more accurately, a cage. It makes boxing rather tame. The contestants hit and kick one another, until one of them usually falls to the mat with his opponent on top of him. He then pummels the man who is down, trying to knock him unconscious. The ultimate fight continues until time runs out or one of the "gladiators" is unconscious or so badly injured he cannot continue. Mixed martial arts is bloody but "spectators pay an average of $276 for a ticket, with front-row seats going for as much as $10,000. The massive pay-per-view television audience generated more than $276 million in 2008."[6]

NASCAR

While the masses are enthralled with the speed of the cars and skill of the drivers, I am cynical enough to believe this huge spectator sport's fan base would drop significantly if there were no big crashes and pileups. That is what makes it exciting. The grandstands at NASCAR races are also good vantage points to see good fistfights between drivers whose cars have been "bumped out of contention." How different is NASCAR from the chariot races of a bygone age in Rome or Spain where center cities were constructed around the ovals of their racetracks and the spectators expected several spectacular pileups?

PAINTBALL GAMES

In paintball, contestants can play on their own in the woods or pay for entrance to a commercial course where they shoot projectiles of paint at one another. Contestants are never up close and personal when the paint explodes on another's body and people are encouraged not to shoot at someone's head. The paint on someone's body stops cold all arguments as to whether or not one has been hit. Some churches sponsor paintball parties for their youth groups because

6. Broyles, "Turn from Violence," 44.

"the kids just love them." There are those who defend paintball games and say guns are not used, but their websites call them guns and the results are obviously the same. I can hear the kids now, "Oh, come on, Mom. It's just a fun game; we just *pretend* to kill our buddies."

HUNTING FOR BAMBI

This is the brainchild of Michael Birdick of Las Vegas and has drawn world attention. It's a new form of adult entertainment. Men are paying anywhere from $5,000 to $10,000 for the opportunity to come to the desert and shoot naked women with a paintball gun. The women are not allowed to wear any protective gear, nothing except tennis shoes. So why do women agree to strip down and run naked around the desert dodging paintballs? One of the women said, "It's good money. I mean it's $2,500 if you don't get hit and it's $1,000 if you do."[7]

ARE THERE DOTS TO CONNECT VIOLENCE LITE WITH WAR AND GUN VIOLENCE?

The consensus of the classes was: we do not like *excessive* violence, but we enjoy violence lite. It makes life more exciting. I plead guilty to being fascinated with it. I'm a regular voyeur. And you? Do you watch crime movies on television? Is there a connection between violence lite and the violence inherent in war? Is there a link between violence lite and the 30,000 gun deaths every year which we say we abhor? Can we coolly dismiss such questions as irrelevant? Is it a stretch to link toys, sports, movies, and videos, etc., to gun violence, murder, and mayhem? Is there more to violence lite than meets the eye? Whenever we talk about violence we are on a continuum. I argue there are dots to connect between violence lite and our fascination for weapons of war and those three million handguns that come off our assembly lines this year.

7. KLAS TV (Las Vegas), July 15, 2003.

Some act as if violence is only an incidental facet of human personality and like a light switch, we can turn it on or off, depending on our needs or whims. Not so. Violence is a pervasive spirit that touches and affects everything we do and everything we are. It is a spirit loose in the world and like the genie that escapes, it cannot be crammed back into the bottle where we can keep it out of sight and out of mind. Violence captivates, thrills and fascinates us, and it starts beguiling us early in life, often when we hear our first boom and watch the first victim fall. Having the power to dominate others is fascinating and addictive. It gives us a thrill even if we are just pretending. On a trip to China in 2008, I picked up a copy of the *South China Morning Post* and read "Philippines Haunted by Its Long Love Affair with Guns." An army private commented, "When you fire a gun, it's like eating delicious food—especially when you hit an enemy. I love guns."[8]

The Rev. David R. Taylor, former pastor of the Simpsonville Presbyterian Church in South Carolina, tells of making a pastoral call on a young family that had moved to the community. As he talked with the parents, their four-year-old boy pulled out two toy guns from his play chest and innocently went around the room play-shooting everyone. That visit was on the very day the video of the killer at Virginia Tech pointing guns at the camera was plastered all over the airwaves. It was more than Taylor could take. He comments: "We say 'boys will be boys,' and most boys don't grow up to be killers. But far too many do. Is there a connection? With forty-one school shootings in the last ten years, can we safely assume there isn't?"[9]

Vernon Broyles, writing in his monthly column for *Presbyterians Today,* asks a pertinent question: "Many people of faith dare with some frequency, to call this a 'Christian nation.' Polls continue to show most Americans hold some religious faith, with Christianity claimed most often. How then does our self-identification as followers of the Prince of Peace relate to what can at least minimally be called a fascination with violence?"[10] Every church officers' group in America should discuss his question.

8. "Philippines Haunted by Its Long Love Affair with Guns," *South China Morning Post,* May 21, 2008.

9. Taylor, "Reflections on the Virginia Tech Massacre," April 22, 2007.

10. Broyles, "Turn From Violence," 44.

6

The Language of
a Gun Culture

The sign over a souvenir shop on a London street read: "English is spoken here. American is understood." If Americans want to understand our fascination with violence, we must also understand that our language is shaped by our gun culture. Indeed, the socialization of violence in America, particularly for boys and men, comes from our language. Sometimes the impact of language on culture is subtle; other times, dramatic. People are increasingly aware that violence in movies, TV, video games, and some rap music has a lasting negative effect on our youth. Violent words and idioms in our everyday speech have a similar effect. The philosopher Jean-Paul Sartre seemed to think violent words encourage violent acts: "Words are loaded pistols," he said.

I confess I can't speak English without garnishing my conversations with words and phrases that refer to guns, killing and violence, and I really try not to. I'm not alone. Recently, the Honorable Hillary Clinton, Secretary of State, who has worked diligently to bring the Palestinians and Israelis to the negotiating table said, "We have a shot at peace in the Middle East."[1] The first time Ms. Clinton used that phrase, she was probably in elementary school and it became habitual. She also learned that "It's a straight shot from First Street to City Hall."

American English is chockablock full of violent terms. I'm not referring to the spicy language of Marine drill sergeants or macho-types, but to the everyday language of office workers, Sunday school teachers, PTA officers, moms, nuns, college professors of English, and

1. CNN Wire Staff, September 8, 2010.

clergy. I'd wager the reader cannot engage in free-flowing conversation without using phrases, idioms and expressions which reference guns, explosions, or killing. A sampling of these words and phrases can be found below.

big shot	shoot for the moon	have gun will travel
supershot	hot shot	going great guns
on a hit list	sharpshooter	I'll give it my best shot.
He's shell shocked.	shoot me for a billy goat	shot to hell
Where is your piece?	You call the shots.	gang bang
gat (slang for a gun)	shoot the works	shoot up the joint
went off like a gun	the target audience	He's packin' heat.
a bang of a good time	right on target	off target
hit the bull's-eye	my aim was off	forewarned is forearmed
Praise Lord, pass ammo	shot down	lock, stock, and barrel
gun shy	the smoking gun	shooting fish in barrel
We reached a stand off.	trigger an idea	trigger happy
Is it a trigger for you?	brush teeth with gunpowder	Don't jump the gun.
a shotgun wedding	she blew me away	go off half-cocked
hire a trouble shooter	She's a pistol.	pistol whipped
pistol-packin' mama	a notch in the gun belt	Stick to your guns.
I'll be a son of a gun	take true aim	sure shot
Go off with a bang.	We dodged a bullet.	The senator is under fire.
going postal	She went ballistic.	shoot to the top
a scattershot approach	It's a long shot.	shooting the bull
It's just a warning shot.	a shot over his bow	At the wrong end of the barrel
pulling the trigger	shoot from the hip	He's a straight shooter,
a shot to the head(boxer)	keep firing	Adam is their big gun.
fast as a speeding bullet	The whole shooting match.	take a shot in the dark

What weapons to use?	High-caliber person	pop a cap
bite the bullet	not with a bang-but a whimper	Who's riding shotgun?
He blew his brains out.	blow it to smithereens	the third bullet on the page
an arm like a cannon	He shot through the line	an explosive personality
pull out the big guns	shot down an argument	shoot holes in one's talk
loaded for bear	He is grace under fire.	Questions? Fire away.
He got flak over that.	Questions? OK, shoot.	What are we aiming at?
He's out gunning for me	He's shooting blanks.	We were outgunned.
we're shooting for gold	ammunition for my talk	shot at from every angle
He's a hired gun	He shot his mouth off	We killed them, 42–0
Nice kill, Sam.	Shoot me an e-mail.	A double-barrel approach
look down the barrel of a gun	blast off	She's a blast
We're having a blast.	torpedo an idea	I bombed out.
We oughta nuke 'em.	give me some cover	bombarded by questions
Now, here's the killer.	Where are the land mines?	Let's get fired up.
aiming to kill	Do that and I'll kill you.	fire at will
fire when ready	a rocket in my pocket	draw a bead on you
Got you in the crosshairs.	sounds like a booby trap	a straight shot to the city
duck and cover	It will backfire on us.	We'll have a shootout.
Got him in our sights.	two shots to the end zone	rapid-fire questions
No magic bullets	the silver bullet	shotgun formation
He's in the gun.	She knocked 'em dead.	the plan of attack
bang-bang play at first	don't shoot the messenger	The guy needs killin'.
fry him in the electric chair	took pot shots at me	not a shotgun approach
go to a gun fight with a knife	more bang for your buck	young gun (new leader)
He's got guns (biceps).	He's a loose cannon.	Bombs away!

Don't retreat—reload	gunboat diplomacy	He was ambushed.
Bang, bang, shoot-em-up	overshot the runway	shoot myself in the foot
I'm all shot (tired).	got a shot at a good job	a shot of whisky
The storm blew up our plans	hit man	open season
We're under the gun	kill the bill	he blew up
a shooting duck	a shooting gallery	shoot the rapids
my back's killing me	he killed the bottle	killing time
it killed the taste	a killer instinct	kill two birds with one stone
want him dead or alive	ready - aim - fire	stand your ground
shoot to kill	shoot 'em up movie	Let's blow this pop stand

George Lakoff, Professor of Cognitive Science and Linguistics at the University of California, Berkeley, has written numerous books on the cognitive unconscious. He says that every word we hear activates a collection of frames in our brains. He contends that "most people are shocked to discover that most of our thought—an estimated 98 percent—is not conscious at all. It is what our brains are doing that we cannot see or hear. This is the cognitive unconscious, and the scientific evidence for its existence is overwhelming."[2]

I read of a little boy who found some flowers in a wastebasket at home. He asked his mother why they were there. She replied, "Because they're dead. I threw them out." He replied, "Well, who shot them?"

The most thrilling part of parenting is shaping the moral imagination of children and helping them to create the frames of a good, new world. "God created the world with words . . . This is the first invocation of the Torah's beliefs in the reality of words which have the power to create and the power to destroy."[3]

I referred earlier to that sign in London that the British speak English and understand American. For the most part Brits understand

2. Lakoff, *Don't Think of an Elephant*.
3. Hayim, *Torah and Commentary*, 4.

the terms listed above and occasionally use them, but colloquial British English has but a few words and phrases that refer to guns, violence, and killing. I've been told neither the French nor the Spanish languages employ such a large volume of violent terms in their every-day conversations.

Yvonne Grandaux Miller, a French educator who works for the United Nations, is a personal friend. I gave her lists of these terms and asked her to compare them with any similar expressions in her own French language. She replied: "I just got back from France. I asked my relatives and friends about daily conversational phrases that would include gun-related language but we did not come up with much. When I told folks about your list of expressions, everyone shook their heads in disbelief before the conversation immediately shifted to a discussion on Columbine or Virginia Tech. People asked, 'Why do Americans feel like they need guns?'"

The words we use are not neutral. It's commonplace to hear a family member say, "I'm so angry I could shoot you," or "She made me so mad I could kill her." Small children, the mentally ill, as well as intelligent, gentle people are influenced by such words. Could violence be so much a part of our culture that we are totally unaware of the explosive power of the words we speak?

And what of the words we sing? Music gives them an even greater impact. Martin Luther often said he cared little about who preached the sermons, for a cleric's words would soon be forgotten, but he cared intensely about who wrote the hymns. Words that are sung long remain in the singer's heart and mind.

D'Angelo, one of the founding fathers of the neo-soul movement in the mid- to- late 1990s has a song called *Forty-four Blues*. It is about a man who walked all over town carrying his .44-caliber gun looking for his lover and the man who stole her away from him. Such sentiments stay in the mind. And what of the little ditties children pick up at school? When my children were in elementary school they sang almost non-stop a nonsensical song that included the words: "I met my teacher at the door with a loaded .44 and she ain't my teacher no more." To be sure, not everyone who sings such lyrics turns into a murderer, but a seed is planted in the mind that guns put authority figures on level ground and solve human problems.

"Jingle bells, Jingle bells, Santa Claus is dead. Rudolph took a .45 and shot him in the head." These were words Dan Giosta sang almost fifty years ago. When I mentioned this subject to him, it took only a split second for him to recall the words and sing them again.

As one of my colleagues said at a National Capital Presbytery meeting, "Words matter. Words can assault or comfort; they can abandon or nurture; words build walls or tear them down; words can control or set us free; words criticize but they can also encourage; words darken, yet illuminate the darkness; words can hide the truth—words can reveal truth; words can kill and words can bring new life; words reject but words also embrace; our words can scatter, they can also gather; words can heal or they can hurt."[4]

USING VIOLENT WORDS TO MOTIVATE SUPPORTERS OR CRITICIZE OPPONENTS

The vitriolic language of national leaders who have turned its use into an art form and become motivational speakers distresses me. Their harsh words can incite a riot. Sarah Palin, former Governor of Alaska, hunter, and NRA Board Member, has been particularly irresponsible: "Don't retreat; reload," she counseled followers and on her website she placed the crosshairs of gun sights on the pictures or names of legislators she wanted to defeat. When one's passionate followers are encouraged to "get in the face" of opponents, some of them plan attacks. On April 11, 2010, Palin added a disclaimer on her website, stating, "And that's not a call for violence."

One of the candidates Ms. Palin was intent on defeating was Arizona Congresswoman, Gabby Giffords, who had voted for Health-care Reform. To show toughness on the issues, Gifford's electoral opponent, Randy Graf, offered financial donors the chance to shoot a fully automatic M-16. After opponents destroyed her Tucson office, Giffords said: "Our national pride is we effect change at the ballot box and not through outbursts of violence. We're on Sarah Palin's targeted list, but the thing is that the way she has depicted it, has

4. Rev. Yena Hwang, sermon fragment, National Capital Presbytery, April 30, 2011.

the crosshairs of a gun right over our district. When people do that, they've got to realize there are consequences to that action."[5]

Representative Giffords was shot on January 10, 2011, as an unstable young man armed with a Glock 19 murdered six of her constituents and staff. There is no hard evidence to link Jared Loughner's murders and attempted murder of Rep. Gabriel Gifford to violent words, but the tragedy in Tucson should make us all aware of that possibility. Are we more aware today after Ted Nugent, NRA Board Member rails, "If Barack Obama becomes president in November again, I will either be dead or in jail by this time next year."[6]

I'm convinced the inflammatory language of talk show hosts have caused the rise of armed militias in America, which have tripled in number in 2009, growing 245 percent. In March of last year nine members of the "Christian militia" in Michigan were arrested for plotting to kill law enforcement officers, whom they said are "the foot soldiers of the federal government." They had hoped their actions would spark a national uprising. These "Christians" are members of only one of the 512 armed militias and hate groups in the country.[7]

We should listen again to the third chapter of James: "With the tongue we bless the Lord and Father, and with it we curse those who are made in the likeness of God. From the same mouth come blessing and cursing. My brothers and sisters, this ought not so to be. Does a spring pour forth from the same opening both fresh and brackish water? Can a fig tree, my brothers and sisters, yield olives, or a grapevine, figs? No more can salt water yield fresh" (Jas 3:9–12).

In the Bible, Job says to Bildad, "How long will you torment me, and break me in pieces with words?" Floyd Patterson, former world heavyweight boxing champion could relate to Job. When Patterson died the New York Times published a lengthy obituary noting what a sensitive person he was. He was once quoted, "You can hit me and I won't think much of it, but you can say something to me and hurt me very much."[8]

5. Representative Gabrielle Giffords, interview by MSNBC, March 25, 2010.

6. Peter Grier, "Decoder Wire." April 17, 2012.

7. Mark Potok of the Southern Poverty Law Center, interviewed on the Diane Rehm Show, National Public Radio, March 31, 2010.

8. "Floyd Patterson, Boxing Champion Dies at 71," New York Times, May 12, 2006.

I challenge us all to think about the words we use in daily conversation and to remove the most violent from our vocabularies. We could take some risks and call attention to one another's use of violent words and phrases. If we confess our own struggles and use humor, raising a question or two about word choices might help create a kinder and gentler society. Who knows? The truth is that where violence is a problem, words really matter.

7

Violence in Our DNA

Our country started keeping records of gun deaths in 1933. Since then, 1.7 million Americans have died at a gun barrel. But the most compelling statistic I know is that more American citizens were killed with guns in the eighteen-year period between 1979 and 1997 (651,697) than all servicemen and women killed in battle in all of the United States' wars since 1775 (650,858).[1] (Should these numbers appear "inflated" or unbelieveable, please consult Appendix 1 for a full accounting.)

VIOLENCE: THE ETHOS OF OUR TIMES

People in other developed countries cannot understand why we not only tolerate the violence but accept it as part of the American way. Nevertheless, gun deaths can never be understood in isolation. They must always be examined in the larger context of violence itself. Biblical scholar Walter Wink says,

> Violence is the ethos of our times. It is the spirituality of the modern world. It has been accorded the status of a religion, demanding from its devotees an absolute obedience to death. Its followers are not aware, however, that the devotion they pay to violence is a form of religious piety. Violence is successful as a myth precisely because it does not seem to be mythic in the least. Violence simply appears to be the nature of things. It is what works. It is inevitable, the last, and often, the first resort in conflicts. It is embraced with equal alacrity by people on the left and on the right,

1. FBI Statistics and Department of Defense Records.

by religious liberals and religious conservatives. The threat of violence, it is believed, alone can deter aggressors. Some would argue the threat of nuclear annihilation has bought the world sixty-six years of peace. Violence is thriving as never before in every sector of American popular culture, civil religion, nationalism, and foreign policy. Violence, not Christianity, is the real religion of America.[2]

We can probably all agree that violence is thriving in the United States as never before. How did we get to this point? Danish theologian Soren Kierkegaard wrote, "Life must be lived forward, but it can only be understood backward."

CLAIMING TO BE A CHRISTIAN NATION GIVES BIRTH TO VIOLENCE

Our trust in violence did not sneak up on us with 9/11 or while we were simultaneously fighting two wars in Iraq and Afghanistan. Our trust in violence is linked to our founding fathers and our curious national myth that Almighty God ordained the United States to be "the trustees of the world's progress," "the guardian of its righteous peace," and even "Christ's light for the salvation of the world."[3]

In 1850, when Herman Melville wrote his novel *White Jacket*, he reminded the world that America held a special place in the heart of God:

> And we Americans are the peculiar, chosen people—the Israel of our time; we bear the ark of the liberties of the world. Long enough have we been skeptics with regard to ourselves, and doubted whether, indeed, the political Messiah had come. But he has come *in us*, if we would give utterance to his promptings.[4]

My first awareness that I too, in the minds of others, was supposed to "bear the ark" of the world's liberties was in a receiving line

2. Wink, *Engaging the Powers*, 13.
3. *The Annals of America*, vol. XII, 343.
4. Quoted in Jewett, *Captain America Complex*, 9.

for newly commissioned Presbyterian missionaries at the Montreat (North Carolina) Conference Center in August of 1965. A lovely, gracious woman shook our hands and said to my wife and me, "We are so glad that people like you are going to Japan to represent the United States of America." We were stunned to hear her equate our missionary work in Japan with advancing the national goals of the United States of America. Our understanding was we were going to Japan as ambassadors for Christ, not Washington.

As American Christians link together our nation and our faith the integrity of both are compromised—not only in American minds, but in the minds of the people with whom we work in other nations. In Japan, my wife and I heard on occasion, "Missionary, go home."

Jakov Jukic, a Croatian sociologist of religion, says, "At the heart of monotheism itself is an exclusivity which is bound to have a violent legacy. The argument goes: 'We,' the faithful, have on our side the one true God and we stand in opposition to 'them,' the infidels and renegades."[5] Believing we were doing God's work gave our Anglo-Saxon forebears the chutzpah to walk through the new world in "ten-league boots," running roughshod over Native American peoples, supporting the institution of slavery, and subjugating peoples of other lands as we attempted to bring them "civilization" and "salvation." Our forebears understood that using our power and deadly force, which itself was believed to be "a gift from God," was not only acceptable, but expected and the right thing to do. Millions of us continue to believe that. It is the spirituality of militarism and a subconscious need to be considered "armed and dangerous."

Robert Jewett says,

> Biblical zeal offers an astounding mystique for violence, which makes it seem plausible that righteous violence could redeem other people, demonstrate one's superiority over rival forces, and even convert the world. This mystique clarifies the proximity of destruction and conversion, and it justifies the most appalling atrocities against alien persons and objects. It is believed that violence can even produce peace. With an appeal of this magnitude, it is logical that the grounds for violence so often seem self-evident. It also

5. Quoted in Volf, "Christianity and Violence," 8.

follows that a culture schooled in this tradition will exhibit extremely high levels of violence in both individual and collective behavior.[6]

Every American of every religious persuasion has been taught, overtly or covertly, that we are "a Christian nation." Actually, the idea itself was *officially rejected* in 1797 when the Senate and President John Adams signed a treaty declaring, "The United States is not a Christian nation any more than it is a Jewish or Mohammedan nation."[7]

For most Americans, it makes little difference that we are not officially a "Christian nation." It *is* a comforting thought for most of us, even for those who never go to church. From elementary school we have learned our earliest settlers came here to worship and serve God. On examination, their motives, however, were not so selfless or devout. "The first English settlers arrived on these shores in search of gold, not God," writes Jon Meacham.[8]

Meacham cites the First Charter of Virginia, which was "lovely, the sentiments warm, the king's expectation clear." Issuing the document to the Virginia Company of London April 10, 1606, King James I said he was "happy to bless so noble a work" in the hope that the mission to the New World would carry the "Christian religion to such people as yet live in darkness and miserable ignorance of the true knowledge and worship of God."

"With the Lord out of the way," writes Meacham,

> James quickly turned to mammon and his immediate concerns. The company was to take possession of "all the Lands, Woods, Soil, Grounds, Havens, Ports, Rivers, Mines, Minerals, Marshes, Waters, Fishings, Commodities"—and on and on, for three paragraphs. Then came the order to "dig, mine, and search for all Manner of Mines of Gold, Silver, and Copper. To defend the enterprise, no Robbery or Spoil would ever go unpunished, and the company was authorized to pursue with hostility, the said offenders in the

6. Jewett, *The Captain America Complex*, 182.

7. President John Adams, quoted in Al Gore, *The Assault on Reason*, 49.

8. Meacham, *American Gospel*, 41.

event of plunder." The charter is 3,805 words long; 98 of the words are about God.[9]

I once saw depicted two Puritans on the deck of a ship about to land in the new world. One says to his friend, "My immediate goal is to enjoy my freedom of worship, but my long-term goal is to go into real estate."

There is little doubt that America's readiness to use violence to keep our nation and/or our homes safe and secure, stems from our confidence that "we are a Christian nation" and a good and generous people whose motives are beyond reproach. Such self-understanding gives birth to a sure sense of privilege to use any means necessary to advance the cause of democracy and freedom as well as to protect our homes and private property. Such is the work of patriots. Because we are a good and generous people, the violence we may be forced to use to accomplish God's purposes is not to be considered deplorable, only necessary. In the final analysis violence can be praised and glorified, even construed as redemptive. Nothing is nobler than defending the honor of our Creator, protecting our precious families, or safeguarding the cause of freedom and democracy. Using violence when necessary in support of these righteous causes is not only justified, it is a moral obligation.

OUR BIBLICAL AND THEOLOGICAL WARRANT TO CONQUER

At the beginning of the twentieth century, a zealous patriotism gripped the country to the point that even the U.S. Congress adjourned so elected representatives could march in the parade of the 1910 Convention of the World Sunday School Association. At the climactic moment of the convention two Sunday school leaders, one American, one British, stood on the platform. Suddenly two other men raced up from the audience and draped the Union Jack around the shoulders of the man from Britain and the Stars and Stripes around the American. The American was moved to say, "We have honor for all the flags of this world, but under these two flags the

9. Ibid., 42.

Anglo-Saxon people have upon themselves the responsibility under God of being the big brother to all the other flags."[10]

Where did these big brothers get their information that England and the United States had been selected by the Creator to be God's General Managers of the world? Even before the Puritans set sail for the new world these devout people believed God would help them conquer the promised land across the ocean, which, like the biblical Canaan, was filled with milk and honey. They realized, however, they would have to fight for it just as Joshua and his armies fought the Amorites, the Hittites, the Perizzites, the Canaanites, the Hivites, and the Jebusites and utterly destroyed them as they claimed the land of Canaan for God and God's people.

One of the bloodiest chapters of the Bible (Josh 11) summarizes these battles and records Israel's faith that God authorized, legitimized, and led them to destroy whole tribes, villages, and peoples. Biblical scholar Walter Brueggemann contextualizes this difficult chapter as he pictures a ragtag band of landless and ill-equipped immigrants having to fight the mighty kings of the region who had horses without number and iron chariots . . . and these poor immigrants won the battles by hamstringing the horses and burning the chariots.[11]

Our forebears of the seventeenth century read these words in Joshua as a literal call from God to go and do likewise. After the Revolutionary War, America's confidence and feelings of superiority over Europeans grew immeasurably. John Adams's letter to Thomas Jefferson on November 13, 1813 claimed almost millennial sainthood on all Americans: "Many hundred years must roll away before we shall be corrupted. Our pure, virtuous, public spirited, federative republic will last forever, govern the globe and introduce the perfection of man."[12]

Josiah Strong, the Secretary of the American Home Missionary Society, in 1885 clearly defined our mission and manifest destiny: "The evangelizing of the American West was to place the stamp of Christ on the *entire world.*" No shrinking violet, Strong declared the

10. *World-wide Sunday School Work*, 46–47.

11. Brueggemann, *Divine Presence Amid Violence*, 20.

12. John Adams, letter to Thomas Jefferson, November 13, 1813. Quoted online: American Heritage.com, October 17, 2006.

Anglo-Saxon peoples represent the great ideas of civil liberty and "pure spiritual Christianity." God is preparing them with their prosperity and their power "to be the die with which to stamp the peoples of the earth." Strong wrote, "This race has been honored not for its own sake but for the sake of the world. It has been made powerful not to make subject, but to serve; Free not simply to exult in freedom, but to make free; exalted not to look down, but to lift up."[13]

Such generous rhetoric, flavored with the powerful sense of cultural and racial superiority, would inevitably lead to warfare against all those who did not want to be subjugated and were therefore described as opposed to civilization and progress. Jewett asks, "What other alternative would there be when lesser nations resisted the 'stamp' of Anglo-Saxon civilization?"[14]

Americans have always been preoccupied with progress of every kind—biological, industrial, technological, and cultural, as well as spiritual and moral. We have assumed our riches, development, and advancements to be further evidence of God's favor and proof of our national virtue.[15] Progress also meant acquiring more territory, such as in the nearby provinces of Mexico and the rich Philippine Islands. It was simply beyond comprehension that the blessings of America's ideals would be contained by national boundaries. Surely a benevolent Creator did not intend such blessings for only a few; expansion was seen as a divinely ordered means of extending enlightenment to despot-ridden masses. As one said, "This was not imperialism; it was a kind of enforced salvation."[16]

When the Filipinos resisted our colonial designs, brutal coercion was used. Estimates of deaths for Filipinos in the Spanish-American War vary widely. Some list them as low as 34,000; others as high as one million.[17] It was brutal enough that scores of Christian ministers challenged our growing expansionism and reminded the nation that Jesus' Great Commission to carry the gospel to all the nations did not mean proselytizing with guns and dynamite.

13. Jewett, The Captain America Complex, 43.

14. Ibid.

15. J. F. Maclear, quoted in Robert Jewett, The Captain America Complex, 42.

16. Quoted in ibid., 188.

17. Steele and Goldenberg, The Guardian, March 18, 2008.

Charles Adams, the great-grandson of our second president, was offended by the clergy questioning national motives and replied with disdain:

> The clergymen have all got hold of the idea of Duty; we have a *Mission*; it is the distinct call of the Almighty. They [the clergymen] want to go out, and have this Great Nation [export] the blessings of Liberty and the Gospel to other Inferior Races, who wait for us, as for their Messiah—only we must remember to take with us lots of shotguns to keep those other Superior Races—all wolves in sheep's clothing —away from our flock. They would devour them; but we won't. Oh no!—such ideas are "pessimistic," you should have more faith in the American people!—Such can't!—It does make me tired.[18]

Adams had a kindred spirit in Senator Alfred Beveridge of Indiana. Speaking before the Union League Club in New York City, he thundered:

> American manhood today contains the master adminis- trators of the world and they go forth for the healing of the nations. They go forth in the cause of civilization. They go forth for the betterment of man. They go forth, and the word on their lips is Christ and his peace, not conquest and its pillage. They go forth to prepare the peoples, through decades and maybe centuries of patient effort, for the great gift of American institutions. They go forth not for imperial- ism, but for the Greater Republic.[19]

Beveridge issued a caveat: "Lasting peace in the Philippines can be secured *only* by overwhelming forces in ceaseless action un- til universal and absolutely final defeat is inflicted on the enemy." If some people charge our conduct of the war has been cruel, one must keep in mind we are dealing with Orientals. They mistake kind- ness for weakness, forbearance for fear. To the protest from other circles that use of such violence was antithetical to the Declaration of Independence, he insisted it "applies only to people capable of

18. Albright, *The Mighty and the Almighty*, 25.
19. *The Annals of America*, vol. XII, 336–45.

self-government, not to these Malay children of barbarism. Almighty God has marked the American people as His chosen nation to finally lead in the regeneration of the world."[20]

It wasn't the first time nations asserted their right to rule others, nor would it be the last. The last Kaiser, Wilhelm II, announced that the German people were the chosen of God, and not this upstart country across the Atlantic. He was convinced he had a divine right to be in charge. In a speech to his troops in Berlin, August 4, 1914, he said: "Remember the German people are chosen by God. On me as the German Emperor, the spirit of God has descended. I am his weapon, his sword, his vice regent. Woe to the disobedient and death to cowards and unbelievers."[21]

Boasting of God's favor and claiming hegemony is not confined to the Anglo Saxon or Teutonic peoples. Holland, Italy, Portugal, Spain and France, among others, were equally driven to bring civilization and salvation to "the heathen" and raise their flags over other's lands. China and Japan are prime examples of Asian hegemony, although they were more moderate in claiming divine guidance. The desire to rule other people is in everyone's DNA. Once people dare to add God's name to those potent genes an even more sinister drive is forthcoming.

The beautiful Saint Francis Cathedral in Santa Fe, New Mexico, houses an evocative statue of the Virgin Mary carried by the Conquistadors who, with their guns and armor, overpowered the native peoples of the Southwest in the name of Spain and the Roman Catholic Church. The statue is called, *Our Lady of the Conquistadors, Our Lady of Peace.* How many look at that statue and think the Conquistadors were there in the name of peace?

I must be honest and confess the first time I saw the statue, I was unable to grasp its meaning. Only after later reflection did I realize I was deaf, dumb, and blind before an outrage. Thousands, like myself, continue to stare at that statue, and only a precious few are troubled, fewer still wonder if violence can ever be a part of God's plans for peace and the world's salvation.

20. Ibid.

21. http://christsassembly.com/literature/reminder_from_the_kaiser.htm.

WHY DO AMERICANS INSIST ON MORE VIOLENCE TODAY?

Why do American people need such enormous levels of firepower in both weapons of war and domestic handguns? Why do we need extended magazines for semi-automatic weapons filled with cop-killer bullets to penetrate so-called bulletproof vests? Why do law-abiding citizens *need* silencers for their guns, or grenades, or the latest assault weapons that are issued to the 101st Airborne and the U.S. Marines?

The late Myrtle Brock, a high school history teacher in Jones County, North Carolina, understood that the past is prologue. She wisely counsels, "To know nothing of the past is to understand little of the present and to have no conception of the future."[22] If Jesus' church can internalize those sentiments and understand there are dots to connect between America's violent past and our current faith in the tools of violence, then, and only then, is there *some* hope Americans may be able to repent (i.e. change direction) and discover what the Apostle Paul called, "a still more excellent way [of love]" (1 Cor 12:31b).

Our country has from its beginnings always publicly declared our goals are not for dominion, but for world peace and security. Nevertheless, right-wing gospel preacher, the Rev. Pat Robertson of the 700 Club, speaks for millions and believes otherwise. In his television programs he has repeatedly proclaimed, "There will never be world peace until God's house and God's people are given their rightful place of leadership at the top of the world."[23]

Jim Wallis of *Sojourners* quotes political analyst William Kristol of the influential *Weekly Standard,* who readily admits the U.S. aspiration to empire: "If people want to say we're an imperial power, fine." Kristol is chair of the Project for the New American Empire, a group of conservative political figures that began in 1997 to chart a much more aggressive American foreign policy. The project's papers lay out the vision of an "American peace" based on "unquestioned U.S. military pre-eminence." These imperial visionaries write, "America's

22. Brock's name and this quote are part of a display in Mattock's Hall of the North Carolina Education Center at Tryon Palace, New Bern, NC.

23. "The Rise of the Religious Right in the Republican Party," www.theocracy watch.com.

grand strategy should aim to preserve and extend this advantageous position as far into the future as possible." It is imperative, in their view, for the United States to "accept responsibility for America's unique role in preserving and extending an international order friendly to our security, our prosperity, and our principles."

Wallis writes, "In the run-up to the war with Iraq, Kristol told me that Europe was now unfit to lead because it was 'corrupted by secularism,' as was the developing world, which was 'corrupted by poverty.' Only the United States could provide the 'moral framework' to govern a new world order, according to Kristol, who recently and candidly wrote, 'Well, what's wrong with dominance in the service of sound principles and high ideals?'"[24]

Infatuation with our power is still alive and well among us, and most of us have not even considered the possibility that this is hubris and that fixation on our power might in the long run carry with it enormous risks for our long-term security. President John Adams, aware of the new nation's large national appetites, wrote Thomas Jefferson in February, 1816: "Power always thinks it has great soul and vast views beyond the comprehension of the weak; and that it is doing God's service when it is violating all of God's laws."[25] More recently George Orwell observed, "We not only do not disapprove of atrocities committed by our side, but have a remarkable capacity for not even hearing about them."[26]

My purpose in writing about our dark side is not to heap scorn upon the country I love, but rather to encourage the church of Jesus Christ to dig deep and examine where our penchant for violence comes from, and to ask why we place such great confidence in weapons of war and defensive handguns. Do we have an excessive need to be in control? Do we trust the tools of violence more than other countries? Those of us who believe in the love of God revealed in the life, death, and resurrection of Jesus of Nazareth must get in touch with our American obsession for dominance, power, and violence. We must admit them. We must confess these "needs" and put in their place a born-again trust in the efficacy of the fruits of the Spirit: love,

24. Wallis, "Bush's Theology of Empire," *Sojourners*, December 19, 2003.

25. Coffman, *Founders v. Bush*, www.foundersvbush.com.

26. Orwell, "Notes on Nationalism."

joy, peace, patience, kindness, generosity, faithfulness, gentleness, and self-control (Gal 5:22–23).

Trusting God and valuing the fruits of the Spirit requires persistent focus and that is doubly difficult because we hear almost daily innumerable self-congratulatory proclamations from the White House, Congress, the Pentagon, and the Gun Empire:

- We are a good and a peaceful people; *and they are half right.*

- We are motivated by the very best of intentions; *and they are half right.*

- We use violence *only* as a last resort; *and they are half right.*

- If the use of violence becomes necessary, we can be trusted to use our weapons judiciously; *and they are half right.*

- Violence we may be forced to use will *always* be in defense of freedom, democracy, and world peace; *and they are half right.*

REDEMPTIVE VIOLENCE

In Walter Wink's trilogy about the Principalities and the Powers (*Naming the Powers, Unmasking the Powers, Engaging the Powers*), he frequently uses a startling term, *redemptive violence,* which sounds like an oxymoron. As if violence against any of God's children can, in fact, *be* redemptive. Herein, God, whom the Bible says, "hates him that loves violence" (Ps 11:5) is perceived as *blessing* violence because the nobility of the cause eclipses any possible revulsion. Can any cause be so worthy as to gain God's favor, when the methods of gaining victory are themselves immoral?

When the Puritans and early settlers came to this land they expected violence and believed faithfulness to God even *demanded* it. The biblical tradition of redemptive violence was popularized in Western culture by the Crusades. The Reformation in England then took it up. Puritanism developed the crusading impulse of the Old Testament to the logical extreme. Puritans visualized God as a God of violent justice, and they called on their people to carry out his purposes in history: a warlike God made warlike men. "Above all creatures [God] loves soldiers," proclaimed a Puritan preacher. "Above all actions he honors warlike and martial design." "Whoever is a professed Christian," declared another, "is a professed soldier." They believed that as there is permanent opposition and conflict in the cosmos, so there is a permanent warfare on earth. "The condition of the child of God," wrote Thomas Taylor, "is military in this life." The saint was a soldier, but so was everyone else; Puritans did not recognize noncombatants. "All degrees of men are warriors, some fighting for the enlargement of religion and some against it."[27]

Redemptive violence is not an abstraction. It has been called by some "the spirituality of militarism," which in essence means controlling others through force of arms. When I first heard the words *redemptive violence* my mind leaped back to the announcement from the village of Ben Tre, Vietnam. That's when the commanding officer reported to his superiors: "It was necessary to destroy the village in order to save it."[28]

Does our fascination with violence today stem from the Gun Empire, which spews out millions of efficient handguns that can shoot dozens of rounds in a few seconds and penetrate bulletproof vests? Or does our faith in violence come from the Military Industrial Complex whose products can obliterate an entire city with sophisticated missiles fired from submarines under the sea or by drones guided to their targets from thousands of miles away? It is a chicken and egg question, for each form of violence is controlled by the same animating spirit. Together they illustrate our national faith in the values and effectiveness of obeying the dictates of redemptive violence.

Redemptive violence is the living theology of gun zealots as well as the U.S. Marines, both of whom, with the best of intentions, maintain that the violence they are ready to use is redemptive in nature. As they shout, "Iraqi Freedom" or "Guns save lives," they tell the world their mission is salvific; they are armed to protect our values and the American way of life . . . to save, to make this world a better place, "a kinder, gentler place," "a more polite and safer place." As the Gun Empire shouts "Guns save lives" they tell us their first priority is not to love their neighbor, but to defend themselves *against* their neighbor, and if the situation demands it, to kill him.

27. Quoted by Michael Walzer, as cited in Jewett, *The Captain America Complex*, 182–83.

28. *Des Moines Register*, February 8, 1968.

Redemptive violence is tough-minded. It understands that the evil in the world must be confronted and controlled. The spirit of redemptive violence must be obeyed because we have enemies who are out to destroy us. The cartoon character Pogo was famous for saying, "We have met the enemy and he is us." Pogo's more humble assessment and willingness to see the contradictions and evil in oneself, is a biblically sound approach to any conflict that might arise, whether in an individual or a national context. However, those who proclaim the values in redemptive violence are convinced that the evil in the world is *because* of our enemy's purposes and plans. That is, "those people" who are not like us are out to destroy us. Redemptive violence stands or falls in its ability to blame others for our problems: the communists, the gays, the straights, the blacks, the whites, the liberals, the conservatives, the Republicans, the Democrats, the Hispanics, and the Muslims. For those who trust redemptive violence, the evil in the world is always someone else's fault.

The blasphemy of redemptive violence is that we consider ourselves to be God's chosen people and therefore responsible and entitled to bring violence upon others whose intentions and purposes are, or *may be*, contrary to ours. When we lead the world in military procurements, it is to maintain the highest of human ideals; when the Russians and Chinese manufacture their tools of violence, it is perceived as warmongering. When we place arms in our bedside tables, we are simply protecting our vulnerable families from "those people" whose values are so out of kilter that they want to do us harm.

The concept of redemptive violence is the motivating force behind the Gun Empire's promotion of concealed carry on college campuses, churches, schools, gas stations, and shopping malls. After the Virginia Tech and Tucson executions, which were both carried out by mentally crazed young men armed with semi-automatic handguns, some students and others sponsored demonstrations with the message: "If students, professors and citizens had been armed these tragedies would never have happened." They asked, "Is there a cause more sacred than protecting human lives?" To have a concealed carry weapons permit (CCWP) is to believe in redemptive violence.

In summarizing the myth of redemptive violence Walter Wink covers all the bases. He writes,

The myth of redemptive violence is nationalism become absolute. This myth speaks for God; it does not listen for God to speak. It invokes the sovereignty of God as its own; it does not entertain the prophetic possibility of radical denunciation and negation by God. It misappropriates the language, symbols, and scriptures of Christianity. It does not seek God in order to change; it claims God in order to prevent change. Its God is not the impartial ruler of all nations but a biased and partial tribal god worshipped as an idol. Its metaphor is not the journey but a fortress. Its symbol is not the cross but a rod of iron. Its offer is not forgiveness but victory. Its good news is not the unconditional love of enemies but their final liquidation. Its salvation is not a new heart but a successful foreign policy. It usurps the revelation of God's purposes for humanity in Jesus. It is blasphemous. It is idolatrous.[29]

SOCIETY'S MOST TRUSTWORTHY CITIZENS

The Gun Empire spreads the myth that those with CCWP are society's most trustworthy citizens and its best defense against dangerous individuals. Between 1996 and 2000, the Violence Policy Center examined those assertions and came to other conclusions. They conducted major studies of permit holders in Texas and Florida. In Texas they discovered CCWP holders were arrested for weapon-related offenses at a rate 81 percent higher than that of the general population aged 21 and older.[30]

A more recent analysis by the *Florida Sun-Sentinel* showed similar results. Of Florida's 1400 permit holders who pleaded guilty or no contest to a felony, 216 of them had outstanding warrants, 128 of them had active domestic violence restraining orders, and six were registered sex offenders.[31] The Gun Empire wants all Americans to believe more guns will stop crime and even provide a polite society.

29. Wink, *Engaging the Powers*, 30.

30. Violence Policy Center, "License to Kill: More Guns, More Crime," 2002.

31. "Investigation Reveals Criminal Pasts of Those Toting Guns," *South Florida Sun-Sentinel*, January 28, 2007.

With more than 300 million civilian guns, almost enough for every man, woman and child, we should have already reached a level of politeness that would be the envy of the whole world.

While the motives of CCWP holders *may* be pure and even though they *may* be loyal and dependable citizens, they are nevertheless *only people* like the rest of us with their own unique problems, stresses, and limitations. In 2009, there were six mass shootings (defined as three or more deaths) in Virginia alone. The shooters were unable to control the chaos in their own lives when their angers, emotions, and fears reached fever pitch. Even highly trained law enforcement SWAT team members are not always calm, cool, and collected when a madman is spraying bullets. How are they to distinguish the good guys from the bad guys?

In Tucson, Arizona, Joe Zamudio tackled and subdued Jared Loughner after he murdered six people and almost killed Congress-woman Gabby Gifford. Zamudio was armed during the incident and revealed he almost fired at the wrong man, providing more evidence that having more guns in these deadly scenes is not the solution, and in fact, might increase the body count.[32]

Other unintended consequences of trusting in redemptive violence should give us pause. In February 2010, an honorable young Marine with a CCWP was watching television and dry firing, i.e., drawing his weapon and aiming at candles on the wall. A round from the weapon discharged as he was preparing to put it back in its holster. The bullet struck and killed his nine-month-old daughter as she sat in her high chair eating fruit. Her father, a combat veteran of three tours in Iraq, told police he carried his concealed weapon with a bullet in the chamber at all times.[33]

On October 11, 2011, Tennessee State Representative Curry Todd was jailed and charged with drunken driving and possession of a loaded handgun while under the influence. Rep. Todd was the sponsor of the guns-in-bars legislation passed in Tennessee in 2009.[34]

32. *The Brady Report*, Winter 2011, 5.

33. Coalition to Stop Gun Violence, "Crimes by Virginia Concealed Handgun Permit Holders," July 1, 2010.

34. Ghianni, "Tennessee Lawmaker," *Reuters*, October 14, 2011.

THE TEMPTATION TO FEEL POWERFUL

Leaders in faith communities must understand the compelling temptation to feel powerful and in charge. The violence of today's movies and video games, dramatic explosions, the pin-point accuracy of an air-strike from a jet or helicopter, an attack by a predator drone guided by computers thousands of miles away, a firefight by the Marines in Afghanistan seen in full color on our television screens, have an immense trickle-down attraction for citizens who feel at risk because of the violence in their communities that is reported daily. Watching a war on television or the evening news convinces many that they too *need* weapons for protection in suburbia or the inner city. Violence begets violence is not a rumor; it is a reality. Violence done *anywhere* escalates violence *everywhere*.

Those who place their faith in weapons often ask derisively, "Can a nation or a home be *too secure*? Can we be *too safe*?" The appeal of redemptive violence is the spirit of the age in which we live and it affects all humanity. It is virulent in the United States as it impacts our foreign policy, dictates what our national budgets will be, governs the military industrial complex and Gun Empire, inspires our media and even televangelism; it fuels our national myth that both our homes and the world can be secure with enough firepower.

Redemptive violence is an attractive but idolatrous trust that weapons and tools of violence can be the means of shalom for nations and individuals, that ultimate good can come from the barrels of *our* weapons. Jesus reminded us: that which we sow, we reap, and we should not expect to gather figs from grape vines.

The Holy One of Israel said,

> Woe to those who call evil good and good evil, who put darkness for light and light for darkness, who put bitter for sweet and sweet for bitter. Woe to those who are wise in their own eyes, and shrewd in their own sight. Therefore, as the tongue of fire devours the stubble, and as dry grass sinks down in the flame, so their root will be as rottenness, and their blossom go up like dust; for they have rejected the law of the Lord of hosts, and have despised the word of the Holy One of Israel. (Isa 5:20–21, 24)

THE DIFFERENCE BETWEEN THE USA AND FORMER COLONIALIST NATIONS

America does not stand alone with its violent past. The history of other powers, commonly called colonialist, has been equally or even more violent. No one could deny the crimes committed by Spain, Portugal, Belgium, Holland, Italy, England, France, China, and Japan, to name a few. All the same, after two centuries their societies are relatively free of gun violence, while ours is the most dangerous in the industrialized world. It's not because their citizens are more loving or kind; it is something else, something simple: these former colonialist powers do not permit easy access to guns.

Should their citizens be able to get a gun as easily as we can, they would suffer the same levels of gun deaths; they would feel entitled to use violence against the immigrants who cross their borders; their children, on occasion, would be afraid to go to school for fear of being shot; they too would grieve over drive-by and mass shootings; they too would worry that fired workers might go postal; they too would spend enormous amounts of money paying medical bills for paraplegics and the exorbitant costs of incarceration for the shooters.

Americans are not meaner or more violent than citizens of Europe, China, or Japan. They too are fascinated with violence. They watch the same violent movies, engage in violent sports, play the same video games, sell the same kinds of toys, read the same comics, etc. The *only* difference is most Americans can get a gun within a few hours or a few minutes. Some of us call such access to guns freedom. As a gun owner who has ministered to gun victims and their families, I call such easy access tragedies getting ready to happen.

The NRA calls any limitations on purchasing guns onerous and burdensome. But what do people of other nations think? In spite of not being able to quickly get their hands on guns, citizens in the other developed countries of the world persist in saying they are happy, fulfilled, and *free people*. Are they delusional? Is it a miracle their streets *are* safe? America should be so blessed.

8

The Principalities
and the Powers

America's Military Industrial Complex and the Gun Empire are present day examples of the principalities and powers about which the Apostle Paul wrote: "Our struggle is not against enemies of blood and flesh, but against the rulers, against the authorities, against the cosmic powers of this present darkness, against the spiritual forces of evil in the heavenly places" (Eph 6:12).

The influence of these principalities and powers is heightened because most of us, even in the church, are uncomfortable speaking about the demonic. Biblical scholar Walter Wink observes, "It is as impossible for most of us to believe in the reality of the demonic as it is to believe in dragons, elves or a flat world."[1] Yet, when one looks at massacres in places like Columbine, Virginia Tech, Fort Hood, and Tucson, Arizona, we move closer to acknowledging its presence.

THE PERSONALITY OF THE PRINCIPALITIES AND POWERS

Ephesians 6:12 is well known to most leaders in the Christian community who are not embarrassed to speak about the presence of evil in human systems and organizations. This one verse is the *locus classicus* for describing sinister powers that mock and destroy all that is just and good in the world. Jesus compared the Holy Spirit with the wind (John 3:8). We cannot see it, but we are aware of its presence and experience its effect. Evil and the principalities and powers are

1. Wink, *Naming the Powers*, 4.

also like the wind. We often don't consciously recognize them, but we feel their destructive power.

Paul repeatedly describes "enemies which are not of blood and flesh," "the rulers," "the authorities," "the cosmic powers of this present darkness," "the spiritual forces of evil in the heavenly places." In these huge constructs he describes the invisible, indefinable, yet all embracing, world-enveloping reach of spiritual networks of powers that are hostile to human life.

Says Wink: "The world rulers are those who have mastery over the world, both those humans who by all the marks of aristocracy, education, political skill, and wealth seem to be of a higher order than ourselves, and those other powers, both above and below the range of visibility. Nor can we leave aside all forms of institutional idolatry, whereby religion, commerce, education, and the state make their own well-being and survival the final criteria of morality."[2]

Wink, who has devoted years to studying the principalities and powers, says, they assume both inner and outer forms. "The invisible inner spirit is the 'spirituality' of institutions, the inner essence of organizations of power; the generating principles of our corporate national culture, sub-cultures, or collective personalities." He describes the outer form of the principalities and powers as the political systems, elected and appointed officials, the chairs of organizations and committees, the laws, buildings, influential people, institutions, Congress, guns, gun shows, financial bottom lines, etc. In short, they are all of the tangible manifestations that power takes. Neither the visible, physical expression, nor their inner guiding spirits are the cause of the other. Both come into existence together and need one another so they can claim to be worthy of human admiration and respect while they do evil in the name of what is good.[3]

The principalities and powers are the super-patriots of our day and claim the highest of human values such as democracy, freedom, and our American way of life. They extol wealth, privilege, and power in the name of God and all that is virtuous. Their greatest strength lies in their ability to deceive people into believing that *in the real world* violence is required in the pursuit of peace and democracy.

2. Ibid., 5.
3. Ibid.

As a case in point, the Czech Playwright and later President of the country, Vaclav Havel, wrote while the communist state was still in power:

> Because the regime is captive to its own lies, it must falsify everything. It falsifies the past; it falsifies the present. It falsifies the future. It falsifies statistics. It pretends not to possess an omnipotent and unprincipled police apparatus. It pretends to respect human rights. It pretends to persecute no one. It pretends to fear nothing. It pretends to pretend nothing.
>
> Individuals need not believe all these mystifications, but they must behave as though they did, or they must at least tolerate them in silence, or get along well with those who work with them. For this reason, however, they must live within a lie. They need not accept the lie. It is enough for them to have accepted their life with it and in it. For by this very fact, individuals confirm the system, fulfill the system, make the system, *are* the system.[4]

In chapter 2 we spoke of the gun industry's intentional use of words such as political and spiritual, which can stop honest conversations about the misuse of guns. Using the phrase *the real world* accomplishes the same. People of faith often hear the phrase, which serves as an instant roadblock when one proclaims the imperatives of love, reconciliation with enemies, trusting others, or working for world peace. The principalities and powers say it is naïve to depend on love and/or seek the fruits of the spirit in the real world because somewhere out there is another Hitler or Osama Bin Laden, and we must be ready at all times to take them on, and eventually to take them out.

It is impossible to plumb the inner psychological depths of the structures and systems of this real world where violence is glorified and trusted. How do you explain America's trust in violence to a junior high school student or an adult Sunday school class? Just as one cannot describe the stench of an abattoir, one can't fully grasp the insidious influence of a principality or power, and that's precisely the point and it is in large measure its power. Its vastness and indescribability reveals subtle, but far-reaching, almost limitless power. One simply cannot comfortably get one's mind around it.

4. Vaclav Havel, quoted in Wink, *Engaging the Powers*, 98.

Chuck Fager, a Quaker from Fayetteville, North Carolina, suggests it would be more accurate to call the Military Industrial Complex the Military-Industrial-Political-Academic-Scientific-Think-Tank-Mass-Media-Entertainment Complex.[5] Neither is the Gun Empire only dozens of isolated factories that make guns: the empire is a huge network of powerful political and social personalities and large conglomerates that supply gun owners with ammunition, targets, hunting and sport's shooting clothes, formal wearing apparel, shoes and boots, color coded pistols (so women can match their guns with their accessories, shoes, and handbags), hunting guides, a large focused hunting press, special liaisons with the police and military services that will field test new guns and extol their virtues to the public, and a large contingent of public relations specialists whose job is to get the latest models of guns into action scenes for television and the movies. There are paid and volunteer lobbyists that visit Congress and every state house in the land. As the name suggests, it is an Empire.

How do these principalities and powers affect the people of America? What is their influence on humankind? How do the idols of power and deadly force impact the traditional values of the United States? How do they impact the entire world? What is the connection between these powers and our yearly arms bazaars, which sell billions of dollars in military materiel to poverty-stricken countries that can't afford to feed their own populations? Or again, how can the mystique of guns so control the minds of intelligent men and women that they would even argue guns don't kill? What is the psychological appeal for our youth in having a gun at one's side? What is America's self-interest in looking the other way when thousands of assault weapons are sold *illegally* to straw purchasers in Texas and Arizona and delivered to drug cartels in Mexico? How do we explain to church partners around the world the United States' massive gun sales to barbarous, dictatorial regimes in Africa and South America, which distribute assault weapons to child soldiers? How do these principalities and powers concoct the necessary conditions and connections that enable their demonic networks to flourish and convince good, God-fearing people they need more guns? How and when does one start explaining the principalities and powers to our children?

5. Fager, *Study War Some More*, 15.

THEIR ART OF DECEPTION

The idols of power and deadly force command immense "spiritual influence" over those who are tricked into believing that power and deadly force are essential for reconciliation between nations and for solving human conflicts here at home. Americans have not always been quite so gullible. I was in high school during the Chinese Cultural Revolution when Chairman Mao Tse Tung issued his famous declaration: "Power comes from the barrel of a gun." From coast to coast we let out a collective gasp. We were furious over the blasphemy. The American church quickly denounced his heresy. We knew *instantaneously* Mao's words were evil.

Alas, in the first decade of the twenty-first century, many of us appear to be converts to Mao's philosophy. When the Gun Empire repeats comparable comments, there is hardly a whisper of dissent. Wayne La Pierre, the chief spokesperson for the NRA, has repeatedly proclaimed, "In America, the ones with the guns make the rules."[6] His friend and colleague, David Kopel of the Cato Institute and adjunct Professor of Law at Denver University adds: "Guns are the tools of political dissent . . . and they should be privately owned and unregulated."[7] Those who are armed will determine what kind of country this will be. As they proclaim the authority of bullets over ballots in our democratic society, there isn't even a whimper from the White House or Congress, and to our shame, the church house is as quiet as its church mice.

There is not a dime's worth of difference between the views of Wayne La Pierre, David Kopel, and Chairman Mao Tse Tung. Lest we forget, the greatest strength of the idol of power and deadly force is deception and the most egregious deception of all is convincing others that evil is good and freedom requires violence.

By transforming freedom and other American values into religious or sacred symbols, and as the people are reminded that "our soldiers are fighting all over the world for the freedoms that make America great," freedom comes to mean "gun rights must be protected." As

6. Speech at the Conservative Political Action Conference, Washington, D.C., February 26, 2009.

7. Horwitz and Anderson, *Guns, Democracy, and the Insurrectionist Idea*, 169.

the tools of violence become more revered, their adherents grow blind to the carnage they bring to our society and block all attempts to find rational solutions. There is always more heat than light as honest discourse gives way to emotional defense of positions that are proclaimed as dogma. How often do the irrational positions receive sacred status and then get defended even more vigorously?

NAMING AND UNMASKING THE IDOLS

For Americans to live free of fear and violence requires God's people to unmask the idols. The unmasking takes place as we expose the true character of the principalities and powers, and shine the light of truth on their deceptions. The unmasking occurs as people of faith summon their courage and *name* the idols and describe what they do. God promises us that once we name the evil, its power to influence us is neutralized, its masquerade is over, its true character is exposed for all to see, and God's power to bring about change is given to those who have heretofore been intimidated by the principalities and the powers. Naming the idols sets us free. Someone has said, "When anyone tells the truth, and lives the truth, she enables everyone else to peer behind the curtain as well."

Says Wink, "The Church is uniquely equipped to help people unmask the powers which are in the midst of earthly institutions, systems and structures. People of faith can bring into the open the idolatrous pretensions of the powers and identify their dehumanizing values, strip away their mantle of respectability, and disenthrall their victims."[8]

Immediately following the Apostle Paul's thumbnail sketch of the principalities and powers, he gives instructions on how to do battle against them. He writes: "Put on the whole armor of God so that you may be able to stand against the wiles of the devil. Fasten the belt of truth around your waist. Put on the breastplate of righteousness. As for shoes, put on whatever will make you ready to proclaim the gospel of peace. Take the shield of faith with which you will be able to quench all the flaming arrows of the evil one. Take the helmet of

8. Wink, *Engaging the Powers*, 164.

salvation and the sword of the Spirit, which is the word of God. Pray in the Spirit at all times. Keep alert and always persevere in supplication for all the saints. Make known with boldness the mystery of the Gospel" (Eph 6:13–20). Note: all of these weapons are nonviolent.

One of the purposes of this book is to reveal the depths of deception and cunning of extremist ideologues within the NRA and the Gun Empire. For decades they have manipulated the structures and systems of our democracy and intimidated legislators to support laissez-faire gun policies. In their wake, they have brought untold suffering and death to thousands of American families and buried them under a mountain of illogical, ridiculous laws, among which:

1. Forbid any gun or piece of ammunition to be examined for safety.

2. Give the gun industry almost total immunity against litigation, including the manufacture of faulty products, mass distributions to rogue gun dealers, and irresponsible straw purchase sales by dealers. This is the only industry that enjoys such blanket immunity.

3. Close the courthouse door to citizens who have no other recourse to justice against irresponsible business practices within the gun industry.

4. Keep law enforcement agencies intentionally weak and ineffective.

5. Erect insurmountable barriers to full scientific inquiry and research on the effects of guns in our society. (See chapter 16)

To believe in God is to gamble that truth is more powerful than lies. Lies cannot last forever because they dishonor God and are an affront to God's people. When people discover they have been lied to and manipulated by powerful elites they grow angry. People will eventually rise up and dismantle the power of the idols that carry within the seeds of their own destruction. Little by little today, the truth about the Empire is leaking out. The fraud and subterfuge under which we Americans have lived for so long is becoming known and their true purposes are being exposed. Their secrets are being announced from a few steeples. Have you heard them yet? If not, you will. Once the American people understand the extent of how much we have bought into their charade, we will be able to say no to the lies that more powerful weapons will lead us to the good life. We will be strong enough and wise enough to say violence is incapable of leading us to the security and peace we really want. A good and powerful spirit is stirring in America today prompting people of faith to start naming and unmasking the idols.

One has said, unmasking the idols requires unusual eyes. Unusual eyes are not the eyes we possess, but rather, the eyes we receive in special situations, in struggles against what has come to be regarded as self-evident truth. Unmasking an idol is a special way of seeing and gaining a special awareness, which comes from God alone.

> Open my eyes, that I may see glimpses of truth thou hast
> for me.
> Place in my hand the wonderful key that shall unclasp and
> set me free.
> Silently now, I wait for Thee, Ready my God, Thy will to see;
> Open my eyes, illumine me, Spirit Divine![9]

9. Scott, "Open My Eyes That I May See," 1895.

9

The Idol's Greatest Need

DIVINE STATUS, A PREREQUISITE FOR AN IDOL

Former NRA Executive Warren Cassidy did his best to give the idols of power and deadly force what they most need: a claim of divine status. He said, "You would get a far better understanding of the NRA if you approached us as if you were approaching one of the great religions of the world."[1]

An idol gains power only when its followers or owners revere it and use religious terms to define or defend it. If Cassidy's comment were an isolated one, it would be difficult to make much over it, but the religious overtones in the speech and actions of dedicated gun zealots reveal we are in the presence of idols. In 1998, after giving his first speech as NRA President in Philadelphia, Charlton Heston was presented with an antique musket. He was thrilled with the gift and mused at the time, "*Sacred stuff* resides in that wooden stock and blue steel when ordinary hands can possess such an extraordinary instrument that gives the most common man the most uncommon of freedoms that symbolize the full measure of human dignity and liberty."[2]

During the 2000 presidential election campaign, Heston repeated the same words as he dramatically raised the musket over his head, adding, "I must say those fighting words especially for you,

---

1. Davidson, *Under Fire*, 44.

2. Speech to NRA members at the 1998 NRA Annual Convention in Philadelphia.

Mr. Gore—'from my cold dead hands!'"[3] The implication: He would die before he would relinquish his gun. Thousands stood and roared their approval. Mr. Heston was proclaiming a widely held belief among gun zealots that guns have ultimate value. Guns, after all, are like God—they are the difference between life and death.

I agree with the suggestion that the erosion of biblical knowledge and theological understanding on the part of average American citizens leaves an open door for the idols of power and deadly force to place a blasphemous "Christian veneer" on their policies and products. Attaching God's name to what people value creates false theological assumptions that God would encourage the purchase of an assault pistol. Such assumptions, loudly publicized, give the idol control over those who are fascinated with violence and its tools. Although the Gun Empire regularly proclaims the social benefits of weapons, the inevitable consequences of their veneration are deaths and injuries.

In December 2006, the *Daily News Journal* of Murfreesboro, Tennessee, ran a series of articles on successful local businessmen and women. One of the success stories was Mr. Ronnie Barrett of the Barrett Manufacturing Company. His enterprise manufactures a .50-caliber rifle that can shoot five miles and accurately for one. He has contracts with the U.S. military and fifty governments world wide, but he would also sell his rifle to any individual who happened to need one.

Barrett, a member of the NRA Board, advertised his rifle this way: "The cost effectiveness of the Model 82A1 cannot be overemphasized when a round of ammunition purchased for less than 10 U.S. dollars can be used to destroy or disable a modern jet aircraft."[4]

Among Barrett's many awards is the Man of the Year from the National Industrial Defense Association. The NRA has established the Barrett Award for Excellence in his honor. Ernst and Young in November 2006 named him a member of an elite group of outstanding entrepreneurs in America. Barrett says of his rifle, "It really is a

3. Speech to NRA members at the annual convention in Charlotte, North Carolina, May 20, 2000.

4. Barrett Firearms Manufacturing Inc., brochure advertising Model 82A1 .50-caliber sniper rifle.

gift from God."[5] *That's* quite an endorsement! The Almighty often gets blamed for various calamities and natural disasters, but nowadays God gets credit for many things that are repugnant. Which God/god is Barrett talking about? Is his statement a figure of speech or does he believe our benevolent Creator would give this needy world a .50-caliber rifle that would enable an ordinary citizen to knock a plane from the sky?

In January 2010, we learned of other Christian evangelists in Trijicon, Inc., a defense contracting firm of Wixom, Michigan. They manufacture gun sights for the U.S. Army and Marines. The effectiveness of their gun sights is due to tritium, a radioactive form of hydrogen, which creates light around the target and helps the shooter to better "service the target."

ABC News reported the company was etching two biblical texts on its Advanced Combat Optical Gun Sight. Both citations referred to light: The first was John 8:12: "Jesus said, "I am the light of the world; he that follows me shall not walk in darkness, but shall have the light of life." The other was 2 Corinthians 4:6: "For God who commanded the light to shine out of darkness, has shined in our hearts to give the light of the knowledge of the glory of God in the face of Jesus Christ."[6]

This use of Scripture assumes Jesus would bless the gun, the gun sight, and the shooter in the task of more efficiently killing another human being. This is blasphemy and a profane use of the Scriptures. Far more than cussing, this is really what it means to take the name of the Lord in vain. Thankfully, after the Associated Press exposed their "Christian witness" voices of protest were raised and the Pentagon stepped in to stop any further etchings.

Did the company really believe God blesses that which God despises? The Scriptures reveal a God who gives life, not death. Guns do not give life; they take life away. The late Richard Shaull, Professor of Ecumenics at Princeton Theological Seminary, observed the only way idols have to meet the challenge of God is to take the very things

---

5. Turner Hutchens, "Aiming for Success." *Daily News Journal*, Murfreesboro, Tennessee, December 24, 2006.

6. Luis Martinez, Joseph Rhee, and Mark Schone, "No More Jesus Rifles," ABC News, January 21, 2010.

God's presence calls into question and make gods out of them, as-
cribing to them a sacred or divine quality of their own, worshiping
them and doing everything possible to get others to do the same.
In this way, the order they create is identified with an all-powerful
and transcendent Good; it is something sacred, and it should not be
questioned.[7]

Because of copyright laws and my reluctance to be sued, I have
not included in these pages any of the dozens of artistic images
available of Jesus of Nazareth holding an assault weapon. For the
millions of gun owners who believe that if Jesus walked our streets
today, he would be armed with the most efficient weapon he could
afford, such pictures enhance their sincere belief that the Lord would
be ready at a moment's notice to use the gun to protect and defend
himself and/or his contemporary disciples. Such images prompt us
to ask an assumed follow-up question: "*Who* would Jesus shoot?"

It is often said, "a picture is worth a thousand words." I wish I
could provide that picture for the reader to experience the blasphemy
it represents. However, using the Internet, the reader can easily locate
such pictures and experience the devotion many Americans have for
the Lord Jesus who blesses the possession and use of the world's most
efficient firearms. It is obvious these individuals see no contradiction
in linking Jesus with the violence which comes from the barrel of an
assault weapon. Here one can see first-hand the essence of idolatry
as "the Savior of the World" holds a "weapon of mass destruction"
and often with a smile.

A TWISTED BIBLICAL ARGUMENT FOR OWNING GUNS

I once debated an Orthodox Presbyterian clergyman whose devotion
to firearms was as strong as his faith in Jesus Christ. The reverend's
beliefs were based on the idea that God ordained the man to be the
head of the household and it is his duty, not only to his family, but
also to God, to protect them in the most effective way. The reverend
unabashedly believes God calls him to carry a handgun at all times,

7. Shaull, *Naming the Idols*, 131.

and he was clear in stating that Jesus would carry a gun if he were walking our streets today.

Bear in mind he was referring to the same Jesus of Nazareth who instructed his disciples to turn the other cheek, to love our enemies, and who laid down his life even for the man who put a spear in his side.

Notwithstanding, this reverend and other Christians in gun cults are certain God does not want the head of the household using a trigger lock on his gun. His duties to protect the family require that he be ready at a moment's notice to come to their defense.

This theology is blasphemous, but it is a theology nevertheless. My friend, The Rev. Rachel Smith, calls it "Gundamentalism." Many modern-day shamans and religious gun enthusiasts proclaim God wants all citizens well armed so they can protect our homes, our values, even our faith. At times, some of these groups make the NRA seem tame. These religious cults have become an integral part of the religion of the Gun Empire that give the idols of power and deadly force what they most need: a divine status. For these men and women the command to love God with all your heart, soul, mind, and strength and your neighbor as yourself, is placed right alongside their new commandment to be ready at all times to *defend yourself against your neighbor*. We are not surprised that the latter gains far more attention than the former in their press and advertisements.

There are many references in the Bible, which on first glance, *seem* to support the use of violence, as in the conquest of Canaan, which we briefly considered in a preceding chapter. Nevertheless, one is hard-pressed to make a solid biblical or theological case that the people of God should be ready at all times to kill one's neighbors. The unmistakable, unifying message of the Bible is God is love; and God's people are not only to *love* God and their neighbors as themselves, but their enemies as well. Someone reminded me recently, "When Jesus told us to love our enemies, he probably meant, 'Don't kill them.'" All morals and ethical behavior that stem from all the world's religions are based on love.

Some theologians have said, "the values and concepts inherent in the terms of freedom, liberty, and democracy would shield America from idolatry." It is apparent that America lost the shield.

The idols of power and deadly force are alive and well. While major faith communities were sleeping or were indifferent to the proliferation of guns in the 1970s, modern-day shamans built an idolatrous religious framework around guns and have worked feverishly to justify biblically their unwarranted fascination with guns and have given the idols of power and deadly force what they covet the most . . . a divine status. Millions worship at this shrine.

WHICH GOD/god DOES ONE TRUST?

The vital question is not whether one believes in God/god, but rather *which* God/god one *trusts*. Many today, even those who say they are Christian or Jewish, do not consider themselves to be religious, i.e., committed to any particular religion, denomination, or theological viewpoint, but they do claim to be "spiritual." They reserve the right to make their own decisions on matters of faith and particularly on behavioral issues. They will not be constrained by any particular dogma or institutional guidelines, religious or otherwise. Their spirituality means they will be open to the teachings of any religion or any valuable insight, regardless of its source.

The number of American adults identifying themselves as more spiritual than religious has increased from 19 percent in 1998 to 27 percent today, according to the General Social Survey. Fully 30 percent of adults under age forty say they are spiritual but profess no religion at all. According to a poll by Marist College, 63 percent of Americans say it's either "very true" or at least "partly true" that they are "spiritual but not religious." In fact, the number of Americans self-identifying as "more spiritual than religious" equals the number identified as Roman Catholics, the largest actively religious body in the United States.[8]

Such wide self-understandings offer innumerable opportunities for various interests, causes, ideologies, *and idols* to exert a spiritual influence over those who are searching for meaning or revere some higher power or someone or something that, in their mind, has intrinsic human or spiritual value. To which spirit does one look to

8. Jack Haberer, "Winning? Losing!" *The Presbyterian Outlook*, April 19, 2010, 5.

make sense of life? Which God or gods will provide a sense of well being? Which God or gods will become one's ultimate concern and what form will such allegiance take?

"It is not enough to believe in God," says Roger Burggraeve, "which remains a formal neutral approach; it is about the manner or form which represents God for oneself. The content of one's faith in God is at stake in the sense that it makes no difference in which god one has faith. One's *image* of God/god makes the difference. The God to which one attaches one's heart also determines the direction in which one's human longing proceeds: for where your God/god is, there will your heart be also."[9]

The Rev. Dr. Howard Moody, Pastor Emeritus of the Judson Memorial Church of Greenwich Village in New York City, knows first-hand the widespread influence of new age spirituality and shares his unique response to those who ask about his personal faith. When asked, "Do you believe in God?" Moody replies, "I refuse to answer on the grounds it might incriminate me." After the questioner defines *which* God/god he/she is talking about Moody is ready to join them in an honest conversation.

For some, new age spirituality represents openness to truth and brings the thrill of discovering a new significance to life. Others regard it as a rejection of the teachings of the Jewish and Christian religions that by and large have formed our national values and identity. Regardless of how one understands the phenomenon, the effect is the same. New understandings and new idols as well, have limitless opportunities to convince the uncommitted of their value. Consequently we hear the unending theological refrains from the Gun Empire: "Gun rights are God-given rights." "Guns save lives." "An armed society is a polite society." "More guns = less crime." "Can your home be too secure?"

---

9. Burggraeve et. al., *Desirable God*, 38.

10

The Idol's Greatest Strength

CREATING FEAR AND ENEMIES

The greatest strength of the idols of power and deadly force is their ability to create fear in the human heart by deceiving those who are afraid. When people are controlled by their fears, those who are different are seen as dangerous. Each of us has experienced fear when informed of threats from peoples across the seas or by other ethnic, racial, or religious groups across town.

There has never been a time in my life when I was not warned of the dangers posed by people of other races, religions, classes, or nations. My first twelve years were spent in Highland Park, Michigan, a section of Detroit with beautiful homes on tree-lined streets. I'm ashamed to admit my family and neighbors were the NIMBYS ("not-in-my-backyard") of the 1940s. We signed a covenant that we would not sell our homes to Jews or Negroes. *Those people* wanted to move into our neighborhood, which would set our property values plummeting. A vivid memory of my childhood is hearing audible gasps as Highland Parkers passed around photographs of inter-racial couples dancing and partying together. God, forgive me. God, forgive my family. God, forgive us all.

I was not "carefully taught to hate before I was six, or seven, or eight" as the song in the musical, *South Pacific* describes racism. Because my mother and father were loving people I was *subtly* taught to be wary of people who were different. I'm not alone. In the presidential campaign of 2008, candidate Barack Obama revealed his white grandmother was afraid of black men who approached her on the sidewalk.

There was nothing subtle, however, as I learned to hate the Japanese and Germans during World War II. My passions and patriotism were bolstered by jingoistic movies, which portrayed every "Kraut" and "Jap" soldier as both stupid and mean. In less than ten years it was patriotic to hate the Russians, the Chinese communists, and North Koreans. In the 1960s, Castro and the Communist Cubans were added to my enemy's list. In the 1970s and 1980s it was the Sandinistas in Nicaragua and the Iranians. In more recent years, those in high places told me of the Axis of Evil and Saddam Hussein who planned to "put a mushroom cloud over New York City." Nowadays, I'm advised to be suspicious of anyone who might have a few drops of Arab or Hispanic blood coursing through their veins, while the Chinese are described as "future enemies." We are still not ready to let down our guard with the Russians. With advancing years, I've come to believe that the most fearful thing in the world is a strong country that is afraid.

Demonic images of enemies have a persistent way of etching themselves into our national consciousness. Although the identification of the enemy may change through the centuries from Cavalier, Royalist, Englishman, Rebel, Yankee, Indian, Spaniard, Hun, Nazi, Jap, or Gook, the form of the stereotype and its apocalyptic solution remains constant.[1]

To keep us safe from threats of enemies near and far is the rationale behind the commissioning of more aircraft carriers and submarines, building more sophisticated jet fighters, refurbishing more nuclear bombs, and selling billions of dollars of armaments to desperately poor countries. Many wealthy people make a lot of money warning us of our enemies or potential enemies.

To promote fear of the other nations increases exponentially the possibility of future conflicts with them. Our fears give birth to suspicion and distrust, which we are told requires the stockpiling of more arms to defend the country against would-be attackers. Meanwhile, our response to protect ourselves with more and more powerful arms

1. Jewett, *The Captain America Complex*, 149.

is regarded as evidence of our hostile intent against them. Time and again we have seen this played out on the world's scene, and it is regularly the content of the evening news.

Consider as well, the vital role an enemy or potential enemy plays in the marketing of semi-automatic handguns and assault rifles. Sales go right off the charts as citizens are warned of the dangers posed by new immigrant populations whose cultures, colors, dress, foods, languages, and religions differ from our own.

David Brooks, in his delightful book, *On Paradise Drive: How We Live Now (And Always Have) in the Future Tense,* describes how America's suburban civilization will shape the world's future. He writes: "One out of every nine people living in America today was born in a foreign country—roughly 32.5 million people. According to the latest census, there are now more foreign-born Americans than ever before in our history." Brooks describes a recent epiphany when reading the winners of the National Scholar Awards as announced in the Loudon County newspaper (outside of Washington, DC) He found such names as Kawai Cheung, Anastasia Cisneros Fraust, Dantam Do, Hugo Dubovoy, and Maryanthe Malliaris.[2] The names of these young scholars reveal ethnic differences, but at the same time testify to common values and goals, which *should* alleviate *some* fears. What is it that holds us back from recognizing we are not *that* different after all? Our diversity makes acceptance more than a virtue; it makes it a requirement for human survival.

God did not create us to live in the prisons of fear of our own making. God made us for life abundant and for joy, love, and peace. The good news is we are not condemned to live in fear. The Christian hope for salvation and God's promise to build a Peaceable Kingdom begins with the messenger from heaven who declared to us all, "Do not be afraid—I am bringing you good news of great joy for all the people: to you is born this day in the city of David a Savior, who is the Messiah, the Lord" (Luke 2:10–11). Again, in the Bible's last book, Revelation, the Christ says, "Do not be afraid; I am the first and the last, and the living one. I was dead, and see, I am alive forever and ever; and I have the keys of Death and of Hades" (Rev

---

2. Brooks, *On Paradise Drive*, 35.

1:17–18). John the Apostle says, "there is no fear in love, and perfect love casts out fear" (1 John 4:18).

In spite of evidence that all God's people have the same hopes and weep the same tears, insecure and fearful people grow anxious when in proximity to those who do not share social norms. When people fear "them," whether the threat is real or perceived, the effect is the same. In her book *Becoming Human,* feminist theologian Letty Russell, discusses the sociology and psychology of exclusivity. She says: "We maintain our identity "over against" other groups . . . the less sure you are of yourself, the more you must have another to be over against. Persons and groups who are anxious about whether they measure up to the cultural standards of superiority usually cut others down to their size."[3] An effective tool for cutting others down to size is a gun.

BLAMING OTHERS FOR OUR PROBLEMS

I'm convinced at least part of the reason why so many of us place faith in guns is related to the decline of cohesive, homogenous communities where everybody knew one another. It has been said, "We used to be a people who depended on our neighbors and didn't worry much about strangers. Today, we've become a people who are totally dependent on strangers and are afraid of our neighbors." Instead of reaching out and getting to know neighbors, far too many of us build walls. As the evening news provokes inordinate fears that foreigners, particularly Muslims and Latinos at this present moment, are destroying or at least eroding "our American way of life," we grow increasingly suspicious, even xenophobic.

For more than fifty years I've listened to the reasons people give for going to war or buying a handgun. They remain essentially the same: "*Those people* don't value human life like we do." "In today's world, violence is 'the only thing *those people* understand.'" "*Those people* don't understand us, but they *do* understand guns and bombs and bullets." "It's too bad we have to buy these guns or go to war, but *in the real world* we have no other choice."

Consider the vehement voices of Americans who blame our problems on the growing Latino population. Many are numbed into

3. Russell, *Becoming Human,* 23.

believing our economic woes, our job losses, the decline of our neighborhoods, the exorbitant cost of medical services, the rise in crime,
and the possibilities of higher taxes are their fault. Some say their
presence will remove English from America's classrooms. Such hyperbole is reminiscent of the probably apocryphal scolding of Texans
by Ma Ferguson, Texas' first woman governor: "Stop learning our
children dirty rotten French and Spanish. If the English language
was good enough for Jesus Christ, it's good enough for Texans."

Others say that America's problems are because of the Muslims
whose religion teaches jihad and hatred of non-Muslims. Despite the
fact that there were several dozen Muslims who were killed in the
attack on the World Trade Center towers and that Muslims live in almost every country, we're told that all 1.5 billion Muslims in the world
want to destroy America. We've all heard inflammatory lies from the
lips of Christian ministers who preach fear and hate as they tell us
all imams are clandestine leaders of terrorist cells and the Koran they
read promises eternal rewards for those who kill Christians and Jews.
Such false, reckless oratory only increases the strength of the idols of
power and deadly force and persuades those governed by fear to buy
defensive firearms. It seldom enters the minds of those programmed
to hate Arabs that in Indonesia alone, there are more Muslims than
in all the Arab countries of the world put together.

Power structures in every land sow seeds of suspicion, fear, and
hatred about people who are different. Those seeds are likely to
sprout into violence even though some of the "would be enemies"
are not even there, but are only figments of our imagination, like the
boogey man who terrified us when we were children.

> Yesterday upon the stair,
>   I met a man who wasn't there.
> He wasn't there again today.
>   I wish that man would go away.[4]

What a contrast to the gracious welcome Jesus would have us
provide our brothers and sisters of other races, nations, cultures,
classes, and religions. Every time Christians celebrate the Lord's
Supper, we are reminded that the Lord died for all peoples; and the
day is coming when peoples from the east and west, and the north

4. Mearns, "Antigonish."

and south will gather at God's throne and sit down and eat together (Luke 13:28–29). What a glorious day when every child of God will know that all of us belong to God's big human family.

EXPLOITING FEAR

Fear sells guns. Fear sells *any* weapon, large or small. Tom Diaz has exposed the gun industry's air of secrecy in creating fear among the American people. In a particular revealing section of his book, *Making a Killing,* he cites Massad Ayoob, who wrote for the magazine, *Shooting Industry.* Ayoob says today's market is based on defensive firearms, particularly handguns, thanks to reformed "shall issue" concealed carry rules in many states. (For those who own legal handguns and apply for a concealed carry permit, the state *shall issue* it without undue delay.) Ayoob advises gun shop dealers *to use fear to sell more guns on impulse*:

> Customers come to you every day out of fear. Fear of what they read in the newspaper. Fear of what they watch on the 11 o'clock news. Fear of the terrible acts of violence they see on the street. Your job, in no uncertain terms, is to sell them confidence in the form of steel and lead. An impulse of fear has sent that customer to your shop, so you want a quality product in stock to satisfy the customer's needs and complete the impulse purchase.[5]

Yet again, *Gun Games* publisher, Wally Arida, offers advice for creative dealers on how they should follow up to sell more guns to the same customer after a first sale is based on scare tactics: "We scare them to buy one gun. Now let's get these people shooting their guns and educate them to buy more guns. We should tell them, 'Now you have your defense gun, now you need to buy a gun to shoot this sport and another one to shoot this other sport.'"[6]

Only a few months after President Obama was elected in 2008, extremist groups railed against our African American President

5. Ayoob, "Trend Crimes and the Gun Dealer," *Shooting Industry,* March 1993, 18.

6. Quoted by Diaz, Making a Killing, 164.

Barack **Hussein** Obama. (Why do they print the president's middle name in bold?) The most powerful lobby in Washington warned those who *loved* their guns in a typical e-mail, which I happened to receive: "the anti-gunners (are) in control of key committees in Congress and the 'gun grabbers' are out for blood. Make no mistake. Our guns and our right to use them could be wiped away at any moment by Barack Obama, the most anti-gun rights president in history. They already are being attacked in Congress, state legislatures and cities and towns from coast to coast." Although President Obama has said repeatedly gun owners have nothing to fear from him regarding their Second Amendment rights, the outcry is loud and constant.

Such rhetoric sold thousands of guns and hundreds of gun stores could not keep ammunition on their shelves. One website showed a smiling picture of Obama with the caption, "America's No. 1 Gun Salesman." Thousands rushed to purchase more guns "before it was too late and they were left defenseless." When Congresswoman Gifford was struck down by an assassination attempt in Tucson, Arizona, the Gun Empire publicly called for a period of official mourning, but behind the scenes they quietly urged people to buy guns while you still can. The gun manufacturers, distributors, and dealers reveled in the hype.

A DUPLICATE COPY OF THE 1960S AND 1970S

The Gun Empire's shrewd manipulation of our fears of diversity provides a duplicate copy of the 1960s and 1970s when the atmosphere was pulsating with hostility. The whole world was talking about MAD, (Mutual Assured Destruction, as in nobody wins a nuclear war). Those were the days when contractors were building combination den and bomb shelters. Unable to truthfully talk peace, the nations of the world settled for detente on Earth. Violence grew in epidemic proportions as our assembly lines disgorged armaments and munitions of every kind to supply the war effort in Southeast Asia, and shotgun and rifle factories retooled in order to produce what our markets demanded: handguns.

Yet, there was another unlikely culprit in the 1960s and 1970s called democracy, which helped fan the flames of America's obsession for security. The very idea of democracy excited oppressed peoples all over the world, who marched and sang "We Shall Overcome." The song gave hope to the oppressed, but produced fear in the affluent who felt they were losing control of the America they knew.

Throughout the United States, increasing numbers of people of color and those on the bottom rungs of our socio-economic ladders were growing more restless. They showed up regularly at city hall to demand their civil rights and a larger portion of the economic pie. They insisted on a seat at the table when their rights were discussed. Freedom Marches and Freedom Rides, bus boycotts and lunch counter demonstrations produced headlines and panic everywhere. The nation was unaccustomed to such things. "They" never made that much noise before.

In the late 1960s, Los Angeles, Detroit, New York City, Newark, and dozens of other large cities exploded into riots that revealed the bitter, deep-rooted divides of centuries of oppression. Whites fled the cities for the suburbs, yet even in those "safe enclaves" residents were fearful of those who demanded equality and equal justice under the law. The wealthy and moneyed classes who "had the most to lose" were jittery and pressured the mayors and police to give them more protection. "Law and order!" they shouted, and the have-nots shouted back, "Whose law and whose order?"

As our armed forces "fought for our freedom" and "to preserve our American way of life" thousands of miles away in Vietnam, many Americans wondered out loud if "those people" would come into their safe neighborhoods to rape and plunder. The more violence was reported in the media, the more fearful people wanted guns for protection. Ironically, the more guns were purchased, the more violence increased and America was caught in the grips of a vicious circle, spinning out of control.

Citizens did not realize then, nor do we realize today, that the most likely person to do us harm already has a key to the house. Strangers or criminals do not commit most of America's murders and assaults; they are committed by family members, friends, and acquaintances, who, in acts of passion, turn to the instruments originally purchased to protect "us" against "them." Guns purchased for protection are eleven times more likely to be used in a murder, an assault, an accident, or to be stolen and used in a crime than they are to stop an intruder.[7]

The gun industry adjusted to the demands of the marketplace, retooled their older factories, and/or built new ones as it changed its focus from making shotguns and rifles for hunters and sport shooters to supplying a panicked public with handguns. In that stormy, fearful atmosphere some of the younger members of the NRA saw dollar signs and an irrefutable business opportunity and made the most of it. A cartoon of the day pictured the wife saying, "I don't want a gun in this house." The husband replies, "Honey, we need one to protect ourselves from all the crazies out there who are buying them."

THE CINCINNATI REVOLT

At its annual meeting in 1977, later to be known as the Cincinnati Revolt, the young Turks in the NRA, led by Harlan Carter and Neal Knox, persuaded their members to replace the leaders of the old guard who were all about hunting and shooting sports and helping police and scouting organizations in their marksmanship with new leaders. Gun ownership was no longer just about recreational pursuits; it was about big business and making lots of money selling defensive handguns.

The head of the new politicized NRA was Harlan B. Carter, who ushered in the NRA's golden age, which saw its membership leap from 900,000 to nearly three million. That was when the association gained its new reputation as the invincible "gun lobby" and adopted unbending policies to stop *any* effort to modify, restrict, or regulate guns to anybody for any reason whatsoever. These unbending policies guaranteed both more gun sales and more gun deaths.

Minutes before his elevation to the supreme post of executive vice-president of the NRA, Carter mounted the podium at the front of the hall and addressed the cheering crowd below: "Beginning in this place and at this hour, this period in NRA history [where things

7. Arthur Kellerman, "Guns for Safety?," *Washington Post.* June 29, 2008.

like hunting clinics, courses on hunting safety, target shooting, and marksmanship contests were the focus], is finished." From this point on, says Osha Davidson, "the new NRA would be devoted single-mindedly—and proud of the fact—to the proposition that Americans and their guns must never, never be parted." And as Carter said before Congress, "We are in this game for keeps."[8]

The coup d'état was a windfall for gun manufacturers, their stockholders and dealers, but a growing catastrophe for the American people and for countries in the developing world. Hunting and target guns for shooting sports remain large market items today, but the gun industry's growth is concentrated in selling powerful handguns, military-style weapons, and assault rifles.

It's no secret that guns are big business. James L. Oberg, President of Smith and Wesson Company, declared "we are focusing on dollars more than anything else."[9] And William B. Ruger, CEO of Sturm Ruger, Inc., boasted, "We have a little moneymaking machine here. All we have to do is keep introducing the correct new products."[10]

THE MANTRA FOR TODAY'S GUNS: POWER, SPEED, AND FIREPOWER

Gary Anderson, recently retired from the NRA, said long ago the market is dominated by the "Rambo factor," a term he coined in 1993. "American shooting activities place a predominant emphasis on large caliber arms that can be fired rapidly." In the past, gun owners spoke of a kind of trinity: "skill, accuracy, and "marksmanship." No longer. The optimal words for guns today are "power, speed, and firepower."[11]

Says Diaz: "Gun manufacturers have been increasing the firepower of guns for over four decades, but they are constantly being

8. Davidson, *Under Fire*, 36.

9. Cox Newspaper Services, FL, 1981, quoted by Tom Diaz, Violence Policy Center Slideshow, September16, 2008.

10. William R. Ruger, CEO, Sturm Ruger and Co., Inc, quoted by Tom Diaz, Violence Policy Center Power Point presentation, September 16, 2008.

11. Gary Anderson, quoted by Tom Diaz, Violence Policy Center Power Point presentation, Sept. 16, 2008.

pushed by entrepreneurs who are busy creating 'wildcat' or hybrid calibers of ammunition and guns to match them. The most enthusiastic gun lovers are never satisfied with what they can buy off the shelf."[12]

It's a dead end street to argue why America needs to produce bigger and better guns. It's un-American not to have new models coming off assembly lines, whether they are from air-conditioners to pickup trucks, to new handguns. The Gun Empire can easily convince gun aficionados that *a greater violence is required today* to protect our freedoms and give us peace of mind. Regardless of consumerism and of love of the latest gadget, questions about the latest guns should linger. Why is America unwilling to keep these powerful weapons out of the hands of terrorists, criminals, and people who are a danger to themselves and society? Why would the NRA craft legislation to make it easier for dangerous people to buy these guns? Why would the Gun Empire protect not only the guns of respectable citizens, but also those of the least desirable elements of our society? Like so many other details in our gun culture, it makes no sense. Could it have something to do with the slippery slope?

THE GUN EMPIRE'S FIRST SOLUTION TO STOPPING GUN VIOLENCE

If you ask the Gun Empire, "How can we stop gun violence in the country?" they will offer three strategies. First and foremost: "We need more guns." It makes crisp slogans such as More Guns = Less Crime. The Empire is fully committed to this approach, although it is akin to the alcoholic who vows over and over again, "just one more drink and I can solve my problems."

One of the most vocal critics of gun control and passionate advocates of increasing the numbers of citizens who carry concealed weapons to deter crime is the economist, Dr. John Lott, formerly of Yale and the University of Chicago. On August 2, 1996, *The USA Today*, under the headline "Fewer Rapes, Killings Found Where Concealed Guns Legal," reported the results of a "comprehensive" study showing that the states with "shall issue concealed carry permits" had

12. Diaz, *Making a Killing*, 24.

substantial decreases in homicides, rapes, and aggravated assaults. Lott and his colleague David Mustard analyzed crime statistics in the nation's 3,054 counties from 1977 to 1992 and published their findings in the January 1997 *Journal of Legal Studies*. There they made the remarkable claims that had all states adopted the "shall issue laws" by 1992, 1,500 murders, would have been avoided annually, along with 4,000 rapes, 11,000 robberies, and 60,000 aggravated assaults. Shortly thereafter Lott published his book, *More Guns, Less Crime*.[13] Lott's work has been challenged by more than a dozen researchers in at least eight published articles.[14]

More recently he was scheduled to give a lecture on his controversial book at the University of Texas Law School in September 2010, but the event had to be canceled. That very day a gunman wearing a ski mask entered the library and fired his gun several times, before taking his own life.[15] The timing for Lott's lecture was just not right. Nor is it unusual for the NRA to pull legislation from consideration when a well-publicized shooting is still in the news. The NRA wants the nation to continue praying for the survivors. Timing is everything and the empire's success in passing the legislation it wants depends on the very short memories of legislators.

THE SECOND SOLUTION TO STOP GUN VIOLENCE: ENFORCE THE LAWS

Whenever a new gun law is proposed in *any* legislature, a lobbyist is sure to holler, "We don't need any more laws. What we need is for the police to arrest criminals and enforce the twenty thousand laws we already have on the books." Pretending there are indeed *twenty thousand laws* has been part of the NRA's repertoire since the 1960s. Many of us have heard this number quoted so frequently we consider it factual. The truth is no one knows where the twenty thousand figure came from. No source is ever credited. Jon Vernick of Johns Hopkins University and Lisa Hepburn of Harvard University learned

13. Lott and Mustard, "Crime, Deterrence, and Right-to-Carry Concealed Handguns," 1.

14. Henigan, *Lethal Logic*, 131.

15. Steven Hoffer, AOL News, September 28, 2010.

through an electronic newspaper search there were more than two hundred uses of the twenty thousand figure from 1998–2002. Thus began their research. The earliest reference they were able to locate appears in the congressional testimony in 1965 by Rep. John Dingell, D-Michigan, then on the NRA Board, but no records are cited and no source is given. Years later, to the delight of the NRA after President Reagan was shot, he rejected the call for additional gun legislation, saying: "there are today more than 20,000 gun control laws in effect—federal, state, and local—in the United States." Numerous books and articles continue to cite the number twenty thousand but *never* the source.[16]

Vernick and Hepburn conclude there are "about 300 major state and federal laws and an unknown but shrinking number of local laws due to the fact that 40 of our states have preempted all or most local gun laws." They end their research with a suggestion: "Rather than trying to base arguments for more or fewer laws on counting up the current total, we would do better to study the impact of the laws we do have."[17]

THE THIRD SOLUTION IS TO PUNISH THE CRIMINAL

Because the tools of the Gun Empire are those of deadly force, it is understandable and consistent that they would insist on severe penalties and punishment to the fullest extent of the law for all those who use a gun in a crime. One of their favorite programs is Project Exile, begun in Richmond, Virginia, in 1997. Exile stipulates that any crime committed with a gun automatically goes to Federal Court and an automatic five years is added to the sentence of the perpetrators. They are exiled from society and punished to the fullest extent of the law. Many law enforcement agencies support the program, which they claim has reduced crime in areas where it is put in place.

We should not overlook the fact that punishment is meted out only *after* a crime has been committed, and too often victims are

---

16. Vernick and Hepburn, "Twenty Thousand Gun Control Laws?"
17. Ibid.

already dead. A city or state cannot punish a mentally ill young man like Seung Hui Cho of Virginia Tech who took his own life *after* killing thirty-two and wounding fifty-seven. The State of Arizona is in a quandary trying to punish the mentally deranged Jared Loughner, who shot nineteen people in Tucson, killing six. Putting people in prison for life or handing out death sentences *after crimes have been committed* does not really help us build a more just society and will not deter others, particularly the mentally ill, from killing in the future.

Delving further into punishing offenders and examining the simple justice of our criminal justice system is beyond the scope of this book, but our cities, states, and federal government must start protecting those persons who are fated to be the gun violence victims of the future. By studying grid maps of our large metropolitan cities, we can predict where the majorities of those deaths will take place. The majority will be in those sections of the cities where the most arrests for serious crime are made, which also happens to be where there is the highest incidence of communicable disease, alcoholism, and drug use, the lowest levels of literacy, the highest number of school dropouts and unwed mothers, and where the most rats are.

We can prevent many of our most vulnerable citizens from being shot or killed if we develop the will to do so. Alas, the Gun Empire rejects prevention because it implies "controlling guns." Prevention in their minds means "gun control" and big government swooping down to take guns away from law-abiding people, which will put us at the mercy of dangerous criminals. At every turn we meet the slippery slope.

Doctors practice preventive medicine; we use preventive measures to keep tainted food and dangerous medicines from our citizens; we prevent automobile accidents by requiring safety inspections; motorcyclists wear helmets to prevent crippling injuries; we prevent sports injuries with good equipment, etc. What is so draconian or un-American about preventing thousands of injuries and deaths by keeping guns out of the hands of those who are a danger to themselves and others?

THE NRA DECEIVES ITS OWN MEMBERSHIP, NEW RECRUITS, AND GUN BUYERS

Another dimension of the Gun Empire's deception is the fear they create within their own members, recruits, and potential customers. For example: when new ballistic fingerprinting technology was offered the ATF and FBI for help in tracing *crime guns*, it was bitterly opposed by the NRA, which called it an incremental step on the slippery slope leading to government confiscation.

This is par for the course. When even a minimal or wise restriction on guns is proposed in Congress, the NRA distributes thousands of letters and e-mails to members and potential members advising them that their gun rights are in jeopardy. They recite the typical shibboleths that are known to provoke fear: Here come the gun haters and gun grabbers again. They want to register your guns and limit how many you can have; they want to fingerprint you like a criminal and take away your Second Amendment rights; they want to confiscate your guns and padlock your hunting lands; they want to take away your God-given right to defend yourself and your family. Stop the gun grabbers. And the letters never forget to ask for a check.

Immediately after the 2010 elections, which changed the face of the House of Representatives, sponsors of The Nation's Gun Show in the Washington DC suburbs, advertised "1000 tables: The size of two football fields. Over 1.5 miles of Guns, Knives and Accessories." The ad continued: "The Present Administration will attempt to make changes to firearms regulations! Get your guns while you still can!"[18]

TWO AND A HALF MILLION DEFENSIVE GUN USES PER YEAR

As John Lott proclaims more guns in more hands will decrease crime, the Gun Empire along with its most innovative dealers praise the scholarship of their own scientist, Dr. Gary Kleck, Professor of Criminology and Criminal Justice at Florida State University. All gun zealots are familiar with Kleck's "academics" and "research" and

18. Advertisement in *The Washington Post*, November 19–21, 2010.

quote him freely in their magazines and on the airwaves. Their admiration is understandable, for his work "proves" their faith that guns actually *do* save lives. As in "figures don't lie." The Empire has its own scholar to prove their point. The research attributed to Kleck reveals there are 2.5 million annual defensive gun uses in America.

The NRA and the rest of the Gun Empire reject the data compiled by the FBI and the CDC, the two governmental agencies responsible for keeping national death records from all sources, and publicize instead their own unique set of numbers for "Defensive Gun Use in the United States." There is logic to their highly inflated figures. The greater the numbers of "successful gun uses," as in stopping a crime, the more compelling the reason for clients to buy the best and most powerful guns. Like any company, the greater the perceived effectiveness of its products, the greater its sales, which is the be all and end all for the Gun Empire. Gun dealers, citing Kleck's research, tell their customers that 6,850 times a day, every thirteen seconds, law-abiding people use their guns to defend themselves and their families against criminals, or 2.5 million times a year.[19]

I put Kleck's "academics" and "research" in quotes for two reasons. First of all, his methodology does not qualify as "scientific inquiry." More than half of the defensive gun uses Kleck cites cannot be verified because they are based on the *assumptions* of gun owners that alluding to the presence of their gun(s) scares off would be attackers. The accuracy of this assumption is impossible to measure. It is similar to a man placing a "Beware of Dog" sign on his fence and boasting that at least fifty robbers or rapists had been scared away from his property in the past year. Can he prove his boast? Who could prove him wrong?

The second reason I put Kleck's "academics" and "research" in quotes is that his work does not stand up to scrutiny. One of the most telling articles that refute Dr. Kleck's "research" is his own interview with author and filmmaker, J. Neil Schulman. In the interview, on September 13, 1993, Kleck asserts that,

> 54 percent of the defensive gun uses involved somebody
> verbally referring to the gun. 47 percent involved the gun

19. Flyer from Realco Guns of District Heights, Maryland; in the author's personal collection.

being pointed at the criminal. 22 percent involved the gun being fired. 14 percent involved the gun being fired at somebody, meaning it was not just a warning shot; the defender was trying to shoot the criminal. Whether they succeeded or not is another matter but they were trying to shoot a criminal. Finally, in 8 percent of the cases, according to Kleck and his sources, gun owners actually wounded or killed the offender.[20]

When we take a closer look at the math, 8 percent of 2.5 million incidents is two hundred thousand, which Kleck says, is the number of undesirable people killed or wounded by responsible gun owners on a yearly basis. The FBI, on the other hand, document only 100,000 persons who are injured by guns and between 150 and 200 whose deaths have been ruled "justifiable homicides" in the country in any typical year. As for the latter, most of those homicides are at the hands of law enforcement officials who are required to make a report every time their gun is fired.[21]

Dr. David Hemenway, professor at Harvard's School of Public Health, dissected the work of Kleck and Marc Gertz (his associate) in *The Journal of Criminal Law and Criminology* and concluded their survey design contained "a huge overestimation bias" and their estimate is "highly exaggerated." Hemenway applied Kleck and Gertz's methodology to a 1994 *ABC News/Washington Post Survey* in which people were asked if they had ever seen an alien spacecraft or come into direct contact with a space alien. He demonstrated by the application of Kleck and Gertz's methodology, one would conclude that almost twenty million Americans have actually seen a spacecraft from another planet and more than a million have actually met a space alien.[22]

Hemenway and his associates sponsored three national surveys to delve more deeply into the issue of self-defense gun use. They discovered that most of the self-defense gun uses reported on surveys

20. "Q and A: Guns, Crime and Self-Defense," *The Orange County Register*, September 19, 1993.

21. Dr. Gary Kleck, interview by J. Neil Schulman, *The Orange County Register*, September 13, 1993.

22. Hemenway, "Survey Research and Self-Defense Gun Use," 1430–31.

were gun uses in escalating arguments, not in response to actual crimes, and that these uses were both illegal and inimical to society.[23]

The cunning of the Empire in bearing false witness has turned deception and misinformation into art forms, which have undoubtedly increased their sales and influence, but they have come at a very high price. Eventually, the deceptions and falsehoods will be brought into the light. Alexander Solzhenitsyn in his acceptance speech in 1970 for the Nobel Prize for Literature, said, "Let us not forget that violence does not live alone and is not capable of living alone: it is necessarily interwoven with falsehood. Violence finds its only refuge in falsehood, and falsehood its only support in violence. Any man who has once acclaimed violence as his method must inexorably choose falsehood as his principle."[24]

The Gun Empire has at this point in American history wagered that an apathetic American public and a timid church would neither check their statistics for accuracy nor their statements for truth. Today, as the public is starting to resent the ever increasing firepower of their guns and mass shootings are growing more unacceptable, I am gambling that people of faith are *almost ready* to start checking their facts and examining their statistics. When the church and their ecumenical colleagues do their homework and have the integrity to tell the truth from the housetops, our elected leaders will write balanced legislation that supports two constitutional rights: the right to keep and bear arms and the right to live in a safe society with commonsense gun laws.

23. Hemenway et al., "Gun Use in the United States: Results from Two National Surveys," 263–67.

24. Solzhenitsyn, Acceptance Speech for Nobel Peace Prize for Literature, 1970.

11

The Idol Can't Keep
Its Promises

All idols that have ever been placed on a pedestal, literally or figuratively, have the same problem—keeping their promises. Think of all the promises a defensive gun pledges its owner: power, protection, self-confidence, self-determination, security, safety, and control in out-of-control situations. If a gun could keep all these promises, its devotee would be omnipotent and fully in control, just like God, but isn't that why guns are sold?

The Apostle Paul boasts of Almighty God, "who by the power at work within us is able to do far more abundantly than all that we can ask or think" (Eph 3:20). That is not the case with idols. No idol has an unlimited storehouse of blessings or power. Jesus instructs us "to give and it will be given to you; good measure, pressed down, shaken together, running over will be put into your lap. For the measure you give will be given to you" (Luke 6:38).

When God is trusted there is always more; when an object made with human hands is trusted, there is always less. That's a dilemma, particularly for the idols of power and deadly force. People place too much trust in them. People expect too much of finite things, human ideas, and ideologies that capture their imaginations and fantasies. In the end, our idols *always* disappoint us.

We all know individuals who are busy acquiring more and more things. It seems to be their reason for being. If friends remind them money won't buy happiness, they reply, "Then you don't know where to shop." When they are buying something new, they expect it to bring satisfaction and happiness. Having been a pastor in affluent neighborhoods for three decades, I've heard countless cries from within beautiful mansions and gated communities: "I love my life-style but I am not happy." I knew a lovely, wealthy widow who lived alone in her beautiful home and refused to travel beyond the city limits. She had drawers of expensive jewelry and her beautifully appointed home was filled with fine silver, crystal, and art. On a beastly hot summer day I said, "Why don't you go to your house up in the mountains like you used to do and enjoy the cool air and get away from this oppressive heat?" She sighed, "I would like to, but it's just too much trouble and I'm not about to leave this house unattended. It is full of silver." She was imprisoned by beautiful idols.

Another friend confessed, "I know about idols. I grew up in a home with a father who was an alcoholic." There is a large difference between one who enjoys a social drink and one who *needs* a drink to get through the day. For the latter, alcohol is not only an illness, but an idol to which one looks for deliverance. An alcoholic trusts a drink to soothe one's nerves, relieve one's anxieties, or provide strength to face a new day.

Sinclair Lewis describes the scene: "A man takes to drink, a drink takes another, and the drink takes the man." The idol cannot deliver what it promises. Serving this idol often leads to divorce, loss of a job, foreclosure, or the forfeiture of relationships with children.

Although we expect miracles from America's idol of world military superiority and spend more than the next 19 nations *combined* on their militaries,[1] it cannot provide the security or peace it publicly pronounces. Although we drop smart bombs on our enemies; direct predator drones from across the ocean to fire missiles in Afghanistan; fly the most sophisticated jets; intimidate the world with 10,000 nuclear weapons, and spend a million dollars a year to deploy a single soldier in the Middle East, the people of the United States remain anxious and live on the edge, particularly after 9/11.

Similarly, trusting that the most powerful semi-automatic handgun or assault weapon will calm one's nerves or bring peace of mind is destined to disappoint. Instruments of death are incapable of bestowing peace of mind and security. They provide only a "controlled fear." Peace of mind and security are spiritual gifts that only

---

1. Stockholm International Peace Research.

God can dispense. They are God's gifts; God's alone. We can't supply them for ourselves.

In thirty-six years of working to prevent gun violence I have observed that those who must be armed everywhere they go are very nervous and fearful people. I once asked a man in Richmond, Virginia, who had a gun strapped to his leg, "Why are you carrying that gun? Are you afraid of someone?" He replied angrily, "You're damn right I'm afraid and I'm going to get him before he gets me." The security and peace promised by tools of violence are a delusion and the concept of security itself in this tenuous world, is really a scam.

Many who buy guns for protection overestimate their capacity for control in intolerable situations. Human beings are only creatures. In God's world, the creature is never in control, no matter how powerful his tools. The creature may *think* he is in control, but the creature is always by nature, limited. Being overtaken by events is part of what it means to be a human being. Thinking one is in control is one of life's greatest delusions. It is scandalous that such fantasies of control are preached with regularity on college campuses, as students are encouraged to obtain a CCWP.

EVANGELISTS ON COLLEGE CAMPUSES AND STATE HOUSES FOR CONCEALED CARRY

In May 2011, the Texas State Senate passed a bill to allow concealed handguns on state college campuses, which proponents believed would increase safety by introducing the option of self-defense for those with state-issued permits. More than twenty other states have taken up similar bills, which have been strongly supported by Students for Concealed Carry.

The organization has over seventy campuses in three states that allow concealed carry by licensed individuals. "We're tired of depending on the cooperation and goodwill of criminals," said Daniel Crocker, Southern Regional Director. "We shouldn't have to sacrifice the right to protect ourselves to pursue higher education." Governor Rick Perry expressed his support for the measure.[2]

2. Online: www.studentsforconcealedcarry.com.

All these efforts to remove "gun free zones" from the premises of higher education fly in the face of Joe Zamudio, the Tucson hero who tackled and subdued Jared Loughner, after he shot Congresswoman Giffords and killed six others. Zamudio was armed during the incident and confessed he "almost fired at the wrong man, giving more evidence that having more guns in a deadly, rowdy shootout, is not the solution, and, in fact, might increase the body count."[3]

There is one indisputable fact that must be taken into consideration by leaders in statehouses and in houses of worship. Wherever guns are in abundance, cumulative deaths by those guns will surely follow. There are more guns in America's Southland than any other section of the country and it is not a coincidence that the South has the highest rates of gun deaths, with New Orleans holding the distinction of being America's per capita murder capital. As more and more students acquire concealed carry permits, we can with certainty predict there will be more murders and heartbreaking accidents. Concealed carry individuals, just like the rest of us, have their own idiosyncrasies, limitations, and breaking points.

On October 11, 2011, Tennessee State Representative Curry Todd was jailed and charged with drunken driving and possession of a loaded handgun. Todd was the sponsor who led the fight in the Tennessee legislature to pass concealed carry laws and give permit holders the right to carry such weapons into bars and other places where alcohol is served. Before the law was enacted he said, "Drinking with your gun is something that no responsible handgun owner would ever do. In fact, it is prohibited under the Tennessee guns-in-bars law. The law was only to let law abiding (sober) citizens carry their licensed weapons into family restaurants [or places where alcohol is served, such as bars, nightclubs, and pizza parlors—brackets mine] to protect all the patrons against any would-be robbers or other armed assailants."[4]

It is particularly troubling to learn that the screening process in many states to keep dangerous individuals from acquiring these permits is almost non-existent. In 2009 in Virginia alone, six people

3. *The Brady Report*, Winter 2011, 5.

4. Eric Schelzig, "Sponsor of Law Allowing Guns in Bars Arrested on DUI, Gun Charges," October 12, 2011, Associated Press, Fox News.com.

with CCWP committed mass murders (defined as three or more deaths.) Virginia permit holders from 2008 through 2011 killed 34 persons and wounded 40. CSGV monitors the shootings of those with CCWP, which the NRA says are the most trustworthy citizens.[5]

My friend, Andy Goddard, whose son Colin is a survivor of the Virginia Tech shooting, made plain how easily one can get a CCWP. When the Virginia Legislature, for the convenience of its citizens, opened a website for applications, Andy logged on, filled out the required data, sent in his payment by credit card, and in a few minutes had his license. Convenient, yes, but Andy Goddard has *never* held a pistol in his hand. Thirty-three states at present issue concealed weapons permits, including Kentucky and Ohio, who have issued CCWP to persons who are blind.[6]

INHERENT DANGERS FOR CONCEALED CARRY PEOPLE

Gun lovers often speak about feeling safe when they are packing heat. However, knowing some uncomfortable truths might save their lives. Even if one carries a state-of-the-art semi-automatic Glock 19, if another is determined to kill you, you *will* most likely die. When one is determined to rob, rape, or kill you he will not announce his presence or intent to give you a chance to meet his deadly force with your own. That is not the *modus operandi* of killers, rapists, or thieves. If one should approach you with gun in hand, you will not be able to take your gun off the table, out of a drawer, or remove it from your holster or purse. Should you try, you will be killed.

Even some in the gun press consider CCWP to be dangerous. One writer described carriers as people "who are looking for trouble." Another showed how an improperly concealed carry handgun creates a lethal risk for the permit holder. Said he: "One of the prerequisites of concealed carry is that people don't know you have a gun. Failure to conceal it properly can be a fatal mistake. I was in a

5. "Mass Shootings by Concealed Handgun Permit Holders in 2009, www .csgv.org/ccwmassshooters.

6. Joseph Gerth, "Blind May Still Carry Weapons After Bill to End Practice Fails," *The Courier Journal* (Louisville), February 1, 2012.

restaurant recently and noticed a man sitting at a nearby table. He was wearing jeans and a jean jacket and every time he reached for a piece of pizza, I could plainly see his SIG P226 in a pancake holster. If I was able to see his pistol, so was everyone else. If there was someone in there planning to rob the place, he would have been identified as a threat and, therefore, he was at risk of being neutralized first by any serious attacker."[7]

Donna Dees-Thomases, the first mom of the Million Mom March, tells of growing up in New Orleans where her father owned a pharmacy in an economically depressed area. He had difficulty hiring other pharmacists to come and work for him because of the store's location, so the family moved to nearby Metairie in hopes of living and working in a safer place. The smaller community, however, turned out to be no safe haven. Though her dad had never been held up in New Orleans, he was robbed at gunpoint many times in Metairie. One of her father's customers asked him why he didn't buy a gun for protection. He replied, "Because I want to live to see the next holdup."[8]

HAVING A DEFENSIVE GUN NEARBY ENDANGERS MANY

Having a gun in one's home for protection, particularly if it is kept loaded and unlocked, endangers everyone. Disagreements, arguments, or family feuds are the precursors of someone pulling a trigger in anger. American women overwhelmingly bear the brunt of gun violence in the home. They are eleven times more likely to be the victims of guns than women in other high-income countries. One-third of all murders of American women are committed by their intimate partners compared to only 4 percent of men.[9] If there is a gun in the home, a woman is five times more likely to become a victim of domestic homicide. Recent research shows a man's access to firearms increases a woman's risk of being killed. From 1995–2003

7. "Picking a Hideout Holster," *American Rifleman*, cited in Diaz, *Making a Killing*, 170.

8. Dees-Thomases, *Looking For a Few Good Moms*, xvii.

9. Julie Samuels, "Findings from the National Violence Against Women Survey," Department of Justice, 2000.

after Canada tightened its gun laws, gun homicide rates for women dropped by 40 percent.[10] One should never tell a woman who is subject to domestic abuse that her intimate partner's gun is going to protect her. In spite of this research, judges and police are reluctant to take away guns from men who have a history of domestic abuse.

Police officers are another segment of society put at risk by always having a gun in close proximity. In 2010, fifty-six of our nation's law enforcement officers were killed in the line of duty. All but one died at the barrel of a gun. Seven were killed with their own weapons. These were highly skilled professionals who were required to spend hours and hours in weapons training, yet their guns were taken from them and used against them.[11] Consider the dangers for those not so highly trained.

Other gun deaths and injuries are accidental. The words of the old song describe an indisputable peril for all those who are careless with their weapons and keep them within easy reach: "I didn't know the gun was loaded and I'm so sorry my friend. I didn't know the gun was loaded and I'll never, never do it again." The website www. Ohhshoot.com monitors accidental gun deaths in America and describes some totally irresponsible, bizarre behavior, even from NRA gun instructors who have shot themselves or their clients during lessons on self-defense.

Newlywed 22-year-old Tianna Gremore, of Marion Township, Michigan, gave her new husband, 20-year-old Dylan Gremore, a 9mm semiautomatic handgun as a gift. Dylan had the gun a little over a month when he was cleaning the weapon and trying to familiarize himself with the gun. According to police, "He made the major mistake of not taking the clip out of the fully loaded gun before he racked it." Not realizing his actions put a round in the chamber, Dylan pulled the trigger. The bullet hit his hand then grazed his forearm and leg before hitting his wife's leg.[12]

10. Scottish Trades Union Congress, Stop Violence Against Women Conference.

11. "FBI Releases Preliminary Statistics for Law Enforcement Officers Killed in 2010," News release, Washington, D.C., May 16, 2011, 1.

12. "New Bride Gives Husband Handgun as Gift; He Then Unintentionally Shoots Them Both." January 26, 2012, Ohhshootblogspot.com.

Human beings make costly mistakes. The Bullet Counter-Points, "Ordinary People" Series (www.csgv.org) monitors the episodes of ordinary people with CCWP whose bad judgment and/or carelessness led to tragic consequences. One such episode occurred on June 9, 2008, in Columbia, South Carolina. A respected government official and grandmother took her four-year-old granddaughter shopping at Sam's Club. When her back was turned, the child got into her grandmother's purse, pulled out her loaded small-caliber handgun and shot herself in the chest. Luckily, the bullet missed her major organs and the child recovered after surgery.[13] Even highly intelligent, law-abiding gun owners, just like the rest of us, are subject to the distractions of everyday life that often lead to serious lapses in judgment. No one plans on accidents; no one plans on being distracted. The woman believed her gun would protect her, but in the end, it almost killed her granddaughter.

Nearly 1.7 million kids under the age of eighteen live in homes with firearms that are both loaded and unlocked, ostensibly to better protect the family.[14] Children, inquisitive by nature, do explore their homes. If they discover a gun in a dresser or closet, *even if they have been told not to touch a gun,* frequently pull the trigger, killing themselves, a playmate, or a family member. Responsible gun owners, for the safety of all concerned, should at a minimum have a trigger lock on each gun. All guns are lethal. It torments me when I hear gun zealots say, "Of course, I keep my gun loaded and unlocked; a gun that isn't loaded and unlocked is like a car in the garage without gas."

If your child is invited to play in a neighbor's home, please, please inquire if they have a gun. If they do, parents must then ask if the gun is locked up. If there is an unlocked gun in your neighbor's home, it is not safe for your child to play there. You can invite the neighbor's child to come play in your home. My friend, Carole Price, who told her young son, "Sure, you can go play at the neighbors," knows firsthand the agony I seek to prevent. She says, "If you think asking your neighbor if there's a gun in the home is hard? Trust me. Picking out your child's coffin is worse."[15]

13. http.://knudsennews.blogspot.com/2008_06_01_archive.html.

14. Sy Kraft, "National ASK Day Promotes Children's Gun Safety," Medical News Today/Pediatrics/Children's Health.

15. Dees-Thomases, *Looking For a Few Good Moms,* 89.

SUICIDE

More than half of the gun deaths in America are suicides, which have outranked firearms homicides for over one hundred years.[16] In most instances, these deaths are by guns originally purchased for protection. Prior to my senior year in college, suicide was an abstract idea, but it became painfully real when one of the most influential persons in my life, Dr. William T. Martin, Jr., Pastor of the First Presbyterian Church of Tallahassee, Florida, took his own life with a gun early one Sunday morning in 1956. The sermon he had planned to deliver that morning was "Facing Life Steadily." For whatever reasons, he was unable to face life steadily. His depression, about which few had a clue, consumed his desire to face life at all, and his death rocked his wife and young children, the city of Tallahassee, and the campus of Florida State University.

As a pastor, I have tried to give encouragement and hope to those who were contemplating suicide; sadly, I have wept with families and friends whose loved ones took their own lives. When a gun is used in a suicide attempt it is almost always successful. The struggle is over for the departed, but the friends and families who survive have an agonizing lifelong path to walk. Their questions never cease. The cruel "if onlys" never go away. They keep on asking, "Why?" "Why?" and there are no good answers.

Suicide is America's third-leading cause of death among young people 15–24 years of age, while the highest rates of suicide deaths are for white men over eighty-five who are despondent over declining health, the loss of a life's partner, or other attendant maladies of aging. Divorce ranks as the number one factor linked with suicide rates in major cities, ranking above all other physical, financial, and psychological factors. Divorced people are three times more likely to commit suicide, as are married people. For all age groups, the most common method and the great facilitator for suicide is a firearm.[17]

16. Garen S. Wintemute, interview by Evan Silverstein, *Presbyterian News Service*, September 20, 2008, 1–2.

17. Kathleen Lawler-Row and Jeff Elliott, "The Role of Religious Activity and Spirituality in the Health and Well-Being of Older Adults," *Journal of Health Psychology*, 43–52.

It is beyond the scope of this book to deal substantively with the root causes or symptoms of depression that drive people to end their lives. The causes and symptoms are varied and run deep, far deeper into our psyches than most of us can assimilate. The late Dr. Karl Menninger, founder of the Menninger Psychiatric Clinic, wrote, "The great sin by which we all are tempted is the wish to hurt others." He asserts, "Suicides are sometimes committed to forestall the committing of murder? There is no doubt of it. Nor is there any doubt that murder is sometimes committed to avert suicide."[18] This is a sobering assessment, which calls for increased social awareness, but for whatever reasons, be it the side effects of pharmaceutical drugs, bullying, or depression, if depression or suicidal thoughts are suspected at any time in our family members or friends, it is imperative to get the person to a doctor immediately and remove all guns from the house with haste.

The New England Journal of Medicine report on "Guns and Suicide in the United States" makes a good case for physicians and other healthcare providers who care for suicidal patients to assess whether people at risk for suicide have access to a firearm or other lethal means and to work with patients and their families to limit access to those means until suicidal feelings have passed. Effective suicide prevention, says the report, should focus not only on a patient's psychological condition, but also on the availability of lethal instruments, which can mean the difference between life and death.[19]

One-third to four-fifths of all suicide attempts, according to studies, are impulsive. Among people who made near-lethal suicide attempts, for example, 24 percent took less than five minutes between the decision to kill themselves and the actual attempt, and 70 percent took less than one hour.[20]

Meanwhile, the NRA persuaded the Florida legislature and Governor to write into law a provision that prohibits doctors from asking patients or parents if there is a gun in their home. NRA's

18. Menninger, BrainyQuote.com, Xplore, Inc., 2011.

19. Miller and Hemenway, "Perspective: Guns and Suicide in the United States," New England Journal of Medicine, 989–91.

20. Simon et al., "Characteristics of Impulsive Suicide Attempts and Attempters," 49–59.

chief Florida lobbyist, Marion Hammer says, "We take our children to pediatricians for medical care, not social judgment, not privacy intrusions."[21] Fortunately, some of Florida's doctors sued to stop such a ridiculous law and prevailed in the courts. This small victory however will not deter the paid lobbyists for the NRA from keeping the courts clogged with other ludicrous proposals to protect guns instead of people.

As the NRA coup d'état in 1977 changed the association from recreational pursuits to making money by selling handguns, a New Jersey Company, Constitution Arms, has successfully completed tests on plans to market a "Palm Pistol" for physically impaired persons and the elderly who suffer from arthritis or other maladies of aging and would have trouble pulling a trigger. The concept allows individuals to shoot the gun by squeezing a trigger device with their thumb. Their website says this gun design is something seniors need to assist them in daily living. "Using the thumb instead of the index finger for firing, significantly reduces muzzle drift, which is one of the principal causes of inaccurate targeting. Point and shoot couldn't be easier." As of September 2010, no start-up dates or retail costs have been made.[22] In America, if a device goes "boom" there is a market for it.

21. Greg Allen, "Florida Bill Could Muzzle Doctors on Gun Safety," National Public Radio, May 7, 2011.

22. "Easy to Use 'Palm Pistol' Aimed at Elderly, Disabled," www.palmpistol .com.

12

The Idol Transforms People and Communities

A NEW CREATION

Exchanging new lives for old has long been the promise of the Christian faith. The Apostle Paul puts it this way: "If anyone is in Christ, there is a new creation: everything old is passed away; see, everything has become new" (2 Cor 5:17). In his Letter to the Galatians, Paul describes the personality traits of those who become new creations: love, joy, peace, patience, kindness, generosity, faithfulness, gentleness and self-control," and calls these the "fruits of God's Spirit" (Gal 5:22–23).

An individual who says yes to God is transformed and is blessed with a new way of looking at life, a new understanding of oneself and his world, and he must reorder his attitudes and priorities. A conversion also takes place in the life of one who believes a gun has the power to save and protect. She too becomes a new creation with a new way of looking at life, a new understanding of herself and her world, and she must reorder her attitudes and priorities. She develops a new spirit, which is akin to the idol itself. The new spirit of the idol captures "the new believer." The gun is only a thing, but it is *a thing with a spirit*. If one loves mercy, does justice, and wants to walk humbly with God, one grows to be like God. That is God's promise. Conversely, if one looks to tools of violence for deliverance, one grows to be like those tools. The psalmist's words ring true: "Those who make idols are like them; so are all who trust in them" (Ps 115:8).

With a 9mm-semi-automatic gun in hand, no longer are you someone others can run over, you are now in the driver's seat. No longer are you controlled; you are *in control*. No longer are you weak and vulnerable; you are *strong*. No longer are you afraid; you are *fearless*. No longer must you take orders; you will *give orders*. No longer will you be bullied and obey your tormentors; *you can make your tormentors pay* for their insults. With gun in hand, no longer will Dr. Amy Bishop be insulted by her fellow biology professors for denying her tenure at the University of Alabama-Huntsville. She can shoot three of them dead. And she did.[1]

With that cold steel in your hands and the overwhelming power it conveys, you become a different person. You have a feeling you can get whatever you want and you have a right to it. In the process you become another person. When Eric Sevareid was a World War II correspondent in Europe, he met two American paratroopers after France was liberated. They didn't have a place to stay so he invited them to his hotel room to relax. A big man from St. Louis, who had been a milk truck driver, said, "I've been reading how the FBI is organizing special squads to take care of us when we get home. I've got an idea it'll be needed. See this pistol? I killed a man this morning, just to get it. I ran into a German officer in a hotel near the edge of town. He surrendered, but he wouldn't give me his pistol. You know, it kind of scares me. It's so easy to kill; it solves all your problems and there's no questions asked. I think I'm getting the habit."[2]

DIFFERING IMAGES AND VALUES OF GUNS

Tom Diaz says the firearm is less a utilitarian tool than an icon, so laden with implicit values its hold over its devotees approaches the mystical. In this context, guns are not simply mechanical devices to be used as means to such ends as self-defense, target competition, or hunting, but function as tribal totems embodying a complex of values that includes manliness (defined in warrior terms), individual

1. Shalia Dewan, Stephanie Saul, and Kate Zemia, "For Professor, Fury Just Beneath the Surface," *New York Times,* February 20, 2010.

2. Sevareid, *Not So Wild a Dream,* 417.

liberty (as against the state), self-reliance (as against everyone else), and the administration of preemptory justice by ad hoc personal means (shooting "bad" people).[3]

Legal scholar Allen Rostron points to the duality of how Americans view guns: the dual nature of guns is reflected in the very different feelings people have about them. For many Americans, guns have overwhelmingly positive associations. To them, guns are about families and traditions, about growing up and spending time learning how to shoot and hunt, and about each generation passing something on to the next. For others, guns have completely different connotations. To a young person in an inner city, guns may be associated only with bad things, like being scared, having grandparents who are afraid to go outside, or knowing someone who was shot.[4]

There is a world of difference between family members or friends going hunting together or a grandfather passing on his shotgun to his grandson as a keepsake and believing that a semi-automatic handgun will keep one safe. When one *trusts* (the most basic of spiritual concepts) a gun for one's well being, the seeds of a disturbing idea are planted in the mind, which can and frequently does turn one's personality inside out and upside down. I've seen it happen to soldiers and civilians alike.

When guns become idols and life seems too dangerous to be without them, one's ability to reason, cherish community, love neighbors, and depend on God for security are often surrendered. One does not think about such things as cause and effect or the value of negotiation over confrontation, or forgiveness instead of revenge. Nor does a gun zealot imagine his young child could be so fascinated by his Daddy's gun collection that he wants to examine them up close, especially the one he keeps in the third drawer of his dresser in the bedroom.

Rather than offering a vision of community in which we are bound together by our common humanity, reverence for guns teaches two paradoxical emotions: omnipotence and fear. Omnipotence as one feels the thrill of being in charge and able to dominate others, and fear as one begins to suspect enemies or potential enemies who might want to take away one's new-found power.

3. Diaz, *Making a Killing*, 50.

4. Rostron, "Cease Fire: A Win-Win Strategy on Gun Policy for the Obama Administration," *Harvard Law and Political Review*, 347–67.

THE OVERWHELMING PRESENCE OF GUNS COMPLICATES THE SEARCH FOR AN IDENTITY

Devotion to a gun clouds one's relationship with God and God's other children. Instead of loving and learning to trust God and neighbor, fear of other people mirrors an anxious inner world. How can one reach out to God and neighbor when one hand nervously clutches a gun and one's spirit is focused on protecting oneself from others? As guns pressure us to live in fear, we grow disoriented and disconnected from our true selves, our core values, and the faith in God we once cherished. We forget the most basic truth of all: all God's children are our brothers and sisters.

My heart goes out to young people who are searching for a strong identity, but live in gun-plagued neighborhoods. They often find their identities in weapons, as poverty provides few viable alternatives. Youth in our inner cities know where they can get a gun if they want to be tough, need some quick money, or must protect themselves from bullies. About one in six high school students (18 percent) carried weapons (such as a gun, knife, or club) in the past thirty days, as of 2009. In 1995, the CDC in Atlanta reported in a one-month study, two in twenty-five high school students nationwide carried a gun to school, 7.9 percent of our high school population. Would it be comparing apples to oranges to suggest that houses of worship and statehouses should take note?[5]

Remember that magic mirror in the story of Harry Potter? For those who stood before the mirror, it reflected them not as they were but as they imagined themselves to be if all their dreams came true. The Mirror of Eresid, as the looking glass was called, had an irresistible power of attraction. Once people have looked in it, they are captivated and long to look into the mirror hour after hour. Many were driven crazy by such a thing. In Harry's school, there was only one such mirror, wisely concealed by the headmaster. In the nonfiction world and in each household throughout our country, there are millions of such mirrors. They allow viewers to escape their own limitations and shortcomings and to dream of unrealized longings.

5. Child Trends Data Bank, Centers for Disesase Control and Prevention, Statistics on Guns in Schools 2008, 1–2.

For many youth today, holding a powerful gun in one's hand is like staring into the mirror of Eresid.[6]

The basic question for our youth is, "Who do I really want to be?" Granted, a gun may make one feel invincible and omnipotent for a few moments in time, but one can never fully relax or be at peace for there is always someone else who is looking to *his* gun and feeling invincible and omnipotent. City streets are not large enough to accommodate all the youth who feel invincible and omnipotent. The medieval saint was right: "The soul can never rest in things beneath itself." When guns masquerade as the quick and final solution for human problems, they put our youth on one of two paths: the cemetery or prison.

LIVING IN AN ATMOSPHERE OF VIOLENCE

The dynamic changes in urban cultures and we confront not only guns per se, but *the mood of violence* under which so many are forced to live. City dwellers in these neighborhoods may escape being shot or killed; but it is impossible to escape the poisonous atmosphere scores of guns create in one's community. An atmosphere of hopelessness, death, and finality casts a pall over everyone and everything. When a community is flooded with guns, the environment resembles that of a war zone and people's psyches are perpetually being scarred.

Professors Robert Johnson and Paul Leighton, writing about the plight of America's poor African American men, make the observation in their discussion of black on black crime that in America, at least, poverty rarely kills directly. Few people drop dead in the streets from hunger or exposure to the elements. But poverty does produce a range of physical and psychological stresses, and some reactions to these stresses are expressed in behaviors that destroy life. Members of the victim group may contribute to their own victimization through adaptations to bleak life conditions that include violence directed at self or others (e.g., suicide or homicide) as well as self-destructive lifestyles (notably, drugs and alcohol).[7]

6. Glamour, "Virtual Violence and Dreams of Happiness" in Burggraeve et al., *Desirable God*, 237.

7. Johnson and Leighton, quoted in "Gun Violence and Gospel Values," 11.

Johnson and Leighton admit the causal connection between the larger social structures and "social pathology" of the inner city is very hard to demonstrate. "The larger society is quite removed from the grim life circumstances and daily degradations experienced by poor blacks, and, hence, the average American has little real feeling for the forces that shape their lives." They point out most of the destruction of black life occurs within the ghetto itself, "whose environment is the functional equivalent to prison."[8]

ROOT (Reaching Out to Others Together Inc.) is an organization in Washington, DC, dedicated to advocacy and intervention on behalf of crime victims and their families. Kenneth Barnes founded the organization nine years ago after a seventeen-year-old runaway from a juvenile facility killed his son. With a grant from the city's Office of Victim Services, ROOT reviewed the violence-related experiences of twenty-nine youths from the community called Cedar Heights. This is what they found:

- All twenty-nine young people had been victimized by violent crime.
- All twenty-nine had experienced or witnessed crimes being perpetrated.
- Twelve, including all the females, were victims of gang violence.
- Nine of the youth (all of them male) had been shot at.
- Seven had witnessed a murder.
- Nine of the youth (all of them male) had been assaulted.
- Fourteen had witnessed an assault.

"Even when there are no longer bodies on the ground, scars from violence remain. The impact of violence on youth is significant," says Barnes, "but for the most part, it is ignored. Attention focuses on the victims and perpetrators, and people have little regard left over for those who survive the shootings and assaults. Yet, they too are damaged by violence."[9] It is not difficult to see the connection between violence and absenteeism in schools that youths are afraid to attend.

8. Ibid.

9. King, "Violence's Scars Run Deep in D. C.," *Washington Post*, October 2, 2010.

The mood of violence multiplies behavioral problems and promotes substance abuse, stress disorders, and domestic violence. When guns are literally everywhere, everybody suffers.

AMERICA'S CHANGING NORMS

Most of us rush through life at such a frenetic pace we seldom consider how our lifestyles and social norms are being transformed because of guns and gun violence. Flannery O'Connor has captured the essence of our predicament: "At its best our age is an age of searchers and discoverers, and at its worst, an age that has domesticated despair and learned to live with it happily."[10] While verbally scorning violence, we suppress our hopes in God and in God's peaceable Kingdom and dream ever smaller dreams for better tomorrows. We casually accept the escalation of violence as an inevitable reality. We simply adapt and change our norms and learn to live with the increased tensions that accompany them. Rather than resist and reject the changes violence demands of us, we psychologically inoculate ourselves to its presence so that it no longer horrifies us, but only makes us nervous. One psychiatrist is reputed to have said, "Anyone who isn't tense these days probably isn't well."

Idols of power and deadly force have bequeathed to us a different kind of America. In my childhood many Americans never locked their doors, they took walks and sat on their porches at night; children played in their neighborhoods after dark in the city. When I was ten years old my parents often gave me a dollar and my buddies and I, all by ourselves, got on the streetcar and made two transfers so we could go to Briggs Stadium to watch the Detroit Tigers. Those are not society's norms today. In our inner cities most people stay inside, children do not go out at night or even play near the windows; they are often afraid to go to school. How could it be otherwise when we merely lament our mass shootings, but do nothing substantive to prevent the acquisition of high-capacity guns that make mass-shootings possible, even probable?

10. O'Connor, *Mystery and Manners: Occasional Prose*, 159.

In most states elementary, middle, and senior high schools participate not only in fire drills, but several times a year they practice "Intruder Drills." We never had those when I was a kid, nor did my children. Sometimes they are called, "Lockdowns," or "Code Red" or "Code Blue Drills." The purposes of these drills are not fully explained to the youngest children, though many of them are wise beyond their years. The teachers are apprised of the wide range of situations the exercises are designed to accomplish, including what to do if a madman with a gun comes to the school or a classroom. They are instructed to lock the doors and pull the shades and tell the children to get under their desks and not make a sound. Dare we ask where twenty or more elementary school children would hide in a classroom if a monster kicked open the door holding an assault pistol with an enlarged magazine of thirty rounds? Are "Intruder Drills" *really* the best solutions America can devise to prevent mass shootings, of which there have been over forty in the last ten years?

Not only are the norms in our schools changing because of guns and mass shootings, office managers are nervous if they must discipline or fire an incompetent employee. We've all heard of irate employees who have been fired and returned to their former place of employment to kill entire staffs. This has happened with enough frequency to be etched in manager's minds and the violent behavior has even earned the name: "going postal," which sadly commemorates the first of those victims and assailants who were postal employees.

Americans have also changed their behaviors regarding horn blowing. Reading about incidents of road rage and talking to neighbors about hair-raising experiences on the highway, keeps drivers from blowing their horns at offending drivers because they just might have a gun. A man with a gun threatened a good friend of mine who was driving in an up-scale shopping center in Northern Virginia because he blew his horn at him.

GLOBAL VIOLENCE TRAVELS HOME

The observation that violence done anywhere increases violence everywhere is lived out in our neighborhoods as the trauma of war in Iraq and Afghanistan comes home, bringing more changes to our lifestyles. Entire neighborhoods are haunted by "post-traumatic stress disorder." Every thirty-six hours another soldier or marine takes his or her own life. Our soldiers who have been surrounded by the violence of war have come back home different people. Their personalities have drastically changed and this has had a devastating, crippling effect on their spouses, families, and friends. Too many are saying, "He is not the same Charley he was before he went to Afghanistan." Or as one child put it, "My Daddy's different now."

In February of 2011 a returned soldier, suffering with PTSD, killed his wife and one-year-old daughter before turning the gun on himself. His brother, when interviewed by *Time* magazine said, "It's not a light switch. You don't train how to kill people and then do a couple weeks debriefing and everything's O.K."[11]

It has been reported that eighty percent of military suicides occur within the first three years of military service. There's got to be a reason. I'm convinced it is more obvious and far-reaching than our military and society are willing to consider at this point in time. I believe many commit suicide because they cannot tolerate the changes that living within the mood of violence has brought to their psyches. Their values, faith, personal identities, and the fruits of the Spirit within them have been sacrificed to the idols of power and deadly force. The tragic irony for the men in this syndrome is that they are made to feel less than a man.[12]

THE ECONOMIC COSTS OF GUN VIOLENCE

Those who agonize over our overwhelming national debt should take a long look at the staggering economic burden we bear because so many violent people get their hands on guns. No economist can place a dollar value on a human life, and there is no way to calculate the cost of living with the fear that your child could be shot or a despondent relative could buy a gun. Trial lawyers may try

11. Mark Thompson, "A Soldier's Tragedy," *Time,* April 2, 2011, www.time .com/time/printout/0,8816,2055169,00.html.

12. Brunswick, "Army Combats Suicide Surge in its Ranks," July 30, 2011.

but they cannot put a price tag on the psychological pain of those whose family members or friends have been killed or injured by guns. For every person killed, injured or threatened by a gun, there are large economic consequences for individuals, families, schools, hospitals, government agencies, work places, and entire neighborhoods. Research in the year 2000 revealed that gun violence cost the American people one hundred billion dollars a year.[13]

A subsequent World Health Organization study in 2004 estimated the cost of interpersonal violence in the United States at more than $155 billion per year or two percent of the Gross Domestic Product. On a per capita basis the costs of gun violence were 36 percent of the American cost.[14]

While I don't have the expertise or the space to deal with those figures, we all know that gun violence is a large part of those costs.

If either of those numbers sound over the top, consider only one expense: security personnel. How many have been hired since the 1970s to provide a measure of safety for public buildings, schools, hospitals, transportation networks, athletic events, banks, and government officials? While the security business is thriving and the factories that manufacture scanners and other security systems reap large profits, the American public is paying a steep price for living in a culture where gun rights and gun violence hold sway.

Some of America's largest expenditures for gun violence are in court costs and the correctional system. Our prison population has soared over the past quarter century. We have 5 percent of the world's population, but 25 percent of the world's prison inmates. In 1982, one in seventy-seven adults were in the correctional system in one form or another, totaling 2.2 million people. In two decades an explosive growth of those on probation or parole has propelled the correctional population to more than 7.3 million, or 1 in every 31 U.S. adults. Nearly 90 percent of state corrections dollars are spent on prisons. This phenomenon prompted one African American leader to say we are content with fifth-rate schools but insist on first-rate

---

13. Cook and Ludwig, *Gun Violence: The Real Costs*, 11.

14. *The Economic Dimensions of Interpersonal Violence*, Department of Injuries and Violence Prevention, World Health Organization, 2004, 24-25; http:2//whqlibdoc.who.int/publications/2004/9241591609.pdf.

jails.[15] It's not a coincidence that prisons have become private enterprise and depressed areas of the country court such business.

Don't be surprised there are dots to connect the Gun Empire with these tremendous costs in our criminal justice system. One of the NRA's constant messages is proclaiming the wisdom of punishing the criminal and ridiculing the idea of preventing crime that they say will never work. The proverb, "An ounce of prevention is worth a pound of cure" is foolishness to those whose guns are idols. Prevention implies gun control, which is, in the words of the Gun Empire, a "draconian measure."

MEDICAL COSTS

We quietly adapt as well to the soaring medical costs of gun violence. Dr. Bill Smock, Professor of Emergency Medicine at University Hospital in Louisville, Kentucky, has created the Gunshot Wound Registry, a database of Louisville's gun violence, one of the few such databases in the country. He has collected information for the past fourteen years on the many aspects of all types of gun violence—homicides, assaults, suicides, and accidents—from when they occur, to who the victims are, to the costs of giving them immediate treatment. His figures do not include victims who are shot in the neck and paralyzed whose long-term care is in the multimillions of dollars.

Who pays for those costs? In Louisville, it's a mix of taxpayers and University Hospital, a private nonprofit, and Louisville's only medical center that treats adults with severe gunshot wounds. In 2008, 63 percent of people who suffered all types of gunshot wounds were uninsured or indigent. The hospital paid $16 million in caring for these victims, which was never recovered. Smock comments, "What a waste. In public health terms, wouldn't it be wonderful to spend $16 million on something other than taking care of victims of gun violence when we've got so many other public health needs?"

In 2008, there were $18.3 million spent to treat 419 gunshot cases, up from $7.6 million for 336 cases in 1996, the first year of

15. "One in 31: Prison Count 2010," The Pew Charitable Trust, April 1, 2010; http://www.pewcenteronthestates.org/report_detail.aspx?id=57653.

Smock's study. In 2007, it was $16.8 million to treat 432 cases. The data for 2009 is not yet available, but during the first eight months of that year, 310 cases of gunshot wounds were treated at the hospital, where the average cost was more than $43,000.[16]

The University of Chicago Crime Lab issued a new report, "Gun Violence Among School-Age Youth in Chicago," to characterize factors underlying Chicago's escalating murder rate. The study expanded upon previous research that every crime-related gunshot wound causes around a million dollars in social costs; the reports of four authors calculated the annual cost of gun violence at $2.5 billion, or $2,500 per Chicago household.[17] This is just for Chicago. Dare we consider the math for the country?

One of the reasons medical care is so expensive is because of the increased firepower of today's weapons and their capacity to fire many rounds in only a second or two. Seldom today does a victim have only *one* bullet wound. And because most of the victims do not have medical insurance, future hospital patients find their bills are increased so the hospital can try and recoup its losses, but taxpayers are expected to pick up the rest of the tab. In metropolitan areas such as Washington DC, some emergency rooms and trauma centers have closed down because they could not absorb the escalating costs. For citizens with heart attacks, those seriously injured in automobile wrecks, and others who need *immediate* medical attention, the trauma center has been literally "shot down." We pay for unrestricted "gun rights" one way or another.

I spoke once before a Rotary Club in Arlington, Virginia, and focused my remarks on the economic costs of gun violence. I was surprised that it was one of the most responsive groups I've ever encountered. People often care more about our bottom lines than our high death rates. Especially today when money is tight, people of faith should be reminding our leaders that we would not need to waste so much money if we kept guns out of dangerous hands.

16. Sean Rose, "Rising Gun Violence Costs Tallied: Treatment Expense Tracked by Doctor," *Courier-Journal* (Louisville), May 24, 2010.

17. "Report: Chicago Gun Violence Coats 2.5 billion a year," *Chicago Tribune*, March 3, 2009.

13

The Idol Requires
Human Sacrifice

Among the dictionary's definitions of "sacrifice" are these: "1. The act of offering something to a deity in propitiation or homage; especially, the ritual slaughter of an animal or person for this purpose. 2. The forfeiture of something highly valued for the sake of someone or something considered to have a greater value or claim. 3. A relinquishing of something at less than its presumed value."[1]

CHILD SACRIFICE IN PAGAN CULTURES

Human sacrifice was viewed as essential for the survival of ancient, pagan cultures. Archeologists write of primitive peoples who loved their children as we do, yet, for the well being of entire communities, sacrificed them to gain favor or to placate the anger of their gods. Practices of child sacrifice in pre-Columbian cultures, in particular Meso-American and South American cultures, are well documented both in archaeological records and written sources. In Mayan cultures, mass graves of one– to two-year-old children have been discovered in the Maya region of Comalcalco, apparently performed for consecration purposes when temples were built at the Comalcalco acropolis. Graphic depictions of sacrificed children are seen on painted jars unearthed in Guatemala. In the Yucatan, child sacrifice continued until the first years of the colonial period.[2]

1. *The American Heritage Dictionary.*

2. Child Sacrifice in Pre-Columbian Cultures, Online: www.wikipedia.org/ wiki/Child_Sacrifices_in_Pre-Columbian_Cultures.

Aztec religion is one of the most widely documented pre-Hispanic cultures. Diego Durán in the *Book of the Gods and Rites* wrote about the religious rites and practices devoted to the water gods, Tlaloc and Chalchiuhtlicue, and their annual rituals which included the sacrifice of infants and young children. According to Bernardino de Sahagún, the Aztecs believed that if sacrifices were not given to Tlaloc, the rain would not come and their crops would not grow. Tlaloc required the tears of the young so their tears would wet the earth. As a result, priests made children cry before they were ritually sacrificed, sometimes by tearing off their nails.[3]

Such is beyond gruesome as is the larger mass grave of forty-two children discovered by archaeologists for offerings for the building of the Great Pyramid of Tenochtitlan. Entire civilizations the world over believed such sacrifices were "required" to have good harvests or to assuage the anger of the gods for sending a thunderstorm or an earthquake. Anglo-Saxon leaders were known to put baby girls in wicker baskets and run swords through their bodies so they could determine by the direction of the blood flow, the will of the gods.

COMPARING OUR HUMAN SACRIFICES WITH THOSE OF PAGAN CULTURES

We are disgusted and repulsed over these "religious rites," but as barbaric as they were, their numbers do not begin to approach the sacrifices of 3,285 children, which is America's average annual number of children and youth under eighteen who are killed unnecessarily by guns. These ancient societies put to death only *a few* of their offspring to "benefit" their entire civilization. Though we recoil at the practices of their religion, we must acknowledge their deaths were for benevolent purposes, that is, their shamans carried them out for the supposed welfare of entire societies. These children and youth were killed to benefit everyone in the community and establish or reestablish relationships with their gods.

---

3. Aztec history, online: www.aztec-history.com/cholula-pyramid.html.

ARE AMERICA'S GUN DEATHS HUMAN SACRIFICES?

Between 82 and 84 Americans, ten of whom are children and youth under eighteen, are killed every day by guns in America and nothing is done to prevent them. Who or what does our nation consider to be of greater value than they? Are they slain for altruistic or benevolent ends like the ancient human sacrifices of Peru? Do their deaths put us in touch with our God? Do they give confidence to our society? Between 82 and 84 persons will die *today* by gun violence and on and on into unknown tomorrows, because our society does not consider preventing their deaths to be of great value. For many in the Gun Empire, the victims do not merit the most basic protection.

Among the writings of then-NRA board member Jeff Cooper's monthly column in *Guns and Ammo* is his comment on the murder rate in Los Angeles. He wrote, "The consensus is that no more than five to ten people in a hundred who die by gunfire in Los Angeles are any loss to society. These people fight small wars amongst themselves. It would seem a valid social service to keep them well-supplied with ammunition."[4]

Unfortunately, such statements from prominent members of the NRA's National Board are not that unusual. "Meet the NRA," a new addition to the Coalition to Stop Gun Violence website, profiles NRA board members and catalogues their statements, opening a Pandora's box of racism, misogyny, homophobia, anti-immigrant animus, religious bigotry, anti-environmentalism, political corruption, and insurrectionism. If people of faith are concerned about our neighbors, we should take a long look at the values expressed by the members of the NRA Board of Directors who write our nation's gun laws.

If we had no choice about protecting those who are destined to die at the barrels of guns, or if no other alternatives were available to keep their deaths from happening, we would simply accept them just as we accept the deaths of those from hurricanes and earthquakes, for they are totally beyond our control. However, our country is more than able to prevent thousands of deaths from occurring by putting in place only a few simple measures that are readily available to us

---

4. Cooper, "Cooper's Corner," *Guns and Ammo*, April, 1991, 104.

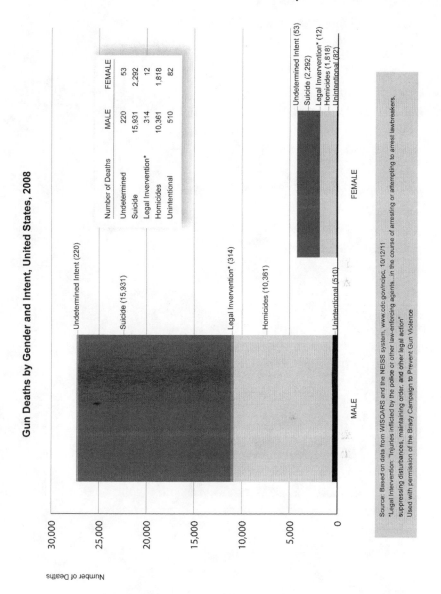

Gun Deaths by Gender and Intent, United States, 2008

Number of Deaths	MALE	FEMALE
Undetermined	220	53
Suicide	15,931	2,292
Legal Inververtion*	314	12
Homicides	10,361	1,818
Unintentional	510	82

Number of Deaths

Source: Based on data from WISQARS and the NEISS system, www.cdc.gov/ncipc, 10/12/11
*"Legal Intervention: "Injuries inflicted by the police or other law-enforcing agents...in the course of arresting or attempting to arrest lawbreakers, suppressing disturbances, maintaining order, and other legal action"
Used with permission of the Brady Campaign to Prevent Gun Violence

and are of minimal consequence to gun owners. To our shame, we have deliberately chosen to do nothing to annually keep 30,000 of our neighbors alive.

In Christian faith such cold-heartedness is unacceptable. In John Calvin's Commentary on the Sixth Commandment, he puts forth his theological perspective on the ordering of society that is

Gun Deaths by Race and Intent, United States, 2008

Number of Deaths	WHITE	BLACK	AM. INDIAN / AK. NATIVE	ASIAN / PAC. ISLANDER
Undetermined	225	41	3	4
Suicide	16,840	1,049	153	181
Legal Invervention*	216	94	10	6
Homicides	5,305	6,569	97	208
Unintentional	479	94	16	3

Undetermined (225)
Suicide (16,840)
LI* (216)
Homicides (5,305)
Unintentional (479)

WHITE   BLACK   AM. INDIAN / AK. NATIVE   ASIAN / PAC. ISLANDER

Number of Deaths

Source: Based on data from WISQARS and the NEISS system. www.cdc.gov/ncipc. 10/12/11
*"Legal Intervention: "Injuries inflicted by the police or other law-enforcing agents...in the course of arresting or attempting to arrest lawbreakers, suppressing disturbances, maintaining order, and other legal action"
Used with permission of the Brady Campaign to Prevent Gun Violence

based on the value of *each* human life who is loved and redeemed by God and is therefore in need of protection. Addressing the commandment, "Thou shalt not kill," he writes,

> . . . since the Lord has bound the whole human race by a kind of unity, the safety of all ought to be considered as entrusted to each. In general, therefore, all violence and injustice, and

every kind of harm from which our neighbor's body suffers, is prohibited. Accordingly, we are required faithfully to do what in us lies to defend the life of our neighbor, to promote whatever tends to his tranquility, to be vigilant in warding off harm, and when danger comes, to assist in removing it.[5]

To be sure some gun enthusiasts will read this statement and reply, "That is *exactly* what we are doing with our guns: defending our neighbor's life, tending to his/her tranquility, warding off harm and removing it from society." So there is no confusion on the point, Calvin was being an advocate for the redemption of individuals and society; he was not commending the heretical fantasy of "redemptive violence."

Caring with compassion for neighbors is the most visible indication of an authentic religion and a viable society. The central point in Jesus' parable of the Good Samaritan (Luke 10:25ff) is how the man showed neighborly love to a total stranger who fell among thieves and was left on the road to die. We are surrounded today by neighbors who appear in a million guises and are left on our roads to die. Jesus' parable teaches us that our neighbors are always worthy of our attention, our time and our money.

The lawyer's question of "who is my neighbor" is pertinent to Main Street. It entered into the British high court in 1932 during the case of a company that bottled a contaminated drink. The court declared "our neighbor is anyone or anything we ought reasonably to think may be affected by our actions."[6] Just imagine the impact of one simple law that would require an instantaneous background check for all guns sold in America! If that were operative, there would be a precipitous drop in the numbers of people killed and assaulted by guns. Cynics will reply: "Do you mean *all* guns will be kept out of criminal hands and our murder rate will be zero?" Of course not! It's not a sin to be realistic in our expectations, and it's honest to say our death rates *would* tumble if such a law were in place.

Only a few proposals for *minimal* regulations on guns are even discussed in state assemblies or in Congress and neighborliness is

5. Calvin, *The Institutes of the Christian Religion*, Book II, Chapter VIII, Number 39.

6. Rumphal, *Our Country, the Planet: Forging a Partnership for Survival*, 211.

not usually part of the discussion. The Gun Empire oversees the early demise of any of these proposals and in their place they insert laws that protect not their neighbors, but guns themselves. The results are a bundle of absurdities that exacerbate crime instead of curtailing it, weaken law enforcement instead of strengthening it, and make it easier for terrorists, domestic abusers, and other dangerous individuals to get weapons. Instead of freeing regulatory agencies of government to monitor terrorists who are on "no-fly lists," the Empire writes legislation that enables them to buy guns and explosives.[7]

The choice America makes to do nothing to keep thousands of people from being killed certifies those who will surely die as "human sacrifices." They are being sacrificed daily for the sake of that which is considered to have a greater value or claim upon us—i.e., "Gun rights."

Richard Shaull reminds us that when guns are made absolutes, an abstract entity that cannot give life to people takes on an existence of its own and becomes an end in itself. When this takes place concern for what happens to women and men has secondary importance, if it is taken into account at all.[8]

The *weaker* America's gun laws become, the more extreme gun zealots applaud those in Congress who vote for them. Because the silent majority of Americans are unaware these laws even exist, the nation tolerates a bundle of absurdities. We surrender our basic security and safety to the idols of power and deadly force that are nourished by death and destruction. Would *any* law stop *all* gun deaths? Of course not. Would *some* rational, even minimal laws, prevent much of the violence and save many human lives? Absolutely.

Prolonging the reign of absurd laws to uphold the mantra of gun rights exists *only in America* and requires the blood of the innocent and the most vulnerable. When five persons are hospitalized in the Southwest with e coli found in spinach, the government *immediately* shuts down the entire spinach industry, putting it under surveillance 24/7 and quarantining suspected farms. When more than 30,000

---

7. Testimony of Eileen R. Larance, Director of Homeland Security and Justice before the Senate Committee on Homeland Security and Governmental Affairs, May 5, 2010, The U.S Government Accountability Office.

8. Shaull, *Naming the Idols: Biblical Alternatives for U. S. Foreign Policy*, 148.

Americans die by gunfire, Congress reacts to *protect* guns, along with their institutions, factories, distribution systems, and private sellers which only guarantees there will be more human sacrifices in the days to come.

Believe me—I'm aware how preposterous using the phrase *human sacrifice* sounds in describing America's astronomical death rates by firearms. Even so, I hasten to add: it is not as absurd as the fifty laws and policies described below that Congress has put in place at the behest of the NRA. These laws and policies show how the effectiveness of the FBI and ATF, our major law enforcement agencies entrusted with overseeing the manufacture, sale, and possession of guns in the United States has been systematically and purposely eroded.

I once had a conversation with a man who loved his guns. I asked, "Don't you have any concern or compassion for the thirty thousand people who die every year by guns?" He responded: "That's the price we have to pay for our freedom. Freedom is not free." Unpacking his creed makes it much clearer for the average citizen to understand: "Thirty thousand Americans must die every year so I can get any gun I want at any time." He speaks not for himself alone; he speaks for an Empire. That Empire is not worried about convicted felons, the mentally deranged, drug addicts, or terrorists getting hold of lethal weapons. What terrifies them is the one in ten million chance that a small restriction could be placed on any gun in America.

Those who rest comfortably in the pocket of the NRA know they must do its bidding to receive their checks. When former Vice-President Dan Quayle heard of the massacre at Columbine High School, he said, "I hope they don't blame this on guns." Donna Dees-Thomases of the Million Mom March countered, "Well, then, Dan, what should we blame it on, the trench coats?" referring to the long coats worn by the shooters.[9]

America is justified in calling attention to human rights abuses of dictatorial regimes and oppressive governments in Africa, South America, the Middle East, Myanmar, and China. Democracy demands we protest such abuses, but can we totally disregard Jesus' counsel? "Why do you see the speck in your neighbor's eye, but do not notice the log that is in your own eye? How can you say to your

9. Dees-Thomases, *Looking For a Few Good Moms*, 17.

neighbor, Let me take the speck out of your eye?' You hypocrite, first take the log out of your own eye, and then you will see clearly to take the speck out of your neighbor's eye" (Matt 7:3–5).

Human rights abuses are unacceptable anywhere, including the United States. When thousands are buried each year *because* nothing is done to prevent mass shootings, ten thousand murders, and twenty thousand suicides, each of the slaughtered has been denied his or her ultimate human right to life, liberty, and the pursuit of happiness. Their deaths are human rights abuses and *they* are the price we pay to keep the idol of power and deadly force on its throne—unquestioned, unexamined, unchallenged, and unchecked. Behind our Christian veneer and the compassionate image we polish for the world to see, in America human sacrifice is expected, even required.

Hear Shaull again:

> In sharp contrast to human sacrifice, the God of the Bible makes human sacrifices unnecessary. This God does not demand of human beings more than they can give. God is at the center of a dynamic movement in history, giving life to those deprived of it as more just structures are being created. To the extent that this happens, there will be no need for immolations or expiations. Jesus Christ as the incarnation of this God, offers his life as a sacrifice on the cross, thus annulling the need for any other sacrifice. There is no further need for human sacrifice since Christ "did this once for all when he offered up himself" (Heb 7:27). Christ takes upon himself all the suffering caused by the injustices and oppressions of history and stands at the center of a community of faith whose members continue the struggle for justice. For them, the sacrifice of the poor and marginal is intolerable, but they know that they can combat it only as they follow the example of Christ.[10]

10. Shaull, *Naming the Idols: Biblical Alternatives for U. S. Foreign Policy*, 150.

14

The Second Amendment
and Freedom

THE NRA'S LOVE FOR HALF OF THE
SECOND AMENDMENT

Have you noticed the NRA seldom, *if ever,* quotes the *entire* Second Amendment to the U. S. Constitution? They must be nervous about it. The amendment is 27 words long and the Gun Empire fights tenaciously to neutralize 13 of them. The Second Amendment reads: "A well-regulated militia being necessary to the security of a free State, the right of the people to keep and bear arms, shall not be infringed."

"A well-regulated militia," the focus in the first half of the amendment is the *last* thing the Gun Empire wants for America. Correspondingly, gun zealots consider any "regulation" to be "a draconian measure" which, if enforced, would rob Americans of their freedom and constitutional rights. It is delusional to think the NRA elite would support any regulations on guns for they are poison to their ideology.

The first half of the amendment is a *dependent clause* which in *Heller v. District* of Columbia, the Supreme Court saw as "prefatory, i.e. preliminary, but irrelevant." Since 1977, when the association ceased being an advocate for hunting and sport shooting to become a corporate giant selling defensive guns, the Empire has fought every proposed regulation of arms. The NRA and the gun lobby want what the amendment itself does not offer: i.e., a totally unrestricted, unregulated right to bear arms. This does not, however, deter them from *claiming* they already have such a right.

As a gun owner, and in company with the majority of NRA members, I endorse it all. For two hundred years the United States Courts have interpreted it as a collective or state's right, but in 2008, the Robert's Supreme Court reversed long-standing constitutional precedent declaring it to be an individual right. In the Supreme Court cases of *District of Columbia v. Heller,* (2008), and *McDonald v. Chicago* (2010), the court ruled that banning handguns for individual possession was unconstitutional. Though I believe they erred in their decision and opened the door for decades of litigation, an "individual right" to own a gun is now the law of the land.

That was a huge victory for gun rights people. One would think such judicial success would make them ecstatic, but they want still more. The Gun Empire is not pleased with Justice Antonin Scalia who wrote for the 5–4 majority, "like most rights, the Second Amendment is not unlimited. It is not a right to keep and carry any weapon whatsoever in any manner whatsoever and for whatever purpose. The Court's opinion, although refraining from an exhaustive analysis of the full scope of the right, "should not be taken to cast doubt on longstanding prohibitions on the possession of firearms by felons and the mentally ill, or laws forbidding the carrying of firearms in sensitive places such as schools and government buildings, or laws imposing conditions and qualifications on the commercial sale of arms."[1]

In spite of these qualifications in the Court's ruling, which in effect negates any claim to unrestricted and unregulated rights to bear arms, *that very claim* remains the goal of a determined Gun Empire as they oppose virtually every proposed gun regulation before every state or federal legislative body and tell the world they have such a right.

INTERPRETING THE SECOND AMENDMENT

In future years I believe America will have three options on *how* to interpret the Second Amendment.

---

1. Scalia, *Heller v. District of Columbia.*

Option One: America can have *a totally unregulated, unrestricted right* to keep and bear arms. No individual, group of individuals, town, municipality, state, or federal government can make *any* law of any kind that would limit, control or constrain *any* person from owning any weapon of choice. This is the ultimate goal and purpose of the Gun Empire.

Option Two: America can have *a poorly regulated right* to keep and bear arms. In effect this is the amendment in force today. There are a host of reasons why the United States does a poor job of regulating our estimated 300 million arms. First and foremost is the drafting of absurd legislation that makes law enforcement agencies weak and ineffective. In addition, federal and state governments have an ineffective patchwork of obscure laws and inconsistent levels of enforcement, which make unified efforts to combat gun crime next to impossible. Hundreds of thousands of people exploit these laws to get guns through private sellers at gun shows, straw purchases at gun dealerships, or through sales "over the back fence." The Second Amendment today is *purposely poorly regulated* and is the interim goal of the Gun Empire.

Option Three: America can embrace the Second Amendment our forebears actually gave us: i.e., the *entire* Second Amendment. All twenty seven words and both clauses: "A well-regulated militia, being necessary to the security of a free State, the right of the people to keep and bear arms shall not be infringed."

Prima facie, this is balanced and recognizes the rights of all law-abiding citizens who have clean records and are of sound mind to have guns for self-defense or recreational purposes; it also assures all citizens that intelligent, reasonable measures will be taken to regulate instruments made to kill.

I find it puzzling when the Second Amendment is discussed that the universal human rights, so beautifully articulated in the Preamble to the Constitution of the United States, are never discussed. The basic human rights described in the preamble supply the context and describe the purpose of the Constitution itself, including the Second Amendment: "to form a more perfect Union, establish Justice, ensure domestic tranquility, provide for the common defense, promote the general welfare, and secure the Blessings of Liberty to ourselves and our Posterity." In that milieu our forebears spoke of "a well-regulated militia" being part of the American social contract.

The "general welfare" and "domestic tranquility" described in the preamble are today systematically denied American citizens, as the rights of the many are subservient to the opinions of a minority of gun extremists. The universal human rights decreed in the Constitution are ignored because little or no attention is paid to *the first half* of the Second Amendment. It appears the Roberts Court regards the amendment as "the private domain " of gun owners and considers it irrelevant to other citizens who seek "the general welfare" and the blessing of "tranquility" in which guns are regulated and one can safely pursue life, liberty, and happiness.

I believe it unjust and shortsighted that the Second Amendment is interpreted within such narrow and exclusive parameters. It should be as much "an ordinary citizen's Second Amendment right" to have sound regulations on guns as it is a right for a person who wants to set up a .50-caliber sniper rifle on his lawn on Main Street. The Second Amendment to the U.S. Constitution belongs to *all citizens*. Recent Supreme Court rulings do not remove the need for good, balanced gun regulations; they enhance them.

I consulted a lawyer friend about my interpretations of the preceding paragraphs. His opinion was that I expressed what was in the minds of our forebears when they drafted the preamble, the Constitution, and the Second Amendment. However, he added, in the court system the preamble to the constitution is treated as an aspirational document, and is not *legally* binding. I must accept that reality even though I find it troubling. Even more troubling is how staunch gun zealots promote "the real purpose of the Second Amendment" and understand the concept of freedom itself.

THE REAL PURPOSE OF THE SECOND AMENDMENT

In the spring of 2007, two American gun zealots praised the Second Amendment and freedom. Gov. Mike Huckabee of Arkansas and former Baptist pastor, while running for the Republican nomination for president, spoke before the Conservative Political Action Conference in Washington, D.C. "The Second Amendment is not about duck hunting," he said.

> I was the first governor in America to have a concealed carry permit; so don't mess with me. But I'm always amused, if not amazed, when some political candidate tries to tell me the purpose of the Second Amendment is largely about hunting. My friends, the purpose of the Second Amendment is to preserve our very freedom. And our founding fathers understood it clearly.

A few days later in New Hampshire, Huckabee exclaimed, "The Second Amendment gives me the last line of defense against tyranny, even the tyranny of my own government."[2]

Then it was Wayne La Pierre's turn at the 2007 NRA convention:

> Threats to freedom are everywhere and the NRA membership must remain fully armed and ever vigilant to fend off those dangers. So no matter what the animal rights terrorists throw at us, no matter what crime wave illegal immigrant gangs cause, no matter what deals are cut in the back rooms of the United Nations, no matter who is slamming gavels at the Supreme Court, no matter who is sitting in the White House, and no matter who wins what election or chairs what committee, if they are enemies of what's in that exhibit hall over there [the NRA Firearms Museum], if they threaten what that great hall preserves, if they dare assault the one freedom that secures all freedoms, this National Rifle Association, millions and millions of members strong, you will rise and stand and we, together, will fight them all.[3]

Charlton Heston often said the Second Amendment is America's first freedom because it is the one right that protects all the other freedoms we enjoy. His disciples continue to call it the "fulcrum of freedom" and state that freedom and the Second Amendment are

2. Horwitz and Anderson, *Guns Democracy, and the Insurrectionist Idea*, 238.

3 Minutes of the Annual Meeting of Members, National Rifle Association of America, April 14, 2007, quoted in Joshua Horwitz and Casey Anderson, *Guns, Democracy, and the Insurrectionist Idea*, 21.

mutually interdependent like the chicken and the egg. Neither can exist without the other."[4] Think about those implications for a moment: The Bill of Rights, freedom of speech, freedom of assembly, freedom of religion, freedom of the press . . . are meaningless without citizens stockpiling lots of guns. Is *that* the significance of the Constitution of the United States of America? Do you believe that without American citizens owning the latest models of firearms freedom has no meaning?

David Kopel, a leading gun rights theorist and Associate Political Analyst of the conservative Cato Institute, calls guns "the tools of political dissent." He contends gun owners have no obligation to obey or respect any law that has been made through our established democratic process, if they happen to disagree with it. An article of faith for hard-core extremists is "people have a right to take whatever measures are necessary, *including force*, to abolish oppressive government." Or again: "armed resistance to government is legitimate and appropriate."[5]

Kopel is talking about Americans, our government, and you and me. His belief is contrary to *everything* I believe about my country. In the America I know, everyone is equal. Kopel's opinions are valid, but so are *mine*, and valid are the opinions of others who disagree with both of us. Who then is ordained to define tyranny on behalf of the people of the United States of America when societal changes have come through an established, electoral democratic process? What Kopel would consider tyrannous, others may view as virtuous. What then? Does David Kopel have a more compelling *right* because he has a gun or a more powerful gun or more guns than I do? Do gun owners rule unarmed Americans? Might makes right is not the way a democracy functions. Isn't America a land with liberty and justice for all? No group, no matter how well armed, has the right to define tyranny on behalf of 300 million other people. Every one of us must respect decisions made by democratic means. Such deference is the glue that keeps our country together and functioning. In the

---

4. "The Second Amendment: America's First Freedom," speech at the National Press Club, Washington, D.C., September 11, 1997.

5. Horwitz and Anderson, *Guns Democracy, and the Insurrectionist Idea*, 169.

United States we make changes to our government through ballots, not bullets.

Famed legal scholar and U.S. Jurist Roscoe Pound wrote in 1957, "A legal right of the citizen to wage war on the government is something that cannot be admitted . . . [because] bearing arms today is a very different thing from what it was in the days of the embattled farmers who withstood the British in 1775. In the urban industrial society of today, a general right to bear arms so as to be able to resist oppression by the government would mean gangs could defeat the whole Bill of Rights."[6]

The Gun Empire is not a defender of basic American values. Its mantra is that if the government does not agree with its understanding of freedom, then it will have no other recourse than to take down the government with stockpiled guns. Should this sound alarmist, remember that I am quoting from the speeches of leaders in the Gun Empire.

To increase their influence in America, the idols of power and deadly force are reaching out to their most ardent right-wing zealots and promoting suspicion and hostility, not only to the Obama administration, but also to America's long-established democratic principles and social institutions. When the Gun Empire cries "freedom," it has in mind preparing for insurrection.

Joshua Horwitz and Casey Anderson, Executive Director and Board Member of the CSGV respectively, in their ground-breaking book, *Guns, Democracy, and the Insurrectionist Idea*, write, "Anyone who doubts the insurrectionist idea now operates as the central animating force behind the modern gun-rights movement need only consider what happens when firearm enthusiasts dare to question the insurrectionist idea in public."[7] They cite the story of Jim Zumbo, one of the country's most famous outdoorsmen, with gun and hunting credentials as long as your arm, who was drummed out of the fellowship because he was critical of those who hunted coyotes and prairie dogs with assault weapons.

In an *Outdoor Life* blog, "Assault Rifles for Hunters," Zumbo saw no place for what he called "terrorist rifles" in the hunting fraternity.

6. Pound, *The Development of Constitutional Guarantees of Liberty*, 90–91.
7. Horwitz and Anderson, *Guns, Democracy, and the Insurrectionist Idea*, 177.

He closed his blog by saying, "As hunters, we don't need the image of walking around the woods carrying one of these weapons. To most of the public, an assault rifle is a terrifying thing. Let's divorce ourselves from them. I say game departments should ban them from the prairies and woods."[8]

What happened next in the gun fraternity? A Web site called "Dump Zumbo" appeared from out of nowhere and demanded his head . . . and got it. Zumbo's sponsors dropped him like the proverbial hot potato. He lost his TV show and magazine and the NRA delegitimized him. One angry response explains the furor: "The Second Amendment isn't about gun ownership for 'sporting purposes' to protect your hunting rifles and shotguns. The spirit and intent of the Second Amendment is about ensuring the current 'arms of the day' are in the hands of the general populace to deter tyranny from enemies abroad and within from depriving any U. S. citizens of our life, liberty, prosperity, and our great country."[9]

Zumbo's story morphed from a discussion of appropriate hunting weapons into an apology for storing up the latest and most powerful weapons to fight the government. Another gun journalist, Pat Wray from Oregon, tried to come to Zumbo's defense and asked his critics to reconsider their actions, which ruined the professional life of one of their most respected hunting authorities. As a result, Wray almost lost his career:

Wrote one:

> Jim Zumbo didn't get it and now Pat Wray doesn't get it. What Zumbo's words amounted to was an attack on your and my second amendment rights, *which was never about hunting*. The second amendment was put in place to guarantee that the Citizens of the United States are armed and to give them a fighting chance in case someone declared themselves dictator of the United States and declared that our Constitution along with all amendments were null and void. Enemies of our constitution want to get rid of the second amendment first because it would in effect pull the

8. Discussion of Zumbo's story. Online: http://armsandthelaw.com/archives/2007/02/Zumbo_controver.php.

9. Ibid.

teeth on the Citizens of these United States. We would no longer have a fighting chance.[10]

GETTING ARMED TO FIGHT TYRANNY

I grew up, as did many of you, believing what I was taught in Civics 101. Namely, the greatest tool of dissent in a free and democratic society is the power of an idea, freely expressed. I believed Americans demonstrated their ultimate power through ballots, not bullets, and our national genius was found in the free and open exchange of public discourse and debate, not in disparaging our institutions of government or taking up arms to fight duly elected representatives, should you disagree with them.

The most *undemocratic or anti-democratic* proposition yet put forward by the Gun Empire is that citizens of the United States should be stockpiling guns to protect their freedom from a tyrannical government. That does not make us safe. That does not enhance our security. That does not keep us free. That is not democracy. That is insurrection.

In my lifetime the most heated rhetoric about fighting tyranny in our own government has surfaced during the administration of our African-American President, Barack Obama. The charges have been unending from the right that he plans to confiscate all guns even as he pursues his socialist agenda (as in "Obamacare") and he has no right to be President in the first place because he wasn't born in the United States, etc., etc. Nevertheless, the ubiquitous Wayne La Pierre has been vigorously preaching the same cause for decades. In 1995 he wrote, "The people have the right, must have the right, to take whatever measures are necessary, including force, to abolish oppressive government."[11]

To give credence to the idea that a few million gun owners with small arms could in fact, hold the 101st Airborne at bay or stop the U.S. Marine Corps, the Empire tells its devotees that had the Jews in

10. Brian Foster, quoted in Horwitz and Anderson, *Guns, Democracy and The Insurrectionist Idea*, 74.

11. La Pierre, *Guns, Crime, and Freedom*, 7.

their ghettoes kept their weapons they would have escaped the gas chambers. Again La Pierre adds fuel to their fire:

> The twentieth century provides *no example* of a determined populace with access to small arms having been defeated by a modern army. The Russians lost in Afghanistan, the United States lost in Vietnam, and the French lost in Indo-China. In each case, it was the poorly armed populace that beat the "modern" army. . . . Each of these triumphs tells a simple truth: a determined people who have the means to maintain prolonged war against a modern army can battle it to a standstill, subverting major portions of the army or defeating it themselves or with major arms supplied by outside forces.[12]

La Pierre and dozens of militias in America believe their cause is so righteous they could defeat the U.S. military. One thing, however, that neither La Pierre nor his collaborators mention is that there are five places in the U. S. Constitution that forbid armed resistance against the government and are appropriately labeled, "treason." Article IV, Section 4 explicitly states the government (which includes the army and marines) shall come to the aid of any of its citizens who are under armed attack.

Timothy McVeigh, who blew up the Federal Building in Oklahoma City, was an active member of a Michigan anti-government militia and incensed that the U.S. Army and ATF, acting as arms of the government destroyed two heavily armed cults that threatened neighbors: Randy Weaver's Idaho compound in 1992 and David Koresh's sect in Waco, Texas, in 1993. Garry Wills described McVeigh as a "Christian anti-authoritarian authoritarian."[13] After the cults were dismantled, McVeigh peddled anti-government propaganda; sold insurrectionist bumper stickers; and took matters into his own hands to show his contempt for an oppressive government that defeated those who had stockpiled arms to fight governmental tyranny. He killed 168 people.

Dozens of militias today are preparing to take up arms against the United States government because they believe it is overreaching,

---

12. Ibid.

13. Wills, *A Necessary Evil: A History of American Distrust of Government*, 204.

authoritarian, committed to more taxes, and *secretly* wants to confiscate the weapons that McVeigh believed were "tools of freedom." These citizen soldiers are convinced the government is too powerful, "doing too much," and has grown repressive as it flaunts its power. On the other hand, there are vigilante groups in the Southwest that are taking the law into their own hands because they believe the United States government is too weak, and "not doing enough" to protect Americans from illegal immigrants. These gun rights individuals angrily complain that, "the government will raise our taxes and take our hard-earned money to pay the medical bills of *those people* who are lazy and illegal and are the ruination of true American values."

These modern "Wild West citizens" recruit their own posses, climb into pickup trucks with night-vision equipment and high-powered guns to stop the "illegals" from crossing the border. They regard themselves as Twenty-First-Century Minutemen who are intent on "taking back our country." Perhaps you have seen the bumper sticker: "It is time to get our muskets and kneel behind a rail fence and take our country back." This is hyperbole, but it is also a treacherous spirit circulating throughout our fifty states.

Joshua Horwitz told me, "When the most visible leader of the gun fraternity, Wayne La Pierre, talks about guns and freedom, he wraps himself in a flag that the NRA is simultaneously ripping to shreds." To further one's political agenda with threats of violence is unacceptable in our constitutional democracy.

FREEDOM AND THE NEED FOR GOVERNMENT

Nothing carries as much freight for gun extremists as their understanding of freedom that is encapsulated in the words "gun rights." They understand freedom to mean an individual has the right to make one's own choices unencumbered by any other person, group, or government. Freedom is also an essential aspect of the Christian faith, which regards it as a blessing that enhances one's relationships with both God and neighbors and gives powerful incentives to citizens to make the right choices for the "common good," "the good society," and the "good life."

The Gun Empire and those who choose to value this biblical understanding of freedom do not agree on what it means to live as free people in a free country. Americans have disagreed on that before. Lincoln spoke about "the shepherd who drives the wolf from the sheep's throat, for which the sheep thank the shepherd as his liberator, while the wolf denounces him for the same act as the destroyer of liberty, especially as the sheep was a black one. Plainly the sheep and the wolf are not agreed upon the definition of the word liberty; and precisely the same difference prevails today among us human creatures."[14]

GOVERNMENT: A PROBLEM OR A GIFT FROM GOD?

It is tempting to idealize "freedom" as a utopian condition in which no person, group, or governmental entity can interfere with someone's ideas, dreams, plans, or lifestyles. It sounds enticing but few of us ever experience it because we live in the real world and in proximity to other people. If we can muster mutual respect for others, life promises to be pleasant. If there can be some "give and take" among the needs, even the wants of differing ethnic and cultural communities, we can live in peace. If we are unable to garner mutual respect, Americans will live with a growing suspicion and hatred of others whose views and goals are different and no one will experience the true blessings of freedom.

All the world's religions speak of living in community with others where each is loved and respected and each has rights, privileges, and responsibilities to work for the good of the whole. St. Paul describes such an atmosphere: "If one member suffers, all suffer together; if one member is honored, all rejoice" (1 Cor 12:26). The most significant words of community are never "I, me, and mine." The most important words of community are "we, us, and our," which

14. Abraham Lincoln, "At a Sanitary Fair," address in Baltimore, April 18, 1864.

prompted Martin Luther to define the Christian as "the most free Lord of all and the most duty bound slave of all." The poet Robert Frost captured both aspects of the above as he wrote: "Freedom is the ability to move easily *in harness.*"

Government is that harness that provides order and structure for all of its citizens, some of whom are often cranky. The harness of government keeps everyone together and moving in the same direction; it prevents chaos; its structures and agencies nurture and protect us, even when we resent protection and the urge is strong to hurt or even kill an adversary. As our national debate on the *value* of government continues *ad infinitum,* we should remember the first thing our founders did when they revolted against the British was to form a government.

My friend and pastor, John Wimberly, in addressing the subject of government, said,

> Among our founders were a number of influential Calvinists who were suspicious of human behavior and insisted on a system of checks and balances. As Calvinists, they also had a deep and abiding fear of chaos and anarchy. They knew that a bunch of individuals left to do what they wanted to do would not produce a positive outcome. There was no naive idealization of the individual among the founders. As a result, they created a government with broad powers and checks and balances that could be expanded and con-tracted as needed in the future. John Calvin never argued for less or more government. He argued for *good* govern-ment with a thirst for justice and peace.[15]

Regrettably, when considering government, many Americans look to the ideology of Ronald Reagan instead of the theology of the Apostles Peter and Paul. We may chuckle at Reagan's taunt: "The nine most terrifying words in the English language: 'I'm from the government and I'm here to help,'" but it does little to clarify the role government *must* play in *any* society.

Historian Garry Wills, argues that large numbers of Americans, *including Bible believing fundamentalists,* believe ours is "a government

15. Wimberly, *Transformation.* Sermon, August 21, 2011.

which is itself against government."[16] To the contrary, Saint Peter instructs his friends, "For the Lord's sake accept the authority of every human institution, whether of the emperor as supreme, or of governors, as sent by him to punish those who do wrong and to praise those who do right. For it is God's will that by doing right you should silence the ignorance of the foolish. As servants [slaves] of God, live as free people, yet do not use your freedom as a pretext for evil. Honor everyone. Love the family of believers. Fear God. Honor the Emperor" (1 Pet 2:13–17).

Saint Paul writes to Christian citizens living under a brutal regime in Rome:

> Let every person be subject to the governing authorities; for there is no authority except from God; and those authorities that exist have been instituted by God. Therefore, whoever resists authority resists what God has appointed, and those who resist will incur judgment. For rulers are not a terror to good conduct but to bad. Do you wish to have no fear of the authority? Then do what is good, and you will receive its approval; for it is God's servant for your good. But if you do what is wrong, then you should be afraid, for the authority does not bear the sword in vain! It is the servant of God to execute wrath on the wrongdoer. Therefore, one must be subject, not only because of wrath but because of conscience. For the same reason you also pay taxes, for the authorities are God's servants, busy with this very thing. Pay to all what is due them—taxes to who taxes are due, revenue to whom revenue is due, respect to whom respect is due, honor to whom honor is due. (Rom 13:1–7)

Romans 13:7 is a verse very few gun zealots will be quoting, for in their minds taxation is the foundation of "big government," which is waiting for the right moment to swoop down on its citizens and confiscate all weapons and padlock hunting lands. That would not be the only reason Grover Nordquist, NRA Board Member, would reject such an admonition.

Most of us, however, have had those moments when we felt government was interfering with our lives. As a young pastor in 1964, I

16. Wills, *A Necessary Evil: A History of American Distrust of Government*, 15.

drove to the Farmer's Feed and Seed Store in Wallace, North Carolina, to visit with the men who every afternoon sat around the pot-bellied stove to talk and drink "coke-colas." It was the day the nation heard from the Surgeon General, Luther L. Terry, who said, "smoking was dangerous for human health and warranted appropriate remedial action." His words hit the state like a tornado. The men around the stove were furious, not only because they smoked, but because they understood their bottom line. Tobacco was their economic engine and declaring it to be unhealthy was an unwarranted government intrusion into their private lives and economic stability.

Shortly thereafter, the government intruded again: seat belts. The older people were, the more seat belts were resented. We grew frantic when buzzers went off reminding us to buckle up. Some of us angrily fastened the belt and triumphantly sat on it; others wrapped it around the seat and buckled it on the backside. Today, blessed with 20/20 hindsight, we recognize that millions of lives have been saved because people stopped smoking and buckled up. We seem to be aware that the government of the 1960s knew something important about which average citizens were clueless. If we paid no attention to the government's advice to stop smoking and didn't buckle up, we did so at our own peril and many paid the ultimate price.

There are legitimate concerns on how extensive the role of government should be. I have long advocated that the government screw its courage to the sticking point and ban once and for all assault weapons. We do not need them in a civil society. I have no illusions however, that the government is going to issue warnings any time soon that assault weapons are "dangerous to all living things and can cause death." Yet, the *remote possibility* that a strong democratic government *could possibly* issue such a warning, or even pass a reasonable gun law, is why gun zealots hold our government in such fear and contempt.

Imagine the blessings of peace and harmony the entire country could savor if our government, with moral and ethical encouragement from the faith community, were able to convince leaders on both sides of our gun divide to come together and craft balanced legislation respecting two constitutional rights: the right to keep and bear arms and the right to live in communities free of gun violence. Wouldn't that be a great day in America? But, should either side say,

"My rights trump your rights," or "It's my way or the highway," we can only expect more discord and thousands more deaths. And no one in America will experience the true blessings of freedom.

FREEDOM FIRST

One of the favorite slogans of the Gun Empire is "Vote Freedom First." It is omnipresent in every election cycle. It summons all gun enthusiasts, not to walk but to run to the polls and vote for all Second Amendment incumbents and candidates who feel that protecting guns is the most important work of our legislatures. Freedom First places gun rights before the economy, education, defense, foreign policy, health, the environment and every other issue. The refrain however, appeals not only to gun lovers but to all who love America, for it is couched in that one word all Americans love the most: freedom. As a result many, particularly those on the bottom rungs of society, are so entranced by the word freedom that they vote against their own self-interest. The word itself is full of promise and rings with such purity and patriotism, it is unimaginable that even the principalities and powers could manipulate good Americans and gain their support simply by using the word, freedom.

A SAMPLING OF "FREEDOM'S LAWS" THAT PUT AMERICANS AT RISK

In 2003 Congress used freedom's good name to expand the reach, sales, and the influence of the Gun Empire as Congress and President George Bush signed into law the sweeping Tiahrt Amendment, which was attached to the Appropriations Bill that funded the ATF. The amendment, named after Representative Todd Tiahrt of Kansas, limits the authority of the ATF to disclose crime gun trace data to the public; codifies the Bush Administration's policy to destroy certain criminal background check records after 24 hours; and bars the ATF from implementing its proposed regulation of requiring gun dealers to conduct annual inventory audits to address the problem of thousands of guns that disappear from gun shops with no record of sales.

In 2004, even though background checks had stopped thousands of felons from purchasing assault weapons for ten years, legislators removed the ban. These weapons have since become the gun of choice in mass shootings.

A year later, the NRA lost several court cases and wanted protection from frivolous lawsuits. The Protection of Lawful Commerce Act was passed, which denies victims of gun violence the right to sue manufacturers, distributors, or dealers for negligent, reckless, or irresponsible conduct. No other industry in America enjoys such blanket immunity and protection.

In 2005, Florida, under Governor Jeb Bush, was the first state in the union to enact expanded provisions of the "Castle Doctrine," which gives one the right to use deadly force if threatened within the home. Six years later Pennsylvania Governor Tom Corbett signed them into law in the Keystone State. Citizens in 27 of our states today not only have the right to use deadly force if threatened within their homes, but with CCWP they now have the right to open fire in other places "if they feel reasonably threatened that harm is going to come to them."[17]

Are the American people freer today because our legislators made it *easier* for criminals and terrorists to buy guns? Do we feel safer because more assault weapons are in our neighborhoods? Do we feel more secure and free knowing *anyone* can go to one of 5,000 gun shows from coast to coast and buy *any* gun from unlicensed sellers with no questions asked? Are we freer because lawmakers moved the courthouse door to make litigation in the manufacture, sale, or possession of firearms almost impossible? Are we better off now that scientific inquiry examining gun deaths at the CDC in Atlanta has been effectively squelched by the NRA?

In the name of freedom our nation's traditional values are systematically eroded; our democratically elected government is labeled tyrannous; and the Gun Empire promotes utter contempt for international law and institutions such as the United Nations. Those who cherish freedom need to be aware when extremists of the Gun Empire shout their "me-first"—Freedom First slogans that their

17. Howard Sheppard, "Governor Tom Corbett Signs Expanded 'Castle Doctrine' Into Law," Fox News, June 28, 2011.

words bear no resemblance to the Bible's understanding of freedom, or even to those of our founders who wrote the Constitution.

Second Amendment author James Madison, wrote, "Liberty may be endangered by the abuse of liberty as well as by the abuses of power. The former rather than the latter is apparently most to be apprehended by the United States."[18]

WE ARE FREE TO LOVE

Christians believe that God calls a person to freedom and stipulates there are *no restrictions or restraints whatsoever on one's call to love.* Freedom is directed to the other. "You were called to freedom, brothers and sisters, only do not use your freedom as an opportunity for self-indulgence, but through love become slaves to one another. For the whole law is summed up in a single commandment, 'You shall love your neighbor as yourself.' If, however, you bite and devour one another, take care that you are not consumed by one another" (Gal 5:13–15).

Biblically speaking, freedom is *always* removed from getting what one desires right now and is placed in the context of considering what one can do for others, or what one can give to *other people.* These two perceptions reveal profound differences, not only in how one understands politics in America, but how one interprets the meaning and purpose of life itself.

She whose mind and heart are captured by a finite thing or idea can see only that which enhances her right to serve it and to follow wherever it leads. The free person, on the other hand, is able to see other's rights and, to at least some degree, "walk in the other's shoes." The one who is bound worries about possible limitations on one's *individual* rights being compromised in the future while the free person is willing to sacrifice a personal privilege or two in acknowledging the community's need for public safety in the present. A free man or woman refuses to live *only* for what is good for me and mine. Albert Einstein got it when he wrote: "The true value of a human

18. Madison, *Federalist Papers* No. 63.

being is determined primarily by the measure and the sense in which one has attained *liberation from the Self.*"[19]

One cannot live with a godly sense of freedom without having an awareness that one belongs to and is responsible for expanding circles of people, even those whom one will never meet. Conversely, believing individual interests or rights trump the welfare of the community, city, state, nation, or world prompt one to say with tongue in cheek: "Absolute freedom is being able to do whatever you feel like doing without giving a single thought as to how your actions will affect your life in the long run, or your wife or husband, your parents, your children, your job, your friends and neighbors, the sheriff, the government, the IRS, your health, your church, and your God."

19. Einstein, "On Good and Evil," line 8.

15

Fifty Laws and Policies That Perpetuate Murder and Disorder

Napoleon Bonaparte observed, "An absurdity is not a handicap in politics." On another occasion the French general added stupidity. Would anyone argue he was wrong on both counts? What a commentary on politics and the human situation! In spite of it all, I choose to bank on God's long-term plans for the world, which exalt wisdom and truth.

> Though the cause of evil prosper, Yet 'tis truth alone is
>   strong;
> Though her portion be the scaffold, And upon the throne
>   be wrong,
> Yet that scaffold sways the future, And, behind the dim
>   unknown,
> Standeth God within the shadow keeping watch above
>   His own.[1]

Surely, Napoleon did not consider absurdity to be momentous only in France. Americans know a thing or two about it. But, why does absurdity find such a warm welcome in the halls of Congress and state houses across the United States when it comes to guns? To argue an absurdity could slip into the political process here and there before leaders could correct or remove it, is only to state the obvious. On the other hand, to argue that a state or nation could assemble its laws and shape its policies for public life on a *foundation* of unending

1. James Russell Lowell, "Once to Every Man and Nation," 1845.

absurdities is a proposition that would be immediately denounced by any people who valued truth and common sense. Government would not work, indeed, *could not work* or serve the common good if its laws and policies were based on absurdities. Nonetheless, when it comes to the manufacture, sale, and possession of guns in the United States, that is exactly what we have. Our state and federal gun regulations are underpinned by literally dozens of farcical laws that defy rational explanation; their *only* effect is to perpetuate murder and disorder by keeping guns available for *all* our citizens and weakening law enforcement from stopping or disrupting sales.

The most common thread of irrationality in the fifty gun laws and policies that follow is the deliberate intent to keep law enforcement (ATF and FBI) weak and ineffective in their task of overseeing the business of guns in America. Most fair-minded persons reading these laws and policies will be able to spot unrestrained greed and a grasp for more power and control by a Gun Empire that has, through Congress, hamstrung law enforcement. Items 41–49 in particular send messages to any ATF or FBI agent to be very careful and cautious about enforcing any laws that would make it more difficult for gun dealers to continue making their sales, even to terrorists. "Gun rights," i.e., the idea that no restrictions or regulations on guns whatsoever are to be tolerated, trumps even minimal restrictions and commonsense measures for public safety, even for gun safety. Because absurdity trumps reason, and commonsense is lacking, we pay a heavy price in unnecessary deaths and injuries, in the devastation of families, in huge economic costs, and in continuing violence in our communities.

That the United States Congress would deny modern law enforcement the tools it needs to be wise, efficient, strong, and effective is fully as absurd as it sounds. Although examples of such laws and policies are legion, only fifty of them below prove Napoleon's point at least at this present time that an absurdity is not a political liability. We are working to put an end to this reality.

1. In most states, a person can buy and own a gun without knowing how to use it and there are no requirements that gun owners be trained in the safe operation of guns.

2. The Consumer Protection Act of 1972 prohibits the Consumer Protection Commission from examining the quality or safety of any gun or any piece of ammunition. Teddy bears, dolls, and toy guns must pass four sets of strict regulations before they can be sold.

3. The ATF keeps records of all gun sales through licensed dealers, but must destroy them after ninety days. The law was enacted in 2001 through the efforts of Attorney General John Ashcroft, a former NRA Board member.

4. The ATF can check gun dealers for illegal sales, but only *once* a year.[2]

5. In July 1996, TWA flight No. 800 exploded in mid-air on a trans-Atlantic flight to Paris. Law enforcement, Congress, and President Clinton suspected terrorism. Potential legislation was proposed to put taggants (small amounts of chemical dyes) into black powder to enable law-enforcement to more effectively trace any act of terrorism where black powder was used. The NRA quickly turned back the efforts and stopped a study on the effectiveness of taggants in stopping terrorist acts. Terrorists often use black powder as triggering devices on explosive bombs, but the NRA reminded Congress that thousands of good, law-abiding American citizens also use black powder in loading their own ammunition. Such procedures would punish these Americans and infringe on their rights.[3]

6. Every year about 500,000 guns are stolen from homes, cars, gun shops, and directly from manufacturers and the military. Eighty percent of guns are stolen from homes. More than 7,000 guns are stolen from cars and 30,000 from licensed gun shops. Police officers say that 10–32 percent of these stolen guns are used in crimes and 17–27 percent of guns which were bought from licensed dealers are used in crimes.[4] Law enforcement agencies also lose firearms. The US Justice Department and the FBI

2. Cheryl Thompson, "The Hidden Life of Guns," *Washington Post*, December 5, 2010.

3. Terrorist Prevention Act—Conference Report, U.S. Senate, April 16, 1996.

4. G. Witkin, "Handgun Stealing Made Real Easy," *U.S. News & World Report*, June 9, 1997, 34–35.

reported 775 firearms missing or stolen between October 1999 and August 2001.[5]

7. In late 2005, the U.S. Congress and President George W. Bush passed the Protection of Lawful Commerce Act, which denies victims of gun violence the right to sue the manufacturers, distributors, or dealers for negligent, reckless, or irresponsible conduct. No other industry in America enjoys such blanket immunity and protection.

8. Barrett Firearms Manufacturing, Inc. is able to advertise its Model 82A1 .50-caliber sniper rifle: "The cost-effectiveness of the Model 82A1 cannot be overemphasized when a round of ammunition purchased for less than $10.00 (U.S.) can be used to destroy or disable a modern jet aircraft."[6]

9. In September 2004, Congress permitted the Violent Crime Control and Law Enforcement Act of 1994 (The Assault Weapons Ban) to expire, allowing these military weapons to once again be sold legally in the country. The weapons were banned for a ten-year period during the Clinton administration.[7]

10. Gun violence costs United States taxpayers more than one hundred billion dollars per year (2000 figures).[8]

11. More than 50 percent of guns acquired at crime scenes come from only 1 percent of gun dealers. The ATF knows who the rogue dealers are, but present law blocks the agency from publicizing their activities or putting them out of business.[9]

12. In 2003, Congress and President George Bush signed into law the sweeping Tiahrt Amendment attached to the Appropriations Bill that funds the ATF. The amendment denies the authority of the ATF to disclose crime gun trace data to the public; codifies the Bush Administration's policy to destroy certain criminal background check records after only twenty-four hours; bars the

5. "Control Over Weapons and Laptop Computers," Department of Justice Summary Report, 2002, 1–2.

6. Grimaldi and Horwitz, "The Hidden Life of Guns," *Washington Post*, December 13, 2010.

7. Bureau of Justice Statistics, background checks for firearms transfers, 1999.

8. Cook and Ludwig, *Gun Violence: The Real Costs*.

9. David Fallis, "The Hidden Life of Guns," *Washington Post*, October 26, 2010.

ATF from implementing its proposed regulation of requiring gun dealers to conduct annual inventory audits to address the problem of guns disappearing from gun shops with no record of sales. (See number 6)

13. Over the strong objections of park rangers and hikers, President Obama in May 2009, signed the law that allows loaded firearms to be carried into national parks and forests where hunting is prohibited.

14. When ballistic fingerprinting technology was introduced to law enforcement that would help identify and trace *crime guns*, it was vigorously opposed by the NRA. Their argument is threefold: "A. It will not curb crime. B. It will lead to a de facto ban on the sale of semi-automatic handguns. C. It is stepping stone legislation toward government confiscation of all guns."[10] (See number 12)

15. In 2010 the Virginia Legislature passed a law which permits persons to carry their guns into bars provided they do not consume alcohol while there. State police chiefs described this legislation as "a recipe for disaster."[11]

16. In many states, an eighteen-year-old can own a handgun but cannot purchase one from a licensed gun dealer. The youth can have a gun, but not a beer.

17. The ten states with the highest crime gun export rates have nearly 60 percent more gun homicides than the ten states with the lowest rates and nearly three times as many fatal shootings of police officers. (This information was released only after a coalition of city mayors and thirty law enforcement organizations lobbied Congress in 2007 to release portions of ATF data which was quarantined since the Tiahrt amendment authored by Rep. Todd Tiahrt [R-Kansas] who said, "I was fulfilling the needs of my friends who are firearms dealers.")[12] (See number 12.)

10. Jessica VanEgeren, *Capital Times* (Madison, WI), December 9, 2009.

11. Virginia Center For Public Safety and Freedom for All. March 19, 2010.

12. Cheryl Thompson, "The Hidden Life of Guns," *Washington Post*, December 5, 2010.

18. Florida's Department of Law Enforcement created a statewide database of pawnshop transactions to aid police officers statewide in tracking stolen property and other crimes. This includes pawned jewelry, televisions, or any other items *except guns.* The NRA's bill stipulates that details of gun transactions are to be purged after forty-eight hours.[13]

19. The ATF identifies gun shows as a major source of illegal firearms nationwide, second only to corrupt licensed dealers. In Virginia, between 2002 and 2005, more than 400 guns purchased at Richmond-area gun shows turned up at crime scenes. These guns originated solely *from licensed dealers* at these events. The numbers of crime guns diverted by unlicensed sellers doing "cash and carry with no questions asked" remains unknown.[14]

20. Licensed gun dealers must keep specific records of sales of firearms, but the law contains extensive restrictions to prevent the ATF from using the records to compile a national database of gun ownership.[15]

21. There are thousands of guns in the country today that do not have a built-in safety mechanism. These and other "cheap junk guns" are likely to fire if dropped from a table. No federal agency is empowered to ensure all guns are designed and manufactured to minimize threats to human life.[16] (See number 2)

22. The automobile industry, tobacco, the airlines, the funeral industry, oil, gas, and coal industries, and manufacturers and distributors of thousands of products are routinely examined by Congress. The gun industry is never examined.

23. As an unprecedented number of American guns flow to violent drug cartels in Mexico, the identities of U.S. dealers that sold guns seized at Mexican crime scenes remain confidential under a law passed by Congress in 2003. All gun tracing data was

---

13. Doris Bloodsworth, *Orlando Sentinel*, 2001.

14. "Gun Shows Are Primary Source of Virginia Crime." Virginans for Public Safety, public document, 2006; http//www.vapublicsafety.com/signup.php.

15. David Fallis, "The Hidden Life of Guns," *Washington Post*, October 26, 2010.

16. "Gun Maker on Mayhem: That's Not Our Doing" *New York Times*, March 19, 1994.

removed from public view by an act of Congress in 2003.[17] (See number 12)

24. The U.S. government bequeathed millions of dollars to a new non-profit organization with strong ties to the NRA. "The Promotion of Rifle Practice and Firearm Safety" received 176,000 old war surplus rifles, worth $53.3 million; 146 million rounds of ammunition worth $9.7 million; and more than $13.2 million in cash and equipment—an endowment worth more than $76 million.[18]

25. We have the technology to include mental illness on all national instant background check lists, but many states, citing privacy and gun rights do not share that information.

26. When all murders of civilians in all the developed countries of the world are tabulated, 86 percent occur in the United States.[19]

27. Through 2008, the laws of only a few states require judges and law enforcement agencies to remove guns from situations where domestic violence has occurred, (or where adjudicated mental illness, drug use, or previous criminal record suggests the possibility of violence). The International Association of Chiefs of Police is a strong advocate on behalf of these measures.[20]

28. States with the highest rates of death and injuries by guns have the weakest gun laws and the largest export rates of crime guns compared to other states with stronger laws.[21]

29. The Bush Administration and Department of Justice announced "the fire sale loophole." The law allows prohibited purchasers to obtain firearms without undergoing background checks and permits a gun dealer who loses his license for misconduct to dispose of his inventory privately without being charged for

17. James Grimaldi and Sari Horwitz, "The Hidden Life of Guns," *Washington Post*, December 13, 2010.

18. Robert Walker, Handgun Control, Inc. quoted on *NBC Nightly News*, May 16, 1996, reprinted in *The Congressional Record*, 1996, S7097.

19. Krug et al., "Firearm-related Deaths," 214–21.

20. Frattaroli, "Removing Guns from Domestic Violence Offenders."

21. Natalie Pompilio, "States With Weak Firearm Laws Lead in Crime Gun Exports," *Philadelphia Daily News*, September 28, 2010.

illegal dealing in firearms. The NRA has worked with members of Congress to codify this measure.[22]

30. One firearm on sale looks like a regular cell phone: same size, shape, overall appearance, but beneath the digital face lies a .22-caliber pistol—a phone capable of firing four rounds in quick succession with a touch of the otherwise standard keypad.[23]

31. Concealed carry permits may be issued to those who are blind.[24]

32. College students who have serious alcohol problems and engage in dangerous behaviors are more likely to have guns with them at school. A study, based on a nationally representative sample of more than 15,000 students at 130 four-year colleges, found students arrested for driving under the influence are twice as likely to have guns compared with students who have not been so arrested.[25]

33. After 9/11, the Justice Department under Attorney General John Ashcroft denied the FBI access to its records to determine if any of the 1,200 people detained after the attacks had bought guns. The FBI had alerts to purchases by those detainees.

34. In April 2005, Governor Jeb Bush of Florida signed into law an expanded provision of the "Castle Doctrine," which gives one the right to use deadly force if one is threatened within the home. The expanded new law, which passed overwhelmingly in the Florida Legislature, gives gun owners the right to open fire on another person *"if you feel reasonably threatened that harm is going to come to you."*[26]

35. In the United States, we register births, marriages, divorces, and deaths; we register cars, trucks, boats, trailers, bicycles, houses, lands, dogs, and cats—*everything but guns.*

22. Ibid.

23. ABC News, London. December 6, 2000.

24. Joseph Gerth, "Blind May Still Carry Weapons After Bill to End Practice Fails," *The Courier Journal* (Louisville), February 23, 2001.

25. "Harvard Study Finds Gun Possession at College More Common among Students with Drinking Problems," press release, July 2, 1999; http://hsph .harvard.edu/cas/Documents/guns-pressrelease.

26. CBS/Associated Press, April 26, 2005.

36. In the mid 1990s, Dr. Arthur Kellerman, MD, Professor and Chairman of Emergency Medicine at Emory University School of Medicine, and Director of the Center for Injury Control at the Rollins School of Public Health of Emory University, did research focusing on injury prevention, with special emphasis on preventing firearm-related injuries and deaths. His findings showed that a gun kept in the home for protection is at least 11 times more likely to kill or wound a family member or friend, or be stolen and used in a crime, than it is to stop an intruder. Kellerman's research was published by the CDC in Atlanta. The NRA said these findings were "political opinion and not medical science," which led Congress to cut $2.6 million dollars from its appropriations; the exact amount the Center spent on firearms injury and prevention research throughout the country. Congress also instructed the CDC that "none of the funds made available for injury prevention and control at the CDC could be used to advocate or promote gun control." Such Congressional forewarning and oversight have all but stopped the accumulation of scientific evidence regarding firearms upon which realistic gun policies can be based. The Gun Empire continues to slash funding for any research that could possibly cast doubt on the claim that guns save lives.[27]

37. Virginia legislators on February 7, 2012 repealed the One Handgun a Month Law, which had stood for more than 20 years and ended the state's reputation as a major supplier of illegal guns on the East Coast. Criminal entrepreneurs can now return to Virginia and fill up the trunks of their cars with assault weapons and resell them to those who could not pass a background check.[28]

38. A gun dealer who sells two or more handguns to the same person within five business days must report the sales to ATF. They are regarded as red flags or significant indicators of trafficking. However, multiple sales of long guns, which include AK 47s (assault rifles), do not have to be reported.[29]

27. "NRA Stymies Firearms Research, Scientists Say," New York Times, January 25, 2011.

28. Sherfinski, "McDonnell Signs Repeal of Virginia's one-gun-a-month law," The Washington Times, February 28, 2012.

29. James Grimaldi and Sari Horwitz, "The Hidden Life of Guns," Washington Post, December 13, 2010.

39. More than five thousand gun shows are held each year in the United States. The ATF's agents are able to conduct investigations at approximately 2 percent of these shows.[30]

40. One thousand two hundred and twenty-eight times individuals on the terrorist watch list have been involved in firearm and explosives background checks since the National Instant Criminal Background Check System (NICS) started conducting these checks in February 2004. In the ensuing six years through February 2010, 1,119 (about 91 percent) of the transactions were allowed to proceed while 109 were denied because of criminal records, histories of violence, mental illness, etc. Result: 1,110 persons who are on the terrorist no fly-list have bought weapons and explosives.[31]

41. The ATF collects data on gun dealers who regularly sell large quantities of guns that end up in crime, but by law cannot make the data known. Investigative reports reveal two-thirds of the guns sold in Virginia since 1998 and recovered by D.C. authorities in criminal investigations came from 40 of Virginia's 3,400 dealers.[32]

42. In 1972, the ATF had 2,500 agents charged with inspecting the nation's gun dealers. There are presently 60,000 dealers and an inspection is likely to take place *every eight years*. In 1972, the FBI had 8,700 agents, the Drug Enforcement Agency (DEA) had 1,500, and there were 1,900 U.S. Marshalls. Today, the FBI has 13,000 agents, the DEA has 5,000 and there are 3,300 U.S. Marshalls. ATF remains at 1972 levels with 2,500 agents. Michael Bouchard, retired former Assistant Director for Field Operations, said, "We were always given just enough food and water to survive. We could barely just keep going. The ATF

---

30. Testimony of Michael Bouchard, Assistant Director of Field Operations of the BATFE before the Sub-Committee on Crime, Terrorism, and Homeland Security, Department of the Judiciary, February 28, 2006.

31. Testimony of Eileen R. Larance, Director of Homeland Security and Justice before the Senate Committee on Homeland Security and Governmental Affairs, May 5, 2010, The U.S Government Accountability Office.

32. "Gun Smoke," *Washington Post*, October 26, 2010.

could never get that strong, because the gun lobby would get too concerned."[33]

43. The 2010 appropriations bill for several major law enforcement agencies reveals the limits Congress imposes on the ATF. For the FBI there are nineteen lines of congressional direction. For the DEA, there are ten. For ATF there are eighty-seven lines, *including the requirement to keep the gun-tracing database hidden from the public.*[34]

44. When firearm dealers close, they are required to box up their records and send them to the National Tracing Center (NTC) in Martinsburg, West Virginia. The center is inundated by thousands of boxes of records that are brought by truck each month. They are stacked high along the walls and between cubicles. In 2009, the backlog of *boxes* waiting to be sorted and digitally copied reached twelve thousand.[35] The center is prohibited from using computers to transcribe these records.

45. Each year the NTC receives three hundred thousand inquiries from police officers trying to track weapons from tens of thousands of gun deaths throughout the country. The NTC is prohibited, by law, from collecting gun ownership records through a modern computerized database. Instead, workers huddle over desks with tape and magnifying glasses trying to decipher the handwritten paper records submitted by the nation's gun dealers.

46. ATF is charged with monitoring 115,000 firearms dealers with six hundred agents—the same number as four decades ago. Meanwhile, the minority of rogue dealers who repeatedly claim lost and stolen inventory—less than 2 percent of retailers—are rarely shut down since lawbreakers are allowed to sell their businesses to family members and continue virtually their same slipshod operations. ATF has been denied a permanent director for over five years.[36]

47. The promoter at one Richmond, Virginia, gun show alleged ATF harassment, then posted the following on the Internet: "After

33. David Fallis, "The Hidden Life of Guns," *Washington Post*, October 26, 2010.
34. Ibid.
35. Ibid.
36. "The Sorry State of Gun Control," *New York Times*, October 31, 2010.

three trips to Washington, DC, hundreds of hours of work and thousands of dollars in attorney's fees, we are in possession of a letter from acting special agent in charge (Washington Division), Jim Cavanaugh, that states in part that, 'BATFE Washington Field Division, *will not* routinely be present at the Richmond Gun Shows.' Prior to the enactment of ATF's new policy, blanket residency checks had shown a 16 percent rate of non-compliance with federal law."[37]

48. In 2003, Congress passed a law that bars federal law enforcement from releasing any information that links guns used in crimes back to the original purchaser or seller.[38]

49. Five hundred and eleven police officers were killed by firearms in the United States from the beginning of 2000 through September 2010. More than two hundred of the shooters were felons, prohibited by federal law from possessing firearms. Many had spent time in prison for illegal handgun possession. At least forty-five were on probation or parole when they killed an officer. At least four were previously convicted of murder or manslaughter, including a Texas man who had done time for two separate slayings and was on parole at the time he killed his third victim—a forty-year-old sheriff's deputy with a wife and three children.[39]

50. In late November 2010, the gun lobby filed two lawsuits in federal court in Lubbock, Texas, to compel the state to allow young people between the ages of eighteen and twenty to buy handguns and carry them concealed in public places. The first suit challenges the longstanding federal law prohibiting licensed gun dealers from selling handguns to anyone under twenty-one years old. The second contests a Texas law setting twenty-one as the minimum age for carrying a concealed weapon. (Youth in this age range commit a disproportionate amount of gun violence.)[40]

37. BATF Investigative Operations at Gun Shows, 35.

38. Ibid

39. Cheryl Thompson, "Officer Shooting: A Father and Son," *The Washington Post*, November 21, 2012, 383.

40. "Handguns for 18 Year Olds?" *New York Times*. November 25, 2010.

Who is responsible that such absurd laws determine the manufacture, distribution, sale, and possession of guns in America? Who is accountable that scores of farcical laws block effective law enforcement? Are we to blame gun extremists and their silly paranoia that the government would or even *could* confiscate 300 million guns? Shall we blame Congresspersons who signed on to laws that effectively perpetuate murder and mayhem? Are ordinary citizens responsible for not caring when absurdity trumps reason? Do church folk have some confessing to do as well? Can people of faith admit we have been lazy and apathetic and afraid to ask questions about guns and violence in America? Can we admit that it was on our watch when Congress, through the NRA, stopped the accumulation of scientific research and evidence regarding the use of firearms that contradicted the Gun Empire's claim that guns save lives?

In spite of the absurd laws that perpetuate violence and murder throughout the nation, some states should be applauded for providing public safety by putting strong legislation into place which restricts access to particularly hazardous types of firearms, sets minimum safety standards for guns, requires a permit to purchase a gun, and restricts the open and concealed carrying of firearms in public. Wise laws save lives and build safe communities. Kristen Rand, Legislative Director of the Violence Policy Center explains it: "The equation is simple," she says, "more guns lead to more gun death, but limiting exposure to firearms saves lives."

The gun lobby will loudly proclaim that gun control will *never* work because "the criminals will always get their guns and *good* law abiding people will be always at their mercy." To the contrary, keeping guns out of dangerous hands *does* work, not only in other countries but in our own. Indeed, it works very well! Strong intentional laws which keep guns out of the hands of felons, terrorists, and the mentally ill save lives. Note the evidence in the chart below: The five states with the strongest gun laws have much fewer gun deaths and the five states with the weakest gun laws have far higher death rates. That not only makes sense; it works!

States with the Five *Highest* Gun Death Rates				States with the Five *Lowest* Gun Death Rates			
Rank	State	Household Gun Ownership	Gun Death Rate per 100,000	Rank	State	Household Gun Ownership	Gun Death Rate per 100,000
1	Alaska	60.6 percent	20.64	50	Hawaii	9.7 percent	3.18
2	Mississippi	54.3 percent	19.32	49	Massachusetts	12.8 percent	3.42
3	Louisiana	45.6 percent	18.47	48	Rhode Island	13.3 percent	4.18
4	Alabama	57.2 percent	17.53	46 (tie)	New York	18.1 percent	4.95
5	Wyoming	62.8 percent	17.45	46 (tie)	New Jersey	11.3 percent	4.95

The VPC defined states with "weak" gun laws as those that add little or nothing to federal restrictions and have permissive laws governing the open or concealed carrying of firearms in public. States with "strong" gun laws were defined as those that add significant state regulation in addition to federal law, such as restricting access to particularly hazardous types of firearms (for example, assault weapons), setting minimum safety standards for firearms and/or requiring a permit to purchase a firearm, and restrictive laws governing the open and concealed carrying of firearms in public. State gun ownership rates were obtained from the September 2005 Pediatrics article "Prevalence of Household Firearms and Firearm-Storage Practices in the 50 States and the District of Columbia: Findings From the Behavioral Risk Factor Surveillance System, 2002," which is the most recent comprehensive data available on state gun ownership.

Used with permission from the Violence Policy Center

MOVING MOUNTAINS

If Christian faith and American democracy mean anything at all, our astronomical number of gun deaths do not have to continue. *It does not have to be this way!* We the people, under God, can move mountains. Have we forgotten that? With faith, even though it is the size of a mustard seed, we can say to the mountain, "'Move from here to there,' and it will move; nothing will be impossible for us" (Matt 17:20).

History shows members of faith communities are often slow in getting started to correct social ills, but once they start moving, they are the world's most effective change agents for they are using the moral authority God gives them. And mountains do move. That is the promise of our God, our faith, and it is the hope of our democracy.

I'm part of the white church that was late to the struggle for human rights, but, at long last we joined our brothers and sisters of color to help move the mountains of slavery and racial segregation; we (the faith communities) cracked glass ceilings and saw women rise to leadership positions in the American church and business. We moved the mountains of big tobacco, sexism, and homophobia. Is it time for us to start moving the mountain of gun violence?

Moving mountains starts with what the Apostle Paul called, a godly grief that produces a repentance, which leads to life (2 Cor 7:10). The mountain of gun violence will not go into the sea if all we do is feel guilty, sorry, or ashamed for what we have done or not done. The apostle doesn't call us to do penance. He calls us to repent. The word Paul uses in Greek is *metanoia*, which means literally to turn around and go in a different direction. To repent means to boldly change our behavior as we exult in the grace and empowering forgiveness of God.

What would today's church look like if we grieved a godly grief and repented and went in a new direction to demonstrate the new life God will give? I think our profile would look something like the following:

1. We would be awake and aware . . . not asleep at the switch when the Gun Empire speaks.
2. We would courageously name the idols and reject the lies and deception of the Gun Empire.
3. We would replace our fears of those who are different with love, which casts out fear.
4. We would with gratitude claim the moral authority God gives the church.
5. We would speak out and work to keep guns out of dangerous hands.
6. We would no longer be intimidated by extremists, but speak the truth in love to them.
7. We would strengthen law enforcement.
8. We would repeal absurd laws and apprise politicians that voting for absurdities *is* a political liability.

16

Expanding and Exporting Our Gun Culture

THE MAJOR SOURCE OF CRIME GUNS IN AMERICA

There are two systems of legal gun commerce in the United States. One is through regulated licensed gun dealers who are required to get positive identification of a buyer, start a background check, keep records of transactions, and (if necessary) observe a waiting period before transferring a firearm. It they do not comply with all the above they could be put out of business by the ATF.

The major source of crime guns in the United States is through licensed, but corrupt, gun dealers who knowingly sell their products to straw purchasers or to those who are a danger to themselves and others. Other rogue dealers are engaged in the highly sophisticated trade of gun trafficking where guns are first sold legally but then resold on the street at great profit by criminal entrepreneurs to those who could never pass a background check. Some of these dealers sell in bulk; others, because of state laws, can sell only one gun a month.

Corrupt gun dealers contribute to crime in other ways: not conducting regular inventories of their stock; storing their weapons in unlocked cases; or hiring employees who have criminal records and are willing to look the other way to make a sale when one does not pass a background check. Some sales at licensed gun shops are literally made out the back door.

As commented earlier, over eighty guns disappear from gun shops every day.[1] To escape getting a citation all a corrupt dealer has to say is: "Oh, that gun must have been stolen." Who knows how it disappeared? According to the law, it's no big deal, and a greedy 1 percent of dealers would rather make a sale than keep guns out of the hands of dangerous individuals.

Over 50 percent of guns found at crime scenes are traced to only 1 percent of gun dealers. This reveals two important facts:

A. Most gun dealers are honest and obey federal and state laws and would decline a profitable sale if they were aware of illegality.

B. Fortunately, for the 1 percent of unscrupulous and dishonest gun dealers, the ATF, because of the Tiahrt amendment, cannot make public the records of gun dealers whose guns end up at crime scenes, nor can they arrest the seller whose sales were "legal." Moreover, in those infrequent cases where the ATF closes down a licensed dealer for infractions of the law, he/she can sell the business to a family member or trusted employee and through a change of "legal ownership" continue to operate the business.

THE GUN SHOW LOOPHOLE: THE SECOND LARGEST SOURCE OF CRIME GUNS

Gun zealots ask, "Why are you gun grabbers always talking about closing the gun show loophole when there is no such thing? It doesn't even exist." Technically, they're right. This other system of gun commerce is by individuals who sell guns, but they are *not engaged in the business of buying and selling guns*. Because there is no definition of what "engaged in a business" really means, unlicensed private sellers are permitted by law to sell privately-owned guns almost anywhere, including gun shows. There is no gun show loophole *per se*. It is legal for anyone who is not in the business to sell guns for cash, without any records, identification, background check, and without any questions whether one is at a gun show or anywhere else. There are 5,000 gun shows every year in America.

1. G. Witkin, "Handgun Stealing Made Real Easy," *U.S. News & World Report*, June 9, 1997, 34–35.

According to the ATF, 25 to 50 percent of firearms vendors at gun shows are unlicensed.[2] A multi-state study by Dr. Garen Wintemute, of the University of California-Davis and a nationally recognized researcher in the field of injury epidemiology and the prevention of firearm violence, found this figure might be a low estimate. Direct observational methods employed in the study revealed as many as 70 percent of gun sellers could not be identified as licensed dealers.[3]

These unlicensed sellers can mingle among the licensed dealers, set up a table alongside them, stroll in the parking lots unimpeded with guns around their necks, and most convenient of all for those who can't pass a background check, they ask no questions of their customers. Their buyers don't even need an ID; it's all cash-and-carry.

The gun show loophole may not exist *per se*, but should a terrorist want to do harm or if one is a felon, domestic abuser, drug addict, or adjudicated as mentally ill and needs a gun what seller would get his business? An honest answer reveals why many of us are concerned about the gun show loophole. All who need guns are well aware of it. The ATF says the five thousand gun shows held annually in the United States are "a major trafficking channel for [illicit] firearms, second only to corrupt federally licensed dealers." An ATF study found that more than 10,000 trafficked guns a year were associated with gun shows—accounting for around 30 percent of all illegal gun trafficking.[4]

In April 2009, family members and survivors of the Virginia Tech tragedy sent an open letter to Virginia's legislators asking them to close the loophole in Virginia law. While Seung-Hui Cho did not get his guns at a gun show, he was able to obtain them because of another gap in Virginia law, which did not include mental illness information on background checks. Congress, to their credit, did pass legislation that made this information available nationwide.

From 2004–2006, because of cuts to staff, inadequate numbers of ATF agents were able to conduct operations at only 195 gun shows

2. Bureau of Alcohol, Tobacco, and Firearms, "Gun Shows, Brady Checks and Crime Gun Traces," 4.

3. Wintemute, "Gun Shows across a multi-state American gun market," 150.

4. Department of the Treasury, Bureau of Alcohol, Tobacco, and Firearms, "Following the Gun: Enforcing Federal Laws Against Firearms Traffickers," June, 2000, 17.

nationwide. In spite of this small number, they arrested 121 individuals and netted 5,345 firearms.[5] Examples of their work include:

- Operation Flea Collar, a two-year investigation into illegal sales at gun shows and flea markets in Alabama, culminated in the arrest of eleven individuals and the seizure of more than seven hundred firearms. The ATF estimated this group had trafficked approximately 70,000 firearms over the last several decades. Those charged had previously sold 267 guns that were linked to homicides, assaults, robberies, drug and sex crimes, and other illegal activities. One of these guns was used in the attempted murder of a Chicago police officer.[6]

- The ATF, San Francisco Field Division, in 2007 cracked down on illegal guns being smuggled into California from gun shows in Nevada. This operation resulted in the confiscation of more than one thousand firearms as well as explosives.

- Between 2002 and 2005, the ATF traced more than four hundred guns purchased at gun shows in Richmond, Virginia, which were later recovered at crime scenes.[7]

The most infamous case involving the gun show loophole concerned Dylan Klebold and Eric Harris, the two shooters at the Columbine High School massacre. They obtained their four guns because of the loophole and a straw purchaser. (One whose age and clean record serves as the qualification to buy a gun(s) on behalf of another who does not qualify.) Gun shows are also a major source of crime guns beyond the United States' borders.

5. US Department of Justice. The Bureau of Alcohol, Tobacco, Firearms and Explosives' Investigative Operations at Gun Shows, iv–v.

6. Michael Bloomberg, "A Gun Probe Yields Hundreds of Weapons Used in Crimes," mayor's press conference, January 31, 2011; http//www.gunshowunder-cover.org/azpressrelease.

7. Statement by Michael Bouchard, Assistant Director of Field Operations of the BATFE, Hearings Before the House Sub Committee on Crime, Terrorism, and Homeland Security, February 28, 2006.

HOW DIFFICULT IS IT TO BUY A GUN AT A GUN SHOW?

Two young men personally involved in the heartbreak of Virginia Tech decided to find out how difficult it is to buy a gun at a gun show. Colin Goddard, who was shot four times and fought valiantly to live, was intent on keeping others safe from the terror and trauma he experienced. The Brady Campaign helped him go undercover with a camera to visit several gun shows in various parts of the country. He captured on film how anyone in a matter of minutes can get a gun with no questions asked. His work is available on YouTube. Goddard says, "Americans should feel outraged knowing this country is not doing all it can to prevent firearms from falling into the wrong hands." He also appears in a compelling documentary, *Living for 32*.

Omar Samaha's sister Reena, a beautiful young freshman, was one of the thirty-two students killed in Blacksburg on that fateful day. To honor her memory, Omar and his family have dedicated themselves to plugging the gaps in local, state, and federal laws that allow dangerous individuals easy access to firearms. In 2009, Omar worked with ABC News to put on film how quickly he could purchase a trunk-load of guns at a Virginia gun show. Without so much as a glance at an ID, let alone a background check, Omar bought ten guns in one hour; all cash-and-carry and with no questions asked. Even as he examined his newly acquired arsenal in the trunk of his car, a stranger approached and asked to buy one of his newly acquired guns.[8]

In spite of ATF identifying gun shows as a major source of crime guns, they are largely unregulated by law enforcement. ATF is able to conduct investigations at approximately 2 percent of all venues. The agency doesn't even have an official gun show enforcement program and such operations "constitute a small percentage of their overall investigative activities."[9] ATF does not have the personnel necessary to conduct significant investigations. Regrettably, that is not because someone in authority failed to notice. It is intentional

8. Virginia Leaders for Closing the Gun Show Loophole Booklet.

9. Statement by Michael Bouchard, Assistant Director of Field Operations of the BATFE, Hearings Before the House Sub Committee on Crime, Terrorism, and Homeland Security, February 28, 2006.

policy; it is the way the gun lobby wants it. In addition, as of this writing, ATF has not had a full time director for over five years.

One of my friends calls gun shows, "Tupperware parties for criminals." Actually, there are some pretty rough customers who attend these events, often advertised as, "Gun and Knife Shows." Trust me: these people are serious about their tools of violence. As well as exhibiting every kind of gun, the gun shows I've attended *always* have a table or two where Nazi paraphernalia, flags, and Aryan reading material are sold and for those who may need it, one can always pick up an instruction manual on how to make a bomb.

As of this writing, seventeen states have closed the Gun Show Loophole; it remains open in thirty-three states.[10]

THE ALLURE OF THE OLD WEST

One of the most popular fantasies of gun enthusiasts is to live in America's frontier days. The Old West conjures up images of cowboys with six guns blazing, fierce battles with Indians, cattle drives, and campfires, fights between the good guys and the bad guys, and just being out on the range where no one is fenced in. These images energize innumerable gun enthusiasts who believe this is what real America and real manhood are all about.

As a child I was caught up in this world when I went to the movies every Saturday afternoon to view the exploits of Roy Rogers, Gene Autry, Tom Mix, Hopalong Cassidy, and Johnny Mack Brown. John Wayne arrived later. During the week, I sat by the radio with my Dad and listened to another episode of the greatest of them all: The Lone Ranger who carried silver bullets and with the help of his faithful Indian companion, Tonto, always got his man. I was impressed that this masked man *never* lost a fight.

Scholars and historians have disclosed the fallacies in Hollywood's glorification of the good guys and their guns. They usually pictured cowboys who carried not one, but two guns in twin holsters. I thrilled as my heroes took a wide stance and fanned the

10. "America's Gun Shows: Open Markets For Criminals," Coalition to Stop Gun Violence, public document.

hammers of their guns in a manner that is mechanically impossible. Although it is impressive on the screen it is a Hollywood myth: another is the U.S. Cavalry riding on the backs of galloping horses shooting their rifles and knocking Indians off the backs of their galloping horses. Pulling the trigger, of course, would have been easy but hitting their targets would have been miraculous. Who cares? Those images stimulated by testosterone had their intended effect as they captured the hearts and minds of macho men and boys who wanted to be a hero, like the Lone Ranger or Johnny Mack Brown. Those same images in 2011, more than half a century removed, still sell lots of guns.

Who cares if the gunfighter in the Old West was a figment of the imagination? Who cares if the infamous Wild West was actually the birthplace of strict gun control laws? Garry Wills writes, "Far from the gun being the tamer of the West, the West had to tame the gun in order to be civilized." Famous Western gun cities such as Dodge City and Durango, required all the cowhands to leave their shooting irons with the sheriff before they could amble off to the saloon.[11] Timid legislators in the Commonwealth of Virginia and other states with lax gun laws should take notes of what the town fathers did in Dodge City, Durnago, and other cowtowns in the old West to save lives.

When I was in my thirties and a missionary in Japan, I was surprised to discover love for the Old West was not limited to Americans. Having some business in Osaka, I visited the 1970 World's Fair. I took a cab to the site and sat in the back seat studying a map of the city that was given to foreign guests. Its cover was a copy of an ancient woodblock print of a horse-drawn street car. The driver said the map embarrassed him because foreign tourists would see the horse-drawn streetcar and think Japan was a backward nation. I replied, "Every foreigner comes to Osaka either by jet plane or on the famous Hikari train and will know immediately how modern Japan is and they will admire the print as art." I said, "the streetcar is part of ancient Japanese history like the pictures of cowboys and Indians in America are a part of our history." The driver was stunned. He pulled the taxi to the side of the road, turned his body around, and asked, "Do you mean cowboys and Indians are not fighting in America today?"

11. Wills, *A Necessary Evil*, 247–49.

The Old West is a compelling image which sells lots of movie tickets, books, guns, and gun accessories. Tom Diaz writes about gun companies, especially Sturm, Ruger and Company, that are reaping great profits as shooters relive the Old West. In 1993 Sturm, Ruger introduced its single-action Vaquero pistol in hopes of capturing the attention of the rapidly growing number of customers who are shooting in Old West and End-of-the-Trail competitions as well as those who participate in costumed cowboy re-enactment events, spending thousands of dollars on clothing and accessories. One gun enthusiast said of the Vaquero, "It fulfills all of my Wild West fantasies."[12]

I met one of those costumed cowboys in July 2005 when I was a Non-Governmental Organization Delegate (NGO) to the United Nations Conference on Global Illegal Arms Trafficking. The man wore a fancy, embroidered dark blue cowboy shirt, stylish pants, and a beautiful pair of shiny boots, but the most distinguishing part of his attire was a huge oval-shaped turquoise belt buckle. He was part of the NRA's NGO team from the United States.

This handsomely attired evangelist proceeded to the microphone and described in detail his recreational pursuits for the international assembly. He told the delegates how he and his friends dress up for cowboy reenactment events and ride their horses and shoot their revolvers at targets and have a wonderful time. He tried valiantly to convince U.N. representatives from dozens of countries that these cowboy events were totally innocent and wholesome family activities, which celebrate American history and tradition. He closed his speech encouraging the delegates not to worry about the presence of guns, but he was not convincing. The delegates were not impressed with adults playing cowboy. They were in the hall to address the *illegal sale of small arms* all over the developing world. The leading nation in these illegal sales was the United States.

UNITED STATES IS NUMBER 1 IN THE SALE OF ILLEGAL ARMS WORLD WIDE

Deaths linked to small arms in the developing world are in the hundreds of thousands and those injured approach one million a year.

12. Diaz, *Making a Killing*, 176.

Adele Kirsten, one of the founders of Gun Free South Africa, said, "We felt the biggest threat to our new democracy was the surplus weapons of war that had saturated our country."[13] Such weapons can always be purchased at bazaars and black markets, and they are present in every country in the world. At least 1,249 companies in more than ninety countries are involved in some aspect of small arms production. Eight million new weapons are produced every year, yet there are no effective international instruments to control this trade.[14]

The United Nations (UN) defines small arms and light weapons (SALW) this way: (a) "small arms" are, broadly speaking, weapons designed for individual use. They include, among other things: revolvers and self-loading pistols, rifles and carbines, sub-machine guns, assault rifles and light machine guns; (b) "Light weapons" are, broadly speaking, weapons designed for use by two or three persons serving as a crew, although some may be carried and used by a single person. They include heavy machine guns, hand-held underbarrel and mounted grenade launchers.[15]

America's delegation at the UN conference was led by members of the NRA's Governing Board, which effectively gutted *every* essential provision of a bill that the representatives cobbled together calling for international cooperation to rid the world of illegal arms sales. Citing national policy, the United States' spokesman refused to endorse any international measure that would cast *any doubt whatsoever* on our domestic "right to keep and bear arms." Delegates from Brazil, Colombia, East Timor, and Mozambique, to name a few of the countries, were angry at the obstructions presented by the United States. Sierra Leone had recently lost 25 percent of its population through terrors wrought by illegal guns, many of which were used by child soldiers. Their delegation was furious at my country.

The Bush Administration quickly dismissed the anger from the developing world: "They are angry because we are successful and democratic," we were told. But the anger in the UN Assembly Hall

13. "The Impact of Guns on Women's Lives," *Amnesty International*, 18.

14. Graduate Institute of International Studies, "Small Arms Survey 2004: Rights at Risk," www.smallarmssurvey.org.

15. UN General Assembly (A/60/88), "Report of the Open-ended Working Group," 7.

that day was because the United States was unconcerned over wide-spread deaths from the proliferation of illegal guns and small arms in their countries and could not or would not hear their representatives who tried valiantly to explain that guns and small arms were the *cause* of their problems, not their solutions.

Most of the countries in the developing world are male-dominated societies where men often justify possessing guns through a stated need to "protect" vulnerable women. This is not because violence against women is natural or inevitable, but because it has been condoned and tolerated as part of historical or cultural practices for so long and it occurs in a variety of contexts and cuts across borders, religions, and class. Actually, women face even greater danger when their families and communities are armed. The bottom line is that the more guns are introduced into a community the greater the risks for women.[16]

Meanwhile, there is lots of money to be made through illegal sales. The United States sells small arms and light weapons all over the world and provides military aid to more than thirty countries that our State Department identifies as dictatorial, unstable and with long records of human rights abuses. We are eager to provide aid to most any nation that says they stand with us in our fight against terrorism.

Our international policy today is not unlike our efforts in the 1960s and 1970s, when we sought the support of dozens of dictators around the globe so we could keep the world safe from communism. Our long list of "friends" included Papa and Baby Doc of Haiti, the Shah of Iran, the Apartheid Regime of South Africa, Fulgencio Batista of Cuba, Idi Amin of Uganda, Suharto Sueharto of Indonesia, Manuel Noriega of Panama, and Augusto Pinochet of Chile, to name only a few who abhorred communism and appreciated our weapons.

Today, to keep the world safe from terrorists, the big five (United States, Russia, China, France, and Great Britain) find it in our collective interest to ignore International Humanitarian Law and Common Article 1 of the Geneva Convention. Even though, as yet, there is no legally binding treaty to control the activities of arms brokers, Americans should not be proud that we skirt the intentions of Article I and have become the world's largest exporter of illegal

16. Frey, "On the Prevention of Human Rights Violations Committed with Small Arms: The Impact of Guns on Women's Lives," 2.

small arms to the developing world, the results of which are counter-productive to our own national interests.

Dr. Reuben Brigety, a recognized authority on the illicit trade in small arms and light weapons, has written:

> A systemic enabler of violent conflict, the illicit proliferation of small arms and light weapons (SALW) represents a triple threat to the security and national interests of the United States. SALW play a pivotal role in terrorist activity, regional conflicts, atrocities and perpetual human insecurity. From Haiti and Somalia to Afghanistan and Iraq, armed groups have used these weapons to kill American soldiers and citizens, attack U.S. allies, and undermine U.S. economic interests, ultimately damaging the United States' effort to win the War on Terror. Indeed, hostile states benefit from arming America's adversaries. By fueling armed conflict, destabilizing states, and spawning criminal networks, the illicit proliferation and trade of SALW undermines U.S. efforts to promote regional stability, encourage democratic and economic development, and counter mass atrocities. Small arms proliferation creates profound humanitarian consequences as well. Estimates suggest that there were between 80,000 and 108,000 deaths as a direct result of violence in armed conflict in 2003. Civilians are indirectly affected by warfare when it forces them to flee their homes, abandon their livelihoods, succumb to disease, and disrupt their normal patterns of social and civic activity. The gravity of the threat to international peace and security and U.S. national interests is matched only by the complexity of the problem. Though the United States pays the most in humanitarian aid and post-conflict reconstruction costs of any country and is deeply concerned with bringing such conflicts under control, both foreign and domestic policy imperatives have led it to oppose treaties or agreements which might conflict with the right of citizens to own arms. The nature of U.S. engagement in multilateral institutions compounds the difficulty of effective policy action.[17]

17. Brigety, "US Small Arms Policy: Security at a Cross Roads," unpublished paper, 4–5.

EXPORTING OUR GUNS TO MEXICO

In Mexico, the intersection of small arms trade and illegal guns is calamitous. These weapons, which include the Barrett sniper rifle that was called, "a gift from God" by the company's president (see chapter 9), have been used by the drug cartels to assassinate police and government officials riding in armored vehicles in Mexico.

In March 2007, the Mexican military and police launched an aggressive crackdown on narcotics traffickers. Both sides were well armed and in the ensuing ten months more than 4,000 people died in drug-related violence. In 2008, the deaths jumped to 6,000.

On the narcotics side, high-tech, high-quality weapons bought in the United States and smuggled south of the border to bolster this industry fuel the violence. The cartels rely on their firepower to sustain production facilities and keep open their supply lines, which both the attorney general and President of Mexico have testified threaten the integrity of the entire country.[18]

Drug gangs seek out guns in the United States because gun laws are far tougher in Mexico. These drug cartel members routinely enlist Americans with clean records to buy two or three rifles at a time, often from different shops or at gun shows where no law requires notification of sale. They then transport the guns across the border. James Ramey, a gun show vendor from Texas, described their methods in border cities: "They send over a scout on Saturday to see if there's anything they want, then they show up on Sunday with a big wad of money and somebody who's got a clean record; who's legal to buy."[19]

Commenting on an investigation conducted between 2004 and 2006, ATF's Phoenix field division reported, "Many U.S. guns shows attract large numbers of gang members from Mexico and California. They often buy large quantities of assault weapons and smuggle them into Mexico or transport them to California. It is estimated that upwards of 80 percent of illegal firearms in Mexico come from the United States."[20]

18. Silverstein, "Freedom Under Fire," interview with Dr. Garen Wintemute, 1–2.

19. Hawley and Solache, "U.S. Guns Pour into Mexico."

20. Graduate Institute of International Studies, "Small Arms Survey 2002: "Counting the Human Cost," Online: www.smallarmssurvey.org.

Three states (Texas, Arizona, and California) account for more than two-thirds of these traced weapons. The region itself is called "the Iron River of Guns," with more than 6,700 licensed gun dealers within a short drive of the two thousand-mile U.S.-Mexican border.[21]

Mexican President Felipe Calderon, on a state visit to Washington, DC, spoke before a joint session of Congress on May 20, 2010, and passionately pled for a revival of the U.S. assault weapons ban. "I fully respect and admire the U.S. Constitution and the purpose of the Second Amendment, which is to guarantee good American citizens rights to defend themselves and their nation," said Calderon, "but believe me, many of these guns are not going to honest American hands." He told the assembled representatives and senators "over the past three years, Mexican authorities have seized some 75,000 weapons used in crime; 80 percent of which came from the U.S." He further stated that "Mexico's surge in violent, drug-cartel related crimes coincided with the 2004 repeal of the assault weapons ban."[22]

In August, 2010, the National Presbyterian Church of Mexico asked the Presbyterian Church, USA, for help in stopping the madness:

> Dear brothers and sisters in Jesus Christ:
>
> The National Presbyterian Church of Mexico is worried due to the high percentage of violence that we are living in our country today. Kidnapping and murders are there every-where, especially, in cities such as Tijuana, Monterrey, Juarez City, Morella, Acapulco just to mention some of them, which are considered to have the highest percentage of insecurity.
>
> That is why; we come to you brothers and sisters in Christ so that you may help us according to your possibilities in transmitting our concerns to those in charge of selling guns to Mexican people. Since, the guns are used by drug dealers to kill, and in many cases—sadly to say—innocent people.
>
> So, as leaders of the National Presbyterian Church of Mexico, we have come to the conclusion that we have to raise our voices against violence; and, together with you

21. "War Along America's Border: The Mexican Drug Cartels," http//perrrya .hubpages.com/hub/War-Along-Americas-Border-The-Mexican-Drug-Cartels.

22. Kara Rowland, "Calderon Presses Congress on Gun Trade," *Washington Times*, May 20, 2010.

all, we might share the same feeling, so that, our presidents may work hard to make stability a reality in our countries. We truly appreciate your gentle attention to this letter."[23]

Christians north of the border cannot ignore our complicity in this violence, nor can we forget our spiritual kinship with those south of the border. Our common faith in Christ demands solidarity with our brothers and sisters in Mexico. Certainly, God wants us to pray for them, but is that all we are willing to do?

23. Letter from the National Presbyterian Church of Mexico to the PCUSA, August 5, 2010.

17

What to Say at the Scene of a Mass Shooting

MOST MURDERS DON'T GET MUCH PRINT

You find the death notices for most of those who have been shot and killed by searching the back pages of your local newspaper. Most of them don't get much print. Hardly anyone notices other than families and close friends whose lives are forever scarred and whose spirits will never be the same.

If there are several homicides in a brief period of time, an editorial or two will appear and the editor is likely to express bewilderment over their frequency. People in the neighborhood will say, "We can't believe it happened here in our town; it is so peaceful and quiet and everyone is friendly." Several members of area churches will learn of the shootings, and word will spread quickly in the community. Someone will ask for prayers during worship and the pastors will pray for God's comfort and healing for the families involved. And, that's about it. For most residents, the deaths will soon be forgotten and people will return to their routines.

Should the victim be a member of a church, the anguish will be visible over a longer period of time. The pastor and officers will be on call 24/7 to try and keep those who grieve from literally falling apart. Church officers will organize efforts to help feed the survivor's families, assist with finances, and take care of the kids. Someone may start a memorial fund for the children's college education. But in spite of the genuine love expressed, the family will never be the same physically, emotionally, or spiritually.

Should the victim be young and live in the inner city, the hopes and dreams of classmates and peers will be shattered once again. They will experience what James Weldon Johnson penned in his unforgettable phrase, "when hope unborn had died."[1] There have been so many young African American males under thirty years of age killed by gunfire in recent years their age group has often been called an endangered species.

One inner city pastor shared with me the story of the funeral of a murdered youth. Instead of the customary six pallbearers, twelve of the victim's closest friends insisted on carrying his body to its final resting place. When they completed their assignment at the graveside, each of the boys put a hand on the coffin while their leader said tenderly, "We'll see you soon, Bro." These were young people who were born not to grieve and shed tears for a friend mowed down by gunfire, but to dream large dreams . . . to fall in love, find a good job and get married, and have children of their own. What hope did these young pallbearers have in tomorrow? How did they envision their future? What a waste of precious young life! It happens every day.

THE SPEECHES OF POLITICIANS AT A MASS SHOOTING

Mass shootings move the storyline to the front pages of our newspapers. We learn much by what is said or not said in these moments of grief. When the largest mass shooting in our nation's history occurred at Virginia Tech in 2007, President George W. Bush spoke at a convocation expressing condolences to the student body on behalf of the country. As he assured the community of the prayers of all Americans he said, "It's impossible to make sense of such violence and suffering. Those whose lives were taken did nothing to deserve their fate. They were simply in the wrong place at the wrong time." Excuse me, Mr. President, these bright young people were precisely in the *right* place at the *right* time. They were in class getting an education. They were exactly where they should have been. The shooter, however, was not where he should have been, and he should not

1. Johnson, "Lift Every Voice and Sing," 1921.

have been armed to the teeth with guns and large capacity magazines that spew out dozens of bullets in a few seconds.

Other local and state political leaders hustled to the scene to express their sympathies and assure the victim's loved ones and friends they were remembered in prayer. The leaders shared their pain. Gov. Tim Kaine of Virginia said it was not the right moment to ask *how* the shooting happened—specifically, why an angry, severely disturbed student with a history of mental illness was able to buy an efficient killing machine, and why it happens over and over again in America. At a press conference, the governor said: "[For] people who want to make it their political hobby horse to ride, I've got nothing but loathing for them. At this point it's about comforting family members and helping this community heal. And so to those who want to try to make this into some little crusade, I say take that elsewhere."[2]

Adam Gopnick, writing for the *New Yorker Magazine,* was not deterred by Kaine's reluctance to discuss *how* the tragedy happened. The magazine pointedly stated, "If the facts weren't so horrible, there might be something touching in the governor's deeply-held American belief that 'healing' can take place magically, without the intervening practice called, 'treating.' The logic is unusual but striking: the aftermath of a terrorist attack is the wrong time to talk about security, the aftermath of a death from lung cancer is not the time to talk about the tobacco industry, and the aftermath of a car crash is the wrong time to talk about seat belts."[3] People did talk about the shooting, of course, but much of the conversation was devoted to musings on the treatment of mental illness in universities, the problem of narcissism, violence in the media and popular culture, copycat killings, the alienation of immigrant students, and the question of evil.[4] Do you find it strange *nobody* in high office wanted to talk about *how* so many bright and beautiful young people died?

State Sen. John Edwards (D-Roanoke), whose district includes Virginia Tech, took his turn a few days later at the Blacksburg microphone, but he was there mostly to defend guns. He talked about

2. Adam Gopnik, "Shootings," *The New Yorker,* April 30, 2007, 28.
3. Ibid.
4. Ibid.

the futility of "gun control within a gun culture." He called gun control a Northern Virginia issue and said neither Republicans nor legislators from the more rural parts of the state would support a change in Virginia's laws to close the gun show loophole despite lobbying by the families of those who had been killed. "It's a cultural issue in this area of Virginia. You've got to be sensitive to cultural values."[5] Yes, he was very sensitive to the culture, the gun culture, that is; it was lost on Edwards that one's culture is more than guns. A remark reputed to be from another rural southerner, the American novelist, William Faulkner, is more truthful. "We all had better grieve for all people beneath a culture which holds any machine superior to any man."

Each elected official who appeared in Blacksburg was elected for the specific purpose of providing order in society and each of them had the power to make society safer by creating safeguards to deny mentally ill people easy access to guns in the future. Instead of taking on that responsibility, they asked for prayers. While their calls to prayer were sincere, what those who were grieving in Blacksburg and all over America really needed from these politicians were promises from the heart that they would *use* every ounce of their authority and influence to keep a disaster like this from ever happening again.

The limousines and police escorts were soon gone. Politicians, as a rule, do not stay long where there has been a mass shooting. They have learned reporters are likely to ask embarrassing questions and put them on the spot about guns.

Do you remember Rudyard Kipling's litany of good questions in his *Just So Stories?*

> I keep six honest serving men.
> They taught me all I knew.
> Their names are what and why and when
> and where and how and who.[6]

There wasn't a soul in Blacksburg who didn't know the answers to four of those "honest serving men." Answers to what, when, where,

5. Tim Craig, "Virginia Tech Families Turn Grief Into Cry for Gun Laws," *Washington Post*, January 5, 2008.

6. Kipling, *Just So Stories*, 83.

and who were well known. Only two of Kipling's questions were left unanswered: why and how. At a tragedy of this magnitude, the most comfortable question a civic leader can address is why? As in *why* such a terrible thing happened. Why was Seung Hui Cho so troubled? Why would he be obsessed with killing his classmates? Why was he so angry? Why didn't someone stop him before this happened? No one has the wisdom to explain why Cho went on his shooting rampage and the most we will ever have is speculation. All we know is he was part of a minority, an outsider, a loner with deep anger and resentment inside; we know he was terribly sick. We have only partial answers as to why and that's all we will ever have.

If we permit our leaders to focus on the question "Why" in such volatile moments, we open up for them the large, safe ground of speculation. It is exactly what they hope for. They can address a multitude of psychological issues: the personal background of the shooter, violence in our society: its movies, video games, rap music, and harsh, vitriolic language etc. When the speech is over, the politician can go home "politically safe" because he said nothing for which he could be held accountable. He was only speculating.

No one can prove or disprove speculation, but it gives politicians, community leaders, and faint-hearted clergy an excuse to side-step making commitments to *do* one single thing to prevent such hideous acts from occurring again.

At a mass shooting, the only *germane* question is *how*. How were thirty-two people killed and fifty-seven injured in just a few minutes? How was Cho able to follow through with this despicable crime? The answer is *very* simple: this terribly sick young man was able to buy two of the world's most efficient killing machines and use them for the purposes for which they were made. *That is how.*

As long as we permit elected leaders to visibly hide on the irrelevant safe ground of speculation and avoid the pertinent questions of how dangerous individuals continue to get guns at the drop of a hat, other mass shootings are waiting to happen. It is not a matter of *if* they will happen; it is *when*. And when these disasters shock the country once more we will all be subject to the same lame speeches from those who refuse to act, but call us to pray fervently for the survivors.

RESPONSIBILITIES OF THE MEDIA

Citizens also need to hold the media to higher standards of account-ability as they cover America's mass shootings. The media needs to ask much tougher questions about the direction gun violence is taking this country ever since the NRA became a business. When they refer to the Second Amendment, reporters can remind the speaker that he/she is quoting only half of the amendment; the other half *requires* good regulations on guns, as in "*a well-regulated militia.*" Or again, on the printed page, editors could easily include the entire amendment alongside the NRA's careful quoting of its second half.

Moreover, the country has never had a substantive national debate about guns in our society. If one or two questions surface about the Second Amendment in the presidential debates, it will be the maximum coverage we have come to expect and we can count on each candidate to affirm his or her solid support for the Second Amendment. This leaves us with a sterile debate by bumper stickers and snappy slogans. The major television networks could perform a great service to America by sponsoring a series of hour-long substantive deliberations led by scholars from each side laying out their respective positions; and closing with an honest debate led by a tough, no-nonsense moderator. Such discussions could help the American people separate fact from fiction and myth from reality. Both sides should be entitled to their own opinions, but not their own facts. Neither side should get a free pass.

In addition, those who select the news items for broadcast and TV anchors themselves must be vigilant and honorable as they choose what stories to air about guns. I have heard several stimulating accounts of vulnerable women, home alone, who shot an intruder in their bedroom, or store clerks in wheelchairs who stopped a robbery in their store by wielding a handgun. Honest journalism requires equal time for the numberless gun accidents that occur daily, such as those several NRA instructors who accidently shot their clients while leading self-defense courses, or the civic official who put her granddaughter in a shopping cart, only for the child to pull a revolver out of her purse and shoot herself in the chest. I've heard several stories of how guns stopped crimes over the airwaves, but I don't recall stories of tragic accidents or ridiculous shootings such as a man killing another for besting him in a Scripture-quoting contest. Such reports are readily available from CSGV and the Brady websites.

I concede that stories of stopping a crime are more compelling. They are like an account of our Navy SEALs killing Osama bin Laden. People hear these accounts and they are energized; they want to cheer, "guns save lives." On the other hand when people hear of gun tragedies they moan. These are "downers," which remind the public that guns actually do kill. The former reveals our human desire to be in control of our life situations; the latter underscores our total lack of control and vulnerability. The facts are: there are between 150–200 justifiable homicides every year, largely carried out by law enforcement. But in 2007 there were 12,632 murders and hundreds of thousands of injuries.[7]

It is not business as usual when we lose between eighty-two and eighty-four persons every day to gun violence. More articles are demanded; more documentaries are needed; and more investigative journalism is required.

Josh Sugarman, the Executive Director of the Violence Policy Center and author of *NRA: Money, Firepower and Fear,* was disgusted with the lack of substantive reporters in the aftermath of Virginia Tech. This moved him to write an article that would provide fainthearted reporters with a template to describe the mass shootings of the future. All reporters need to do is fill in the blanks.

"Yet Another Mass Shooting"

A heavily armed gunman, (insert name) opened fire yesterday at (circle one) an office building/church/school/shopping mall leaving more than 10/20/30 dead and 15/ 24/30 others wounded before taking his own life. Authorities have yet to cite a motive. Armed with a high capacity pistol/ AK-47 type assault rifle/ AR-15 type assault rifle, the gunman, (name), opened fire on the office workers/ worshipers/ students/ shoppers in a rampage that lasted less than 5/10/15 minutes. Police report that the shooter fired more than 50/100/150 rounds of ammunition and that the gun was legally/ not legally owned.

7. "The Facts About Firearm Violence," Illinois Council Against Handgun Violence

The shooter was described by neighbors as <u>a quiet/ an-gry/ friendly</u> man who kept to himself. "<u>I didn't even know he owned a gun/ but he did own a lot of guns,</u>" one said. One onlooker, standing next to an impromptu memorial, told reporters, "I can't believe it happened here in <u>name of town or community</u>. We have such a close-knit community."

Gun control supporters cited yesterday's rampage and the number of annual deaths in the United States from gun violence as over 30,000, or 82 people each day—as proof of the need for tighter controls on the increasingly high-powered firearms available to all Americans. One witness yesterday said, "Thirteen murdered at Columbine, 32 killed at Virginia Tech, now you can add <u>town</u> to the list."

A National Rifle Association spokesman stated, "<u>this is the time to grieve, not to talk about gun control</u>" / "<u>the appropriate focus is enforcement of the 20,000 gun laws already on the books</u>"/ had no comment.

Spokesmen for Senate Majority Leader Harry Reid (D-NV) and House Speaker Nancy Pelosi (D-CA,) citing the in-fluence of the NRA, said that despite the increase in such shootings, they did not anticipate any gun control mea-sures, including a ban on semiautomatic assault weapons and high capacity ammunition magazines, being consid-ered during this session of Congress.[8]

8. Sugarman, "Yet Another Mass Shooting," Violence Policy Center.

18

A Message to Peacemakers and Most Members of the NRA

OUR GOALS ARE COMPATIBLE

It is imperative that the church and people of faith be clear about our goals of keeping dangerous weapons out of dangerous hands if we would reach out to two noteworthy constituencies that share the same values. Those constituencies are the members of nonviolent peace fellowships and the silent majority of the NRA. If we could discover ways of working together, we could become a powerful influence in building a safer and saner America. If we can join hands, together we can save thousands of lives and prevent much of the violence that has become routine in too many places.

First of all, let it be known, churches and faith communities are not opposed to guns and/or gun rights. If one examines the statements made by major denominations over the last forty years, one will discover gun rights are affirmed, not denied. In spite of these moderate proclamations, gun zealots have misinformed the public and said the church cannot be trusted and is secretly working to confiscate all guns. Such falsehoods have made lots of gun owners nervous over the church's intentions. No one can honestly say the church has a secret agenda. We have been up front in our statements and we have not hidden our convictions that military assault weapons should be banned for civilian use. We make no apologies for that stance.

Most of America's faith communities recognize two basic American rights: (1) the right to keep and bear arms and (2) the right to public safety with safe streets, schools, and communities. We endorse the findings of Republican pollster, Frank Luntz, and 80 percent of gun owners in America, who believe "gun rights and public safety are not irreconcilable positions. In our democratic society, they are complementary."[1] Neither gun rights people nor public safety people can have the America of their dreams without giving stature to both of these fundamental American constitutional rights.

AMERICA'S GUN VIOLENCE REQUIRES A SPIRITUAL, ETHICAL, AND MORAL SOLUTION

Then again, it is important that the church be up front and vocal about America's broken legislative process as it concerns guns. The United States Congress is presently in sync with a small, extreme minority of gun owners, who along with manufacturers, distributors, and dealers, consider any regulation on guns, no matter how wise, to be a denial of gun rights. Our Congress is out of sync with the majority of Americans who favor balanced gun laws, including the majority of NRA members. The latter, along with the church, other faith communities, and members of peace fellowships must keep the issue alive and work for measured changes in the law by keeping the letters, e-mails, tweets, and telephone calls coming to our out-of-sync representatives.

Increasing numbers of churches and peoples of faith understand that the solution to America's epidemic of gun violence is not fundamentally a political one. Violence and unnecessary death require spiritual, ethical, and moral solutions. I confess in the past, I looked *first* to the political arena and ignored or bypassed the resources of my God and my faith. So did my denomination and others as well. We did a great job of putting the cart before the horse. We spent our time and energy writing and calling our legislators to remind them

1. Steve Klingman, "Poll: Gun Owners Not in Lockstep with NRA," January 14, 2010; http://open.salon.com/blog/steve_klingman/2010/01/13/poll-gun-owners-not-in-lockstep-with-nra.

of the horrible statistics. Only a few of our nation's leaders seemed to understand our angst; even fewer could see the danger ahead as increasing numbers of people were turning to guns to solve personal and community problems.

For decades church folk pleaded with elected leaders to enact balanced legislation, but they turned a deaf ear. They listened only to those whose guns had become idols and whose checks made it into their coffers. They believed supporting *any* restriction on guns was a losing political strategy. Knowing what we know today of the pervasive power of misinformation, we are not surprised when we learn that the total effect of Congress' inattention to guns made it easier for violent people to buy guns and harder for law enforcement to arrest them or those who sold them weapons illegally.

In spite of some evidence to the contrary, I still believe in the power of truth and the lasting strength of what is morally right. One can't work in this business without that faith. "Though the wrong seems oft so strong, God is the Ruler, yet." In that confidence, and in the name of Jesus' Christ and His Church, I issue heart-felt invitations to peacemakers and members of the peace movement and the NRA to join those of us who work to prevent gun violence. Imagine the power of such a coalition that would rally the American people to use their spiritual, ethical, and moral power to keep those who are a danger to themselves and others from getting their hands on the world's most efficient firearms.

AN INVITATION TO MEMBERS OF PEACE FELLOWSHIPS

In the past, efforts of peace fellowships have usually focused on protesting our nation's wars of choice and/or its foreign policy. Issues of peace were related to what was happening overseas. In June 2010 peace issues became domestic issues for the Presbyterian Peace Fellowship. When we recognized we were losing more people on our own streets through guns than in wars, gun violence became a major priority for us. We hired a part-time person to educate and mobilize Presbyterians to be pro-active in keeping guns away from youth, felons, domestic abusers, and terrorists and we endorsed a faith-based

ecumenical program called Heeding God's Call. (Check it out: www
.heedinggodscall.org.)

In the six years and nine months since the U.S. invasion of Iraq
in March 2003, through December 2009, 4,400 American servicemen and women lost their lives. In the same timeframe approximately 202,500 Americans lost their lives through gun violence on
our own streets.[2] It's small consolation to be told, "We are fighting
over there so we don't have to fight over here." Accurate statistics of
the enormous numbers of Iraqis killed in this wholly unnecessary
conflict are not available, yet each of their deaths must not be over-
looked for they too are God's children. While we mourn the deaths of
all persons in our nation's wars, our immediate grief and concern is
for our own countrymen and women.

Why are those in peace fellowships willing to travel hundreds
or thousands of miles to protest American deaths in war at the ends
of the earth, but are not equally passionate to protest *infinitely more
deaths* by guns in America? Because my wife and I have stood with
you in the past, we are asking you to stand with us in the future. We
need your energy, intelligence, imagination, and love!

AN INVITATION TO THE MAJORITY OF NRA MEMBERS

America needs to hear *directly* from nearly three-quarters of NRA
members who favor balanced laws that protect both one's right to
have a gun and at the same time, keep guns out of the hands of
those who are a danger to themselves and others.

Most Americans mistakenly believe that all NRA members
think the same and agree with your Executive Vice-President, Wayne
La Pierre, that law enforcement agencies such as ATF, which monitors the manufacture and sales of guns, must be rendered powerless
in order to protect your gun rights and deny government plans to
confiscate all weapons and padlock your hunting lands.

2. "Reports on U.S. Military Casualties During the U.S. Led War in Iraq,"
www.globalsecurity.org/military/ops/iraq_casualties.htm.

Many of my friends who are NRA members know there is no truth in that. Nevertheless, the general public perception of the NRA is that all members think alike. If this land is to be healed the silent majority of NRA members must become the vocal majority. Responsible gun owners have a special obligation to join the struggle of keeping guns out of dangerous hands both here at home and in the developing world.

My friend Andy Goddard, surrounded by public safety and gun rights proponents, made this appeal in front of the U. S. Supreme Court:

> I see today that not everyone present shares my opinion on this subject but I would like to point out some common ground amongst us all. I am sure nobody here is comfortable with seeing the daily litany of death and injury brought about by the misuse of firearms. Nobody is comfortable knowing this threat could take our lives or those of our loved ones and it is that basic human instinct for self-preservation that we all share. The difference between us comes in our response to this threat. Many of you see the only logical response being to arm yourself with guns to protect yourselves and your families. You are comfortable with carrying around a deadly weapon and you firmly believe you will be present with your family members at any time they should be threatened and that you will be ready and able to respond effectively in their defense. I, on the other hand, do not feel that way. I don't expect to be close by my family members at all times and I seriously doubt my ability to react in a controlled and effective way under the stress of a gun attack. My first priority is to seek ways to prevent such an attack from happening in the first place. What I am trying to point out is neither of our responses is wrong and also these differing responses do not necessarily have to be mutually exclusive. I do not seek to remove your right to defend yourself by force of arms and you should not seek to restrict my efforts to keep guns out of the hands of those who would use them for harm. In fact, the most logical and effective response to this situation may be to combine our efforts rather than use them to work against each other.[3]

3. Goddard, an unpublished speech before the Supreme Court, April 16, 2008.

If NRA members comprehend that gun rights and regulations to keep guns out of the hands of terrorists and violent people are complementary, but say nothing about it, the only message the people of the United States will hear is the extremist, fear-mongering voice of a minority of paranoid people who think the government wants to take away all their guns and forbid our people to hunt.

In the course of this book I have frequently referenced the solid agreement between the majority of NRA members, those who work in gun violence prevention, and the American people by citing the nationwide poll of Republican Frank Luntz in December 2009. Here are five areas of common ground:

1. Eighty-two percent of NRA members support "prohibiting people on the terrorist watch lists from purchasing guns."
2. Sixty-nine percent favor "requiring all gun sellers at gun shows to conduct criminal background checks of the people buying guns."
3. Seventy-eight percent back "requiring gun owners to alert police if their guns are lost or stolen."
4. Eighty-six percent of all gun owners and NRA members agree with Frank Luntz's core idea that gun rights and gun regulations complement each other: "We can do more to stop criminals from getting guns while also protecting the rights of citizens to freely own them."
5. Sixty-nine percent of NRA members oppose the idea behind the so-called Tiahrt amendment passed by Congress, which prevents law enforcement officials from having full access to gun trace data from the ATF and requires the FBI to destroy certain background-check records after just twenty-four hours.

Are there differences between us? Of course, there are. Luntz showed 59 percent of NRA members are opposed to registration and are worried President Obama will try to ban the sales of guns in the United States at some point while he is president. Commenting on the poll, Luntz said, "There are too many public officials taking an absolutist position when they don't have to, and they're taking it not because they want to, but because they're scared into doing it."[4]

4. E. J. Dionne, Jr., "Making Gun Safety (Politically) Safe," December 9, 2009, http://www.truthdig.com/report/item/making_gun_safety_politically_safe _20091209.

Wayne La Pierre and the NRA's highest paid lobbyists and hard-core extremists will *never* allow gun rights and public safety to be mentioned in the same breath. They go to work every day *in your name* to derail every piece of reasonable minimal legislation both in Washington, DC, and in state capitols. They are motivated and controlled by irrational fears and use simplistic slogans such as "the slippery slope" and "the camel's nose in the tent" to explain away grave national problems that clamor for immediate solutions. They are convinced that a retired minister like myself who has loved hunting for over fifty years is in cahoots with the government and conniving to take away your guns, padlock your hunting lands and deny you a right to own a firearm. That's utter nonsense. If you are part of the NRA's silent majority, you know that. Well, why not say so?

THE SCARIEST SLIPPERY SLOPE OF ALL

I'm not a psychologist, but I *think* I understand the paranoia of the slippery slope argument upon which the NRA and the Gun Empire base their ideology that *any* gun law, no matter how wise or minimal in scope, is but the first step to enable big government to knock on every door in America and confiscate all our guns. For them, the slippery slope is a clear and present danger. Beyond the Gun Empire, however, literally no one else believes this is even a remote possibility.

Those who live in the mountains are most aware that every mountaintop has more than one slope. The purpose of this book is to alert people of faith and others of good will of another slippery slope on which we are living today and it is far more dangerous. It is a huge threat to our children and grandchildren because we as a society are obediently following the advice and counsel of the idols of power and deadly force. We are living as prisoners of the principalities and powers and have forsaken the ways of the loving God who has redeemed us and placed our trust in sophisticated weapons to "guarantee" our security and preserve our nation's most cherished ideals. We live on this slippery slope because we as a people find it almost impossible to shake free of our fascination with and devotion to violence in all its forms. We say, "violence has worked for us in the past, why search for other ways to solve our human conflicts?" That is the slippery slope that scares me.

Biblical scholar Walter Wink is right and his words bear repeating:

> Violence is the ethos of our times. It is the spirituality of the modern world. It is accorded the status of a religion, demanding from its devotees an absolute obedience to death. Its followers are not aware, however, that the devotion they pay to violence is a form of religious piety. Violence is successful as a myth precisely because it does not seem to be mythic in the least. Violence simply appears to be the nature of things. It is what works. It is inevitable, the last, and often, the first resort in conflicts. It is embraced with equal alacrity by people on the left and on the right, by religious liberals and religious conservatives. The threat of violence, it is believed, alone can deter aggressors. Violence is thriving as never before in every sector of American popular culture, civil religion, nationalism, and foreign policy. Violence, not Christianity, is the real religion of America.[5]

Enough people believe more guns will resolve human conflicts to make this country the most dangerous in the developed world. With 300 million guns in private hands and three million more coming off our assembly lines every year, our citizens are armed and dangerous. The guns we purchase for self-defense inevitably become the instruments of murder and suicide among family and friends.

Not only does the Empire tell us we need more guns, but we need more powerful guns. Every year they increase in firepower and in killing potential even as they shrink in size and concealability. We've come a long way from the introduction of the six-shooter pistol to extended magazines for assault pistols that can fire more than thirty rounds in a few seconds. Other weapons are also available. The Barrett Sniper Rifle 82A1 is already on the market, which, according to advertisements, "can destroy or disable a modern jet-aircraft." Should citizens be able to buy a machine gun, a shoulder-fired missile, some grenades, or a sawed off shotgun, which was banned from public sale in 1939?

---

5. Wink, *Engaging the Powers*, 13.

There have been only a few anemic words of protest from the American public and the church. Meanwhile, gun rights trump reason in the halls of Congress, law enforcement is hamstrung in its oversight on guns, and the scientific community no longer can report its research to the CDC when it conflicts with NRA slogans. American people are already living on a slippery slope. It is not a threat of guns being confiscated in the future; it is a threat for the future of America and its traditional Constitutional values.

How much longer will NRA members let the extremists of their organization trivialize and monopolize every NRA message on guns to the country? How many more deaths will be required before responsible persons on both sides of this issue can join hands and lead our nation to acknowledge that gun rights and keeping guns out of the hands of those who are a danger to themselves and others are complementary and not a threat to anyone's freedom?

Every American today lives on the slippery slope of gun violence and each of us is endangered because public safety is not a national priority. Many Americans are armed with powerful guns and shoot their fellow citizens with increasing regularity. The total number of people shot in the United States each year has risen significantly from the beginning of the new century to 2008, the latest year for which complete federal data is available. Between 2000 and 2008, a total of 272,590 people died of gunshot injuries in the United States—an average of 30,288 per year, a number shocking by comparison to any other developed country. During that same time period, an estimated 617,488 people suffered nonfatal gunshot injuries in the United States. The total number of people shot in 2008 totaled 110,215—the highest total recorded during the nine-year period surveyed by the Violence Policy Center.[6]

Non-fatal injuries are, of course, preferable to death, but many with spinal cord injuries might dispute such an assertion. For them it is a living death. Many victims will never walk again or will carry wounds that will not heal; For others, their injuries lead to different kinds of death: the death of a free spirit, the end of feeling in control; and forfeiting the confident pursuit of life, liberty, and happiness. Post Traumatic Stress Syndrome is not only for returning military

---

6. Kristen Rand, Violence Policy Center. Public Paper. January 8, 2012.

personnel; it is a spiritual disorder peculiar to everyone who has ever been a target. The shootings will continue to rise until people of faith and good will step out front and convince our leaders, it does not have to continue.

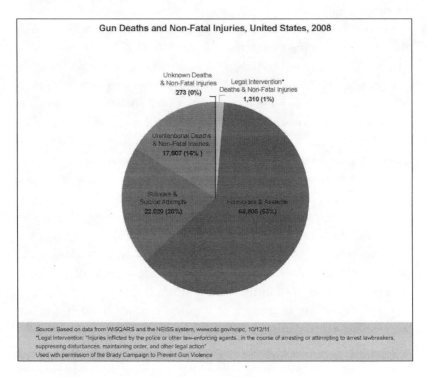

Gun Deaths and Non-Fatal Injuries, United States, 2008

Source: Based on data from WISQARS and the NEISS system, www.cdc.gov/ncipc, 10/12/11
*Legal Intervention: "Injuries inflicted by the police or other law-enforcing agents…in the course of arresting or attempting to arrest lawbreakers, suppressing disturbances, maintaining order, and other legal action"
Used with permission of the Brady Campaign to Prevent Gun Violence

BOB RICKER: A PROFILE IN COURAGE

Before Bob Ricker became a personal friend of mine he was the Assistant General Counsel for the NRA. Hired in 1981, as a promising young lawyer, Ricker represented the NRA in many important federal and state legislative battles and gained a deep understanding of political and legal processes. Eventually he was appointed Executive Director of the American Shooting Sports Council (ASSC), the gun industry's leading trade organization at the time.

In this position, Ricker participated in a series of high-profile gun industry meetings between 1992 and 1997, during which manufacturers questioned whether they should take voluntary action to better control the distribution of guns. Ricker later stated, "Makers of guns had long known the diversion of firearms from legal channels of commerce to the black market takes place principally at the distributor/dealer level." This is because corrupt dealers make it easy for criminals and juveniles to buy guns by allowing practices like "straw purchases," in which an individual with a clean criminal record buys a gun on behalf of someone who is prohibited under federal law from doing so (i.e., a convicted felon, domestic abuser, mentally ill person, drug addict, etc.).

During these industry meetings, Ricker began to question the marketing practices of manufacturers and had the moral resolve to change his mind. He proposed strict standards and guidelines to his industry colleagues wherein manufacturers would sell guns only to distributors and retailers who could demonstrate they had a firm understanding of applicable laws, safety rules, and warning signs for illegal firearm trafficking. Dealers would no longer be able to sell multiple guns to a single individual. Unsurprisingly, his plan was rejected.

As Ricker described it, "The prevailing view was if the industry took action voluntarily, it would be an admission of responsibility for the problem." Ultimately, the industry's lawyers decided that even holding the meetings was dangerous and the meetings were stopped altogether.

Ricker did not stop trying to reduce unnecessary deaths. Following the mass shooting at Columbine High School in 1999, he traveled to the White House on behalf of ASSC to meet with President Clinton to see if something could be done to prevent future school shootings. For the NRA leadership, this was the last straw. Ricker was forced to resign and the ASSC was disbanded in favor of the more conservative National Shooting Sports Foundation (NSSF).

In 2003, Ricker would go public with his concerns about the gun industry when he provided testimony in an affidavit for a lawsuit by twelve California cities and counties against the gun industry. A few months later he appeared on *60 Minutes* to tell his full story. When he was asked why he would risk his reputation and the wrath of gun rights activists by coming forward, Ricker stated, "I don't want to have to come home some night from the office and have my wife tell me, 'Your son was shot in a drive-by shooting,' or, 'The neighbor's kids were killed.'" Ricker concluded, "These people who sit up there

19

A Wake Up Call for the Faith Community

C. S. Lewis wrote, "Christianity is a statement which, if false, is of no importance, and if it is true, of infinite importance. The one thing it cannot be is moderately important."[1] When violence and guns are destroying the character and moral fiber of our nation, it is of infinite importance that the faith community wake up and boldly negate the nonsense that is noised that guns do not kill and the answer to gun violence is more guns.

For citizens to carry their guns everywhere (homes, schools, college campuses, bars, churches, athletic contests, and courthouses) is not an acceptable solution. If the signs for gun free zones are removed from our schools, bedlam will ensue. Relying on more firepower to reduce violence is not a message that faith communities, peace fellowships, the majority of NRA members, or the general populace could embrace. Our faith traditions, should they be honestly consulted, provide much more effective alternatives.

However, while faith communities are *thinking about* taking action, there is vigorous evangelizing by the Gun Empire for CCWP on college campuses nationwide. With every mass shooting, their heated, irrational rhetoric grows louder: "The more guns we have on campus, the safer we will be," they say. "More guns=less crime," and "Guns Save Lives," read their signs.

1. Lewis, *God in the Dock*, 101.

THE GUN EMPIRE CANNOT LONG ENDURE

To enhance its image the Gun Empire boasts of pure American values, yet preaches insurrection and plots the overthrow of a democratically elected government. It asks to be approached as one of the great religions of the world, yet lies to the American public. It claims God-given rights to be armed, but refuses any public responsibility for safety. Such pronouncements may in the short run wield significant power over a minority of gun zealots and a majority of apathetic citizens, but in God's long run, it is doomed: "The Kingdoms of this world shall become the Kingdoms of our Lord and of His Christ and He shall reign forever and ever" (Rev 11:15).

The Gun Empire carries within the seeds of its own destruction, particularly in its classic overreach and promotion of violence. As it seeks more power through devious means and grasps for more exclusive privileges, it sets in motion undeniable and unconquerable spiritual forces that will inevitably lead to its own defeat. Its outrageous methods will eventually bring about its own demise. It will die as all Empires die, by claiming way too much. God still "scatters the proud in the imagination of their hearts, puts down the mighty from their thrones, exalts those of low degree, fills the hungry with good things, and sends the rich and powerful away—empty" (Luke 1:51–53).

Signs of the Gun Empire's demise are increasingly evident as people of good will grow sick and tired of its endless assertions that bigger and more sophisticated weapons will bring security. Albeit slowly, people are gaining new understandings that instruments which bring only death are incapable of providing peace.

The day draws near when people and nations that have invested so much money, blood, and tears acquiring weapons, will realize how grievously they have been deceived by the idols of power and deadly force. The day is coming when all the nations will testify that security and peace are God's gifts, and are not really ends in themselves, but rather the by-products of living in just and loving relationships with God and neighbors.

THE POWER OF THE LAMB THAT WAS SLAIN

Most of the Bible's graphic references to struggles with idols are in the Book of Revelation, where the Roman emperor and his empire, known as "the Beast," and "the New Babylon" make war on Jesus' followers. They are face to face with the seemingly invincible power of Rome, which demands allegiance and savagely kills those who will not bow down and worship the Beast. The blood of the martyrs flows as Christians are fed to wild animals and burned alive as human torches to amuse the powerful.

Even so, John encourages those who were about to die to hold on to their trust in an even greater power—the power of God, which raised Jesus from the grave and conquered death. Nursing only a faint hope that they would be spared a violent end, these believers died confident in God's ultimate promise to dethrone the Beast and conquer every evil power.

Using apocalyptic language John proclaims the defeat of the Beast and "wicked Babylon," which are symbolic of every principality and power. The Conqueror is the risen Christ or Christus Victor. John calls him by another name as well: "The Lamb that was slain." Hear his stunning vision of the Lamb that conquers evil:

> Then I looked, and I heard the voice of many angels surrounding the throne and the living creatures and the elders; they numbered myriads of myriads and thousands of thousands, singing with full voice, "Worthy is the Lamb who was slain to receive power and wealth and wisdom and might and honor and glory and blessing." Then I heard every creature in heaven and on earth and under the earth and in the sea, and all that is in them, singing, "To the one seated on the throne and to the Lamb, be blessing and honor and glory and might forever and ever!" And the four living creatures said, "Amen!" And the elders fell down and worshiped. (Rev 5:11–14)

The violent power of the Beast is overcome not by a more brutal power, which is history's norm, nor are these principalities and powers crushed by a cataclysmic event. The Beast is laid low by the power of One who renounces violence altogether. The old has passed away and God's new earth has arrived. The natural order of things is turned on its head. Life is different now. It is the way it is supposed to be. The Beast and Wicked Babylon are overwhelmed by the Lamb that was slain. To believe in God is to know that what ought to be done *will* be done.

Can we get our sophisticated twenty-first-century minds around that image of the triumphant Lamb of God, who "was led to the slaughter and did not open his mouth" (Isa 53:7)? Can we envision all the idols of power and deadly force lying silently at the feet of him who was crucified, dead and buried, but now is risen?

We don't usually attribute victory and power to lambs, do we? Neither does the National Football League. It has Lions, Bears, Bengals, Broncos, Jaguars, Raiders, Buccaneers, Chiefs, Vikings, Cowboys, Giants, and Redskins, to name a few, but no lambs. Arena football, major league soccer, lacrosse, baseball, basketball, and hockey have no team called "the Lambs." There is no street gang or United States Marine unit called "the Lambs." Yet, when time is no more and all the books are closed and all the armies and navies of the world are mustered out forever and every government and parliament which ever sat is dismissed for all time, when all the nations gather at God Almighty's throne to celebrate the final victory, *every knee* will bow down and fall prostrate before the gentle Lamb that was slain.

"Worthy is the Lamb that was slain to receive power and wealth and wisdom and might and honor and glory and blessing forever and ever! Amen!" (Rev 5:12–13).

I began working to prevent gun violence in 1975. I was motivated largely by rage over a friend's tragic death and my country's sanction of 30,000 deaths per year. I began in anger, but I stayed at it because of my hope in the Lamb of God who will usher in the full and final victory over violence and death. Christian faith steers us to affirm that love is stronger than hate; life is more powerful than death; peace is more compelling than violence; and God's promises are more influential than guns. Guns can only kill. Love can bring new life; love can bring a resurrection.

Many times in my ministry when violence seemed overwhelming, I have turned to *The Declaration of Faith* for renewed energy:

We do not know when the final day will come,
In our time we see only broken and scattered signs
that the renewal of all things is under way.
We do not yet see the end of cruelty and suffering
in the world, the church, or our own lives.
   But we see Jesus as Lord.
As he stands at the center of our history,
   we are confident he will stand at its end.
He will judge all people and nations.
   Evil will be condemned
and rooted out of God's good creation.
There will be no more tears or pain.
All things will be made new.
The fellowship of human beings with God and each other
will be perfected.[2]

Many of us over the years have found it easier to curse the darkness than to light our candles. We may have made our theological statements condemning the carnage, and some of them have been quite good, but our words have been stronger than our deeds. Having been in hundreds of Session, Presbytery, Synod, and General Assembly meetings and committees of the same, I've noticed that Presbyterians, especially, often feel if we "say it just right," we have done our job. Not so.

The Apostle writes to early Christians: "Little children, let us love, not in word or speech, but in truth and action" (1 John 3:18). Making statements about gun violence in the anonymity of district, state, and national assemblies, interacting with folk we are not likely to see again, is an easy task compared to bringing those statements back home and putting them on the home-church agenda.

Part of the reason gun violence is rampant in America is because the subject itself is seldom raised from our pulpits, discussed in officer's meetings, debated in Sunday school, and considered at our fellowship dinners and pot-luck suppers. Yes, these are venues where words are plentiful, but the truth and action that faith requires always begins with words. Even God needed words to create the world. "Let there be light," the Creator decreed and creation happened.

2. Presbyterian Church, US, *Our Confessional Heritage.*

Creation always happens, for good or ill, whenever words are spoken. Every war, every movement to degrade people by nation, race, ethnicity, or sex began with words. Likewise every public measure to rescue the needy, every social advance of the human race, and every stand for justice began with words. Words are never the end of our witness, but our witness always begins with words. If gun violence declines in America, it will be because the church starts *talking* about it—and thinking and arguing about it—using words. When is the last time your church had in-depth conversations about gun violence and made conscious decisions to do something about it?

Somewhere I read an article on what love means. The author prophetically said, "You and I belong, good friends, to a group that gets up early. We get up early because we don't sleep much. And we don't sleep much because the world doesn't let us sleep. And in turn, we try our best not to let the world sleep. When people suffer anywhere, either we shout or we whisper, but at least we try to wake it up."

The most pathetic words I ever hear are from people who listen to the innumerable ways the Gun Empire deceives us and perpetuates murder and mayhem, only to sigh: "The only thing we can do is pray." That is code for "there is nothing we can do." What a denial of God's love. What a rejection of discipleship and the power of Christ in our lives. Prayer unaccompanied by attempts to awaken listless people or congregations, or pouring out one's blood, sweat, and tears to stop the violence, will *never* satisfy the imperatives of love. The church's prayer without accompanying action is really a cop-out.

One of the most loving things one can do to prevent violence, or honor those who have needlessly suffered and died, is to welcome a holy rage. When violence is destroying human beings, those who love are enraged. When injustice reigns, rage is often the first step of love. Jesus was angry when worshipers were exploited in the temple. In an act of love he turned over tables and threw out the moneychangers. William Wilberforce, member of the English Parliament, was enraged by the cruelty of the slave trade. With love in his heart he went public in his denunciation and became a major figure in the abolitionist movement. Sojourner Truth was so angry over the indignities of slavery that with insightful love she walked thousands of miles to help slaves "follow the drinking gourd" to freedom. When

Dutch Christians witnessed Nazi atrocities against Jews, they were outraged and started smuggling Jews to safety. Freedom riders were incensed "the colored" could not eat at lunch counters in five- and ten-cent stores, sit in the front of the bus, or use toilets in gas stations. Out of love for their brothers and sisters, they boarded buses and helped break the chains of segregation. People who love do not sit back and watch when terrible things are happening to neighbors or friends. Those who love welcome within a holy rage.

During France's brutal anti-Muslim war in Algeria, the philosopher Jean-Paul Sartre admonished French commanders and intelligentsia to accept responsibility for crimes against humanity:

> It is not right, my fellow countrymen, you know very well all the crimes committed in our name. It's not at all right that you do not breathe a word about them to anyone, not even to your own soul, for fear of having to stand in judgment of yourself. I'm willing to believe that at the beginning you did not realize what was happening; later you doubted whether such things could be true, but now you know, and still you hold your tongues.[3]

God forbid people of faith hold our tongues any longer over what is reprehensible to God. Our churches and faith communities have ample Scriptural warrant, communication skills, financial resources, critical masses of people, and more fact-finding committees than we know what to do with. What we lack are *fact-facing committees* and a holy rage that too many people are dying so unnecessarily.

THE CALL TO LOVE IN CHRIST'S NAME

Loving is not conjuring up warm, fuzzy feelings; love requires tough, focused public action. It's quite simple, really, and Jesus said it was the most important thing in the world. In our hearts we all know God wants us to be good lovers: "to love God with all our heart, soul, mind and strength and our neighbors as ourselves" (Luke 10:25–28). I hope I'm wrong, but I sense within many churches a kind of dumbing down on God's command to love God and neighbor today. I've

---

3. Sartre, Preface to Franz Fanon's *The Wretched of the Earth*, 25.

seen too many churches that are governed by a kind of creeping sentimentalism that pretends to be love. Are we permitting Jesus' world-changing agape love to morph into schmaltziness and the gushy stuff of greeting cards?

"To believe in God," says Dorothee Soelle, "means to take sides with life and to end our alliance with death. It means to stop killing and wanting to kill, and to do battle with apathy which is so akin to killing . . . Taking sides with life is not an easy or simple thing. It involves a never-ending process of change whereby we constantly renounce the self that is dead and enamored of death and instead becomes free to love life."[4]

For a host of reasons, many congregations today are threatened by declining memberships. One can understand why some pastors and governing bodies might want to "keep everybody happy" and not "rock the boat" by raising anything controversial. To keep the membership rolls intact and the budget in the black, leaders sometimes "back off" from addressing difficult subjects like guns in America and feel it necessary to exchange agape love for a bit of "pleasant togetherness" where Jesus' disciples talk about the weather, our grandchildren, and the football game. If our faith is as important as we declare in our creeds, perhaps we might reexamine our reasons for being a church in the first place.

At the beginning of his national ministry, Martin Luther King wrote in his memorable *Letters From a Birmingham Jail*:

> More than the fire hoses and the police dogs of Bull Connors (Chief of Police of Birmingham, AL), I fear the silence of the churches. The contemporary church is so often a weak, ineffective voice with an uncertain sound. It is so often the arch-supporter of the status quo. Far from being disturbed by the presence of the church, the power structure of the average community is consoled by the church's silent and vocal sanction of things as they are. But the judgment of God is upon the church as never before. If the church of today does not recapture the sacrificial spirit of the early church, it will lose its authentic ring, forfeit the loyalty of millions, and be dismissed as an irrelevant social club with no meaning

4. Soelle, *Death by Bread Alone*, 10.

for the 20th century. I am meeting young people everyday whose disappointment with the church has risen to outright disgust.[5]

Having spent nine years as a missionary in Japan and thirty years as a pastor of three churches in North Carolina and Virginia, I understand the need for an occasional time-out from addressing tough issues. And so I am not dismissed as a hypocrite, I confess I have an idolatrous need to be liked. Consequently, I'm pretty good at knowing when to back off from saying too much when I sense someone is getting upset. I don't pretend to be a model of pastoral courage. Nonetheless, "There is a time to keep silence and a time to speak" (Eccl 3:7).

In 2010, my state and others passed laws that permit gun owners to take their weapons into bars and other places that serve alcohol *provided they do not drink.* (And just why is it people go to bars?) I wonder why some pastors in Virginia and elsewhere are unable to say, "In the name of God, Jack Daniels, Virginia Gentleman, Samuel Adams, and a Glock 19 should not be seen together in a bar; Friends, martinis and guns do not mix." Even the NRA would agree with that. If the shepherds of Jesus' flock are unable to make such an innocuous statement, I wonder if they have anything else of consequence to say to their people.

Those of us in faith communities should jog our memories and recall some great victories for justice and peace in which the church was privileged to participate because we refused to back off from the imperatives of love and be silent: Freedom Marches and Freedom Riders challenged unjust laws and dismantled segregation; women insisted that their call from God to preach the Gospel be honored; Protestors stopped a disastrous war in Southeast Asia; faithful black and white Christians in South Africa turned what appeared to be a bloody war into the peaceful dismantling of apartheid; the Berlin Wall and the Iron Curtain came tumbling down like the walls of Jericho, remember? Public opinion brought Big Tobacco to its knees; and mothers and students working through Mothers Against Drunk Driving and Students Against Drunk Driving brought a significant drop in the number of teens killed by drunken drivers. More recently

5. King, *Letters from a Birmingham Jail*, 12.

mainline churches insisted that gays and lesbians have equal rights. These are miracles that raised the spirits and brightened the lives of millions. People who trust God do not simply believe in miracles; we *depend* on them.

OUR CHOICE: TO BE INTIMIDATED OR SPEAK THE TRUTH IN LOVE

Local congregations may have a member or two whose guns have become idols and even if the issue is raised in a respectful, conciliatory manner, they are likely to get angry and say, "This is a church and it is inappropriate for us to be discussing *political matters* like guns." Should such comments deter a church school class or a congregation from loving God and neighbors and working to prevent unnecessary gun deaths?

Church leaders who are tempted to think Christ's agape love means keeping everyone happy have given some gun zealots the boldness to intimidate whole congregations and keep them from even talking about the violence which plagues their entire communities. Too many people are dying for the church to pretend the elephant in the living room really isn't there. It is *not* love when a pastor, church leaders, or a Sunday school class surrenders to extortion in order to keep the peace. It is the opposite of love when 98 percent of the members in a community permit one person or a small handful to block a discussion or a ministry that could literally spell the difference between life and death. Isn't the church the very place where we can speak the truth in love to one another (Eph 4:15)?

Only a small portion of NRA members and/or gun owners are extremists, but if they are part of one's congregation, they *could* be a disruption. Yet in only a few churches would gun zealots comprise a majority. It is possible that even responsibly addressing the problem might cause a few zealots to leave the membership and take their pledge elsewhere. It is *also* possible that those who have left the congregation because they were bored or offended by a timid, irrelevant church, might start coming back because they see Christ's agape love once again taking form in the world.

John Calvin bet his life and committed his writings to the proposition that there is a direct connection between God's intentions for the world, the prophet's visions, Jesus' teaching, and the implications of love that are to guide our own actions. God's people are compelled to order society in ways that defend citizens, promote peaceful communities, and "ward off and remove harm." How we love others is not through our good feelings or individual acts of charity, but through advocating for policies, which will extend protection to the greatest number of people.

As we earlier noted, John Calvin underscored the importance of social order as he spoke about the sixth commandment, "you shall not kill." "The purpose of this commandment," he wrote,

> is, that since the Lord has bound the whole human race by a kind of unity, the safety of all ought to be considered as entrusted to each. In general, therefore, all violence and injustice, and every kind of harm from which are neighbor's body suffers is prohibited. Accordingly, we are required faithfully to do what in us lies to defend the life of our neighbor, to promote whatever tends to his tranquility, to be vigilant in warding off harm, and when danger comes, to assist in removing it.[6]

Scripture and experience tell us that those who are armed to the teeth cannot build a peaceful society; neither can sentimental people who are satisfied with "a little bit of togetherness," shape Jesus' peaceable Kingdom. Only strong lovers can build a peaceful society. That's the way God designed the world and why Jesus called peacemakers "the children of God" (Matt 5:9).

Church folks need to remember that time is on our side. Over 75 percent of the American people are on our side; America's mainline denominations are on our side; 75 percent of NRA members are on our side. The only thing that could possibly stand in our way is for us to forget who we are and why God put us here.

John Dear has defined violence in those exact terms:

> Violence is the act of forgetting who we are; brothers and sisters of one another, each one a child of God. Violence occurs

6. Calvin, *The Institutes*, Book 2, Chapter 8, 39.

in those moments when we forget and deny our basic identity as God's children, when we treat others as if they were
worthless instead of priceless and cling to our own selfish
desires, possessions and security. In the effort to claim our
inheritance as God's children, we must love one another,
even our enemies. We must remember who we are.[7]

I'm happy to report several faith communities are remembering
and reclaiming who they are. I thank God spiritual alarm clocks have
been awakening increasing numbers of people to address gun violence as one of the greatest spiritual threats to our church and nation.
Surprisingly, the General Assembly of the PCUSA in 2010 by a unanimous vote called its members and judicatories to a spiritual awakening and social mobilization to prevent gun violence.[8] (Trust me, a
unanimous vote in a Presbyterian General Assembly is unusual.)

That awakening includes a call to faith communities to participate in a new faith-based, ecumenical strategy called Heeding God's
Call, which is active in Philadelphia, other cities in Pennsylvania,
and Greater Washington, DC. Other chapters are in formative stages.
HGC is endorsed by the PCUSA, the National Council of Churches
of Christ in the USA, the Council of Bishops of the United Methodist
Church, and the Church of the Brethren.

Heeding God's Call organizes ecumenical efforts to confront
gun dealers and gun shows whose guns routinely show up at crime
scenes, indicating *illegal* sales practices. Central to its strategy is asking dealers to adopt a code of conduct, of non-burdensome business
practices, which will all but eliminate straw purchases and illegal
gun trafficking. The code was originally an agreement with the nation's largest gun dealer, Wal-Mart, and the Mayors Against Illegal
Guns Coalition.

If you are wondering what you and your faith community can
do to move the mountain of gun violence, please have a look at www
.presbypeacefellowship.org/gunviolence and pay particular attention to the toolkit, which was developed by Rev. Maggie Leonard of
the Presbyterian Peace Fellowship. The kit is full of step-by-step practical help in getting the program off the ground in your community.

7. Dear, *Disarming the Heart: Toward a Vow of Nonviolence*, 33.

8. *Gun Violence, Gospel Values: Mobilizing in Response to God's Call*, 9.

If you are ready to go to work, consider the following fifteen specific *actions* the Presbyterian Church, USA, encourages you and others in your faith community to take to save lives.

1. Take responsibility to build public awareness of gun violence and the epidemic of preventable gun-related deaths.

2. Address the temptation to gun suicide and murder-suicide among both old and young people. Pastors especially should present practical theologies of peace as alternatives to fantasies of power, idolatries of force, strategies of vengeance, and the gravitational pull of nihilism or depression.

3. Design liturgies that call for periodic preaching on gun violence and include prayers for the victims and perpetrators of gun violence and confession of our own complicity in the perpetuation and toleration of violence in all its forms in our culture.

4. Develop focused initiatives that build urban-suburban ecumenical partnerships in order to better understand the problem of gun violence and take more effective action.

5. Lead and join ecumenical gatherings for public prayer at sites where gun violence has occurred. With appropriate law enforcement guidance, support models such as "ceasefire" and other urban gang intervention strategies based on the public health model of addressing the most vulnerable populations.

6. Work with local law-enforcement agencies and community groups to identify gun shops that engage in retail practices designed to circumvent laws on gun sales and ownership. Encourage full legal compliance, support higher marketing standards, and if necessary, take nonviolent action against gun shops and gun shows that are known to sell guns that end up in crime, using the faith-based campaign of "Heeding God's Call."

7. Cooperate with colleges, universities, and seminaries to sponsor regular educational and summer conference events on gun violence and its prevention, in order to raise the awareness of the faith community and call it to informed action.

8. Display signs that prohibit carrying guns onto personal or church property. Due to recent expanded provisions in concealed carry laws in many states that now allow guns to be carried openly,

including into houses of worship, we recommend that these provisions be employed.

9. Encourage citizens, hunters, and law-enforcement officials who
   regularly handle weapons properly to be wise examples in reducing risks and teaching how to prevent the misuse of deadly force.

10. Support state and national advocacy bodies in advocating for
    policies that receive wide public support to:

    a. limit legal personal gun acquisition to one handgun a month;

    b. require licensing, registration, and waiting periods to allow
       comprehensive background checks, and cooling-off periods,
       for all guns sold;

    c. close the gun show loophole by requiring background checks
       for all gun buyers;

    d. ban semiautomatic assault weapons, armor piercing handgun
       ammunition, and .50-caliber sniper rifles;

    e. advocate for new technologies to aid law-enforcement agencies
       to trace crime guns and promote public safety;

    f. raise the age for handgun ownership to twenty-one;

    g. eliminate the Tiahrt Amendment attached to annual appro-
       priations for ATF that impedes local law enforcement agencies
       in their use of gun traces and requires the Justice Department
       to destroy within twenty-four hours the records of buyers
       whose NICS (National Instant Criminal Background Check
       System) check were approved.

11. Follow the recommendations of the International Association of
    Chiefs of Police and support laws to "require judges and law en-
    forcement to remove guns from situations of domestic violence,
    as well as from people whose adjudicated mental illness, drug
    use, or previous criminal record suggests the possibility of vio-
    lence," and to increase police training in nonviolent proactive
    intervention.

12. Urge corporate church structures to develop a corporate engage-
    ment strategy for working with corporations in which the church
    may be invested that are producers or distributors of weapons
    that do not comply with its policies on gun violence prevention,

recommending shareholder proposals and divestment actions appropriate to the integrity and effectiveness the church seeks.

13. Include means through which church-wide faithfulness to these commitments can be monitored, supported, encouraged, and resourced, in order to strengthen especially those congregations most exposed to gun violence. Remain vigilant so that appropriate resources continue to be made available to help in worship, pastoral care, and public policy work.

14. Partner with other faith institutions to create and sustain a national, activist faith-based social movement to save thousands of lives yearly.

15. Distribute studies and information on a regular basis for councils, congregations, and other educational and advocacy use.[9]

While we take some of the steps above and are convinced we are following God's call, we must never demonize our Christian brothers and sisters whose views about guns are the polar opposite of our own. We must never claim we are closer to God than they for there are earnest Christians on both sides of this issue. We need to walk together into the future in order to build the America we all want for our children and grandchildren. Neither side can have what it most desires for our society without respecting and accommodating the other. But again, isn't that how God made the world? We must learn to speak the truth in love to those whose views are different. We must take heart because the polls tell us the vast majority of Americans are not far apart on guns and gun violence. Eighty-six percent of all gun owners and NRA members agree that Second Amendment Rights and keeping guns from criminals and terrorists are complementary, not contradictory. What are we waiting for? Let the discussions and the healing begin!

9. *Gun Violence, Gospel Values: Mobilizing in Response to God's Call*, 28–29.

Bibliography

Adams, John. Letter to Thomas Jefferson, November 13, 1813. Online: http://www.americanheritage.com, October 17, 2006.

Advisory Committee on Social Witness Policy. *Gun Violence, Gospel Values: Mobilizing in Response to God's Call.* Presbyterian Church, USA. Louisville: 2010.

Albright, Madeline. *The Mighty and the Almighty: Reflections on America, God and World Affairs.* New York: Harper, 2006.

Allen, Greg. "Florida Bill Could Muzzle Doctors on Gun Safety." National Public Radio, May 7, 2011.

American Heritage Dictionary of the English Language. Edited by William Norris. Boston: Houghton Mifflin, 1980.

American Rifleman. "Picking a Hideout Holster." September 1993.

Annals of America, The. Vol. 7. Edited by William Benton. New York: Encyclopedia Britannica, Inc.

———. Vol. 12. Edited by William Benton. New York: Encyclopedia Britannica, Inc.

Arida, Wally. "Gun Games Publisher Wants Change in Industry." *Firearms Business* (July 1, 1995) 3–4.

Ayoob, Massad. "Trend Crimes and the Gun Dealer." *Shooting Industry*, March, 1993, 18.

Aztec-history.com/Cholula-pyramid.html.

Babcock, Maltbie Davenport. "This is My Father's World" Hymn 293, *The Presbyterian Hymnal.* Louisville: Westminster/John Knox, 1990.

Baum, Don. "Packing Heat: My Concealed Weapon and You." *Harpers* (August 2010) 29ff.

Barrett Firearms Manufacturing Co. Murfreesboro, TN. Ad for Model 82A1 .50-caliber sniper rifle.

Beard, Michael. "Mondays With Mike: 'A Profile in Courage.'" The Coalition to Stop Gun Violence. Public document, December 1, 2009.

Bloomberg, Michael. "New York City Mayor Proves How Easy It Is to Buy Guns in Arizona." Press Conference, January 31, 2011. Online: http://www.gunshowundercover.org/azpressrelease.

Bouchard, Michael. Testimony in Hearings Before the House Sub Committee on Crime, Terrorism, and Homeland Security. February 28, 2006.

Brady Campaign to Prevent Gun Violence. "More Americans Killed by Guns Than by War in the 20th Century." December 30, 1999.

Brady Report, The. Winter 2011.

Brigety, Reuben. "US Small Arms Policy: Security at a Cross Roads." Unpublished working paper, December 31, 2007. In possession of the author.

Brooks, David. *On Paradise Drive: How We Live Now and Always Have in the Future Tense.* New York: Simon and Schuster, 2004.

Broyles, Vernon. "Turn from Violence." *Presbyterians Today* (October 2009) 44.

Brueggemann, Walter. *Divine Presence Amid Violence: Contextualizing the Book of Joshua.* Eugene, OR: Cascade Books, 2009.

Bureau of Alcohol, Tobacco, Firearms and Explosives. "Background Checks for Firearms Transfers." Washington, DC: 1999.

———. "BATFE Investigative Operations at Gun Shows Report." Washington, DC: 2000.

———. "Following the Gun: Enforcing Federal Laws Against Firearms Traffickers." Washington, DC: June 2000.

———. "Gun Shows, Brady Checks and Crime Gun Traces." Washington, DC: 1999. Online: http://www.atf.treas.gov/pub/treas_pub/gun_show.pdf.

Burggrave, Roger, et al. *Desirable God: Our Fascination with Images, Idols and New Deities.* Leuven, Belgium: Peeters Press, 2003.

Burnett, David. "Who Is the Armed Citizen?" *America's First Freedom* (NRA magazine), November 2009, 1–3.

Bush, George H. W. "1992 Speech Before the Religious Broadcasters of America After the First Persian Gulf War." *Christian Social Action Journal* (1992) n.p.

Calvin, John. *The Institutes of the Christian Religion.* Vol. 1. Philadelphia: Westminster, 1960.

———. *The Institutes of the Christian Religion*, vol. 2. Philadelphia: Westminster, 1960.

Canadian Union of Public Employees Report to the Standing Committee on Public Safety and National Security on Bill C-19. "Facts on Firearms and Domestic Violence." (November 24, 2011) 4

Centers for Disease Control and Prevention (CDC). "Injury Mortality Reports 1999–2007."

———. "Child Trends Data Bank, Statistics on Guns in Schools." 2008.

Center for Health Statistics. "Mortality Report Online 2010." http://www.cdc.gov/nchs/fastats/deaths.htm.

Champion, Marge, and Marilee Zdenek. *God Is a Verb.* Monkey Cat Books, 1974.

Chicoine, Luke, *Exporting the Second Amendment: U.S. Assault Weapons and the Homicide Rate in Mexico.* Notre Dame: University of Notre Dame Press, 2011.

Child Sacrifice in Pre-Columbian Cultures. www.wikipedia.org/wiki/child_sacrifices_in_Pre-Columbian Cultures.

Coalition to Stop Gun Violence. "America's Gun Shows: Open Markets for Criminals." Public document.

———. "Crimes by Virginia Concealed Handgun Permit Holders." July 1, 2010. Public document.

———. "Investigative Operations by BATF at Gun Shows." Public document.

———. "Mass Shootings by Concealed Handgun Permit Holders in 2009." Public document. Online: www.csgv.org/ccwmassshooters

———. "The Gun Show Loophole: Frequently Asked Questions." Public document.

———. "The Hidden Handgun: Bullet Counter Points: Ordinary People." Public document.

Coffman, Steve. *Founders v. Bush: A Comparison in Quotations of the Policies and Politics of the Founding Fathers and George W. Bush.* Los Angeles: One World Studios, 2007.

Congressional Record. 1996, S7097.

Constitution Arms. Description of the Palm Pistol. http://www.palmpistol.com/.

Cook, Phillip, and Jens Ludwig. *Gun Violence: The Real Costs.* New York: Oxford University Press, 2000.

Cooper, Jeff. "Cooper's Corner." *Guns and Ammo* (April 1991) 104

Cuen, Lucrezia. "Cell Phone Guns Discovered." ABC News, London. December 6, 2000.

Davidson, Osha. *Under Fire: The NRA and the Battle for Gun Control.* Iowa City: University of Iowa Press, 1998.

Dear, John. *Disarming the Heart: Toward a Vow of Nonviolence.* Scottdale: Herald Press, 1993.

Dees-Thomases, Donna. *Looking For a Few Good Moms: How One Mother Rallied a Million Others Against The Gun Lobby.* New York: Rodale, 2004.

Department of Justice Summary Report. "Control Over Weapons and Laptop Computers." 2002.

Diamond, Marie. "Radical Right-Wing Agenda: Florida Bill Will Come Between Doctors and Patients by Prohibiting Pediatricians from Asking about Guns." *Think Progress,* May 10, 2011.

Diaz, Tom. *Making a Killing; The Business of Guns in America.* New York: New Press, 1999.

———. Power Point Presentation at the Gun Violence/ Gospel Values Conference. Stony Point Center, Stony Point, NY. September 16–18, 2008.

Dionne, E. J., Jr. "Making Gun Safety (Politically) Safe." December 9, 2009. Online: http://www.truthdig.com/report/item/making_gun_safety_politically_safe_20091209/.

"Easy to Use 'Palm Pistol' Aimed at Elderly, Disabled." www.palmpistol.com.

Einstein, Albert. *The World As I See It.* www.Einsteinandreligion.com/goodevil.html.

Fager, Chuck. *Study War Some More: If You Want to Work for Peace.* Fayetteville, NC: Quaker House, 2010.

Federal Bureau of Investigation. "FBI Releases Preliminary Statistics for Law Enforcement Officers Killed in 2010." Public document. May 16, 2011.

———. "Federal Laws Against Firearms Traffickers." Public document. June 2000.

Founders v. Bush. "A Comparison in Quotations of the Policies and Politics of the Founding Fathers and George W. Bush." www.foundersvbush.com.

Frattaroli, Shannon. "Removing Guns from Domestic Violence Offenders: An Analysis of State Level Policies to Prevent Future Abuse." Johns Hopkins Center for Gun Policies and Research, October 2009.

Frey, Barbara. *The Impact of Guns on Women's Lives: On the Prevention of Human Rights Violations Committed With Small Arms.* Amnesty International, The International Action Network on Small Arms (IANSA) and Oxfam International. London, 2005.

Ghianni, Tim. "Tennessee Lawmaker." *Reuters,* October 14, 2011.

Giffords, Representative Gabrielle. Interview by MSNBC. March 25, 2010.

Global Security. "Reports on U. S. Military Casualties During the U. S. Led War in Iraq." www.globalsecurity.org/military/ops/iraq_casualties.htm.

Goddard, Andy. Speech Given in front of U. S. Supreme Court. Unpublished.

Gopnik, Adam. "Shootings." *New Yorker* (April 30, 2007) 27–28

Graduate Institute of International Studies. "Small Arms Survey 2002: Counting the Human Cost," United Kingdom: Oxford University Press.

Grossman, Lev and Evan Narcisse. "Conflict of Interest Video Games Based on America's Real Wars are Big Business." *Time* (October 31, 2011) 70–72.

Haberer, Jack. "Winning? Losing!" *The Presbyterian Outlook* (April 19, 2010) 5.

Harvard University Study. "Study Finds Gun Possession at College More Common Among Students With Drinking Problems." Press Release, July 2, 1999; http://www.hsph.harvard.edu/cas/Documents/guns-pressRelease/.

Havel, Vaclav. *Living in Truth.* Boston: Faber and Faber, 1987.

Hayim, Etz. *Torah and Commentary.* New York: Jewish Publication Society, 2001

Heller v. The District of Columbia.

Hemenway, David, et al. "Gun Use in the United States: Results from Two National Surveys." *Injury Prevention* 6 (2000) 263–67.

———. *Private Guns, Public Health.* Ann Arbor: University of Michigan Press, 2006.

———. "Survey Research and Self-Defense Gun Use: An Explanation of Extreme Overestimates." *The Journal of Criminal Law and Criminology* (June 22, 1997) 1430–31.

Henigan, Dennis A. *Lethal Logic: Exploding the Myths That Paralyze America's Gun Policy.* Washington, D.C.: Potomac Books, 2009.

———. "For the Gun Lobby, Ignorance is Bliss." *The Huffington Post.* October 23, 2009. Online: http://www.huffingtonpost.com/dennis-a-henigan/for-the-gun-lobby-ignoran_b_331577.html.

Heston, Charlton. "The Second Amendment: America's First Freedom." Speech at the National Press Club, Washington DC: September 11, 1997.

Horwitz, Joshua. "Discovery Building Tragedy Affirms Illegitimacy of Political Violence." Coalition to Stop Gun Violence. September 3, 2010. Public paper.

Horwitz, Joshua and Casey Anderson. *Guns, Democracy, and the Insurrectionist Idea.* Ann Arbor: University of Michigan Press, 2009.

Hurley, James. "Property Crimes and Pawnshops: Coincidence or Correlation." *Police Magazine.* (May, 2000) 1–6.

Hwang, Yena. Sermon fragment. National Capital Presbytery. Washington, DC: April 30, 2011.

Illinois Council Against Handgun Violence. "The Facts About Firearm Violence." Undated public document.

Janzon, F. Sam. *Getting Into Luther's Large Catechism: A Guide for Popular Study.* St Louis: Concordia Publishing House, 1978.

Jewett, Robert. *The Captain America Complex: The Dilemma of Zealous Nationalism.* Philadelphia: Westminster, 2003.

Johnson, James Weldon. "Lift Every Voice and Sing." Hymn 563, *Presbyterian Hymnal.* Louisville: Westminster/John Knox, 1990.

Johnson, Robert and Paul Leighton. "Reality of Justice and Black Genocide." *The Journal of African Men,* http://www.paulsjusticepage.com/reality-of-justice/blackgenocide.htm.

King, Martin Luther, Jr. *Letters From a Birmingham Jail.* Philadelphia: American Friends Service Committee, 1963.

Kipling, Rudyard. *Just So Stories for Little Children.* New York: Doubleday, 1902.

KLAS TV. Las Vegas, Nevada. News item on Michael Birdick's Paintball Game: "Hunting for Bambi." July 15, 2003.

Klingman, Steve. "Poll: Gun Owners Not in Lockstep with NRA." January 14, 2010. Online: http://open.salon.com/blog/steve_klingaman/2010/01/13/poll_gun_owners_not_in_lockstep_with_nra.

Kraft, Sy. "National ASK Day Promotes Children's Gun Safety: 'Puppies not Firearms.'" *Medical News Today/Pediatrics/ Children's Health.* www.medicalnews.com.

Krug, E. G., et al. "Firearm Related Deaths in the US and 35 Other High- and Upper-Income Countries." *International Journal of Public Opinion Research.* (1998) 214–21.

Lakoff, George. *Don't Think of an Elephant.* White River Junction, VT: Chelsea Green, 2004

La Pierre, Wayne. *Guns, Crime, and Freedom.* New York: Harper Perennial, 1994.

———. *Shooting Straight: Telling the Truth about Guns in America.* Washington, DC: Regnery, 2002.

Larance, Eileen R. Testimony before the Senate Committee on Homeland Security and Governmental Affairs, May 5, 2010. The U.S Government Accountability Office.

Lawler-Row, Kathleen and Jeff Elliott. "The Role of Religious Activity and Spirituality in the Health and Well-Being of Older Adults." *Journal of Health Psychology* (January 2009) 43–52.

Lewis, C.S. *God in the Dock: Essays on Theology and Ethics.* Grand Rapids: Eerdmans, 1970.

Lincoln, Abraham. "At a Sanitary Fair." Public address, Baltimore, April 18, 1864.

Lott, Jr., John R and David B. Mustard. "Crime, Deterrence, and Right-to-Carry Concealed Handguns." *Journal of Legal Studies* 26:1 (January 1997) 1–68. Online: http://www.lib.uchicago.edu/~llou/guns.html.

———. *More Guns, Less Crime: Understanding Crime and Gun Control Laws.* Chicago: University of Chicago Press, 1998.

Lowell, James Russell. "Once to Every Man and Nation." Hymn 361, *The Hymnbook.* Richmond, VA: Presbyterian Church, 1955.

Luntz, Frank. National Poll of Gun Owners, Including NRA Members. Sponsored by Mayors Against Illegal Guns. December 10, 2009.

Madison, James. *Federalist Papers* No. 63. March 1, 1788.

Meacham, Jon. *American Gospel: God, the Founding Fathers, and the Making of a Nation.* New York: Random House, 2007.

Mearns, William Hughes. "Antigonish." From the play, *Psyco-ed,* 1922.

Menninger, Karl A. BrainyQuote.com, Xplore Inc, 2011. Online: http://www.brainyquote.com/quotes/quotes/k/karlamenn115987.html.

Miller, Matthew and David Hemenway. "Guns and Suicide in the United States." *New England Journal of Medicine* (September 4, 2008) 989–91.

———. "Guns and Gun Threats at College." *The Journal of American College Health.* (September, 2002) 57–65.

Miller, Patrick. *The Ten Commandments.* Louisville: Westminster John Knox, 2009.

Nagler, Michael N. *America Without Violence.* Washington, DC: Island, 1982.

National Presbyterian Church of Mexico. Letter to the Presbyterian Church, USA, August 5, 2010.

NPD Group Market Research. February 12, 2008.

Ohhshootblogspot.com, "New Bride Gives Husband Handgun As Gift, He Then Unintentionally Shoots Them Both." Online: http://ohhshoot.blogspot.com/2012/01/new-bride-gives-husband-handgun-as-gift.html.

O'Connor, Flannery. *Mystery and Manners: Occasional Prose.* London: Faber and Faber, 1972.

Orwell, George. *Notes on Nationalism; England, Your England, and Other Essays.* London: Secker and Warburg, 1953.

Perlo-Freeman, Sam, et al. *Stockholm International Peace Research Institute Yearbook.* London: Oxford University Press, 2011.

Perry, Ya. "War Along America's Border: The Mexican Drug Cartels." Onine: http://perrya.hubpages.com/hub/War-Along-Americas-Border-The-Mexican-Drug-Cartels.

Pew Charitable Trust. "One in 31: Prison Count 2010." Report compiled from Justice Department and U. S. Census Bureau Statistics 2009. April 1, 2010.   Online: http://www.pewcenteronthestates.org/report_detail.aspx?id=57653

Potok, Mark. Interview on the Diane Rehm Show, National Public Radio, March 31, 2010.

Pound, Roscoe. *The Development of Constitutional Guarantees of Liberty.* Westport, CT.: Greenwood, 1957.

Presbyterian Church, US, *Our Confessional Heritage: Confessions of the Reformed Tradition With a Contemporary Declaration of Faith.* Atlanta, 1978.

Presbyterian Church, USA. 202nd General Assembly Minutes, 1990.

Rostron, Allen. "'Cease Fire: A Win-Win.' Strategy on Gun Policy for the Obama Administration." *Harvard Law and Policy Review* (August 24, 2009) 347–67. Online: http://www.hlpronline.com/Vol3_2-Rostron_HLPR.pdf.

Rumphal, Shiridath. *Our Country, the Planet: Forging a Partnership for Survival.* Washington, DC: Island, 1992.

Russell, Letty. *Becoming Human.* Philadelphia: Westminster, 1982.

Samuels, Julie. "Findings From the National Violence Against Women Survey." Department of Justice, 2000.

Sartre, Jean-Paul. Preface to Franz Fanon, *The Wretched of the Earth.* New York: Grove, 1961.

Scott, Clara. "Open My Eyes That I May See." Hymn 324, *The Presbyterian Hymnal.* Louisville: Westminster John Knox, 1990.

Scottish Trades Union Congress. "Stop Violence Against Women Conference." http://www.stuc.org.uk/.../stop-violence-against-women-Conference.

Sevareid, Eric. *Not So Wild a Dream.* New York: Knopf, 1946.

Shaull, Richard. *Naming the Idols: Biblical Alternatives for US Foreign Policy.* Oak Park, IL: Meyer-Stone, 1988.

Simon, O.R., et al. "Characteristics of Impulsive Suicide Attempts and Attempters." *Suicide Life Threat Behavior* 32:Suppl (2001) 49–59.

Small Arms Survey 2004. "Rights at Risk." Online: http://www.smallarmssurvey.org.

Soelle, Dorothee. *Death by Bread Alone.* Philadelphia: Fortress, 1975.

Solzhenitsyn, Alexander. Acceptance Speech for Nobel Peace Prize for Literature, 1970.

Steele, Jonathan and Suzanne Goldenberg. "Report on Iraqis Killed in the War." *The Guardian* (March 18, 2008) n.p.

Swomley, John M. "One Nation, Under God." *Christian Social Action Journal* (May 1992) 12–15.

Taylor, David R. "Reflections on the Virginia Tech Massacre." Sermon. April 22, 2007.

Terrorist Prevention Act—Conference Report, U.S. Senate. April 16, 1996.

Theocracy Watch. "The Rise of the Religious Right in the Republican Party." Online: http://www.theocracywatch.org.

Thompson, Ernest Trice. *Through the Ages: A History of the Christian Church.* Richmond, VA: CLC , 1965.

Thompson, Mark. "A Soldier's Tragedy" *Time* (April 2, 2011) n.p. Online: http://www.time.com/time/printout/0,8816,2055169,00.html.

UN General Assembly. "Report of the Open-Ended Working Group on the Prevention of Human Rights Violations Committed with Small Arms." A/60/88. New York: June 27, 2005.

———. "Report of the Open-ended Working Group to Negotiate an International Instrument to Enable States to Identify and Trace in a Timely and Reliable Manner, Illicit Small Arms and Light Weapons." New York, 2005.

U. S. Department of Defense. "U. S. War Casualties. Military Data Dating Back to 1775."

U. S. Statistical Abstract. "An Annual Report on Trends in Health Statistics: Internet Publishing and Broadcasting and Internet Usage." Online: http://www.census.gov/compendia/statab/cats/information_communications.html.

Vernick, Jon and Lisa Hepburn. "Twenty Thousand Gun Control Laws?" Center on Urban and Metropolitan Policy. Research brief. Washington, DC: Brookings Institution, 2002.

Violence Policy Center, "Arm Teachers? The Facts Argue Against It." Public paper.

———. "License to Kill: More Guns, More Crime." Public paper. June 2002.

———. "Yet Another Mass Shooting." Public paper. April, 2007.

Virginia Center for Public Safety and Freedom for All. Public paper. March 19, 2010.

Virginia Leaders for Closing the Gun Show Loophole. Undated pamphlet.

Virginians for Public Safety. "Gun Shows Are Primary Source of Virginia Crime." 2006 public paper. Online: http://www.vapublicsafety.com/signup.php.

Volf, Miroslav. "Christianity and Violence" In *War in the Bible and Terrorism in the Twenty-first Century*, edited by Richard Hess and Elmer Martens, 1–18. Winona Lake, Indiana: Eisenbrauns, 2008.

Walker, Robert. Interview. *NBC Nightly News.* May 16, 1996. Reprinted in *The Congressional Record,* May 17, 1996.

Wallis, Jim. "Bush's Theology of Empire." *Sojourners* (December 19, 2003) 20–26.

Wilhelm II, Kaiser. Speech at Berlin, Germany, August 4, 1914. Online: http://www.stormfront.org/forum/t123801.

Wills, Garry. *A Necessary Evil: A History of American Distrust of Government.* New York: Simon and Schuster, 1999.

Wimberly, John. *Transformation.* Sermon at Western Presbyterian Church. Washington, D.C. August 21, 2011.

Wink, Walter. *Engaging the Powers: Discernment and Resistance in a World of Domination.* Minneapolis: Fortress, 1992.

————. *Naming the Powers: The Language of Power in the New Testament*. Philadelphia: Fortress, 1984.

————. *Unmasking the Powers: The Invisible Forces That Determine Human Existence*. Philadelphia: Fortress, 1986.

Wintemute, Garen S. "Gun Shows Across a Multi-State American Gun Market: Observational Evidence of the Effects of Regulatory Practices." *Injury Prevention* (2007) n.p. Online: http://injury prevention.bmj.com/cgi/reprint/13/3/150.PDF.

————. "Homicide, Handguns and the Crime Gun Hypothesis: Firearms Used In Fatal Shootings Of Law Enforcement Officers, 1980 to 1989." *American Journal of Public Health* (April, 1994) 561–64.

————. "Freedom Under Fire." Interview by Evan Silverstein. *Presbyterian News Service* (September 20, 2008) 1–3.

Witkin, G. "Handgun Stealing Made Real Easy." *U.S. News & World Report* (June 9, 1997) 34–35.

World Almanac, 1994. "Table for Casualties for Principal Wars of the U.S." http://www.infoplease.com/world.html.

World Health Organization. "The Economic Dimensions of Interpersonal Violence." Geneva, 2004.

World-Wide Sunday-School-Work: The Official Report of the World's Sixth Sunday School Convention, Held in the City of Washington, USA. Edited by William N. Hartshorn. Chicago: World's Sunday School Association, 1910.

Zakaria, Fareed. "Be More Like Ike." *Newsweek* (August 16, 2010) 70–75.

Zumbo, Jim. "Assault Rifles for Hunters." Outdoor Life Blog Web address no longer active, but copies of comments on the blog are in possession of Joshua Horwitz.

————. "NRA Publications Suspend Ties to Jim Zumbo." Feb. 22, 2007. Online: http://www.nraila.org/news/read/inThenews.aspx?ID=8952.

APPENDIX

Deaths in Wars vs. Gun Deaths

TABLE 1. WARS OF THE UNITED STATES[1]

WAR	Years[2]	Battle Deaths[3]
Revolutionary War	1775–1783	4,435
War of 1812	1812–1815	2,260
Mexican War	1846–1848	1,733
Civil War	1861–1865	140,414 (Union)
		74,524 (Conf)[4]
Spanish-American	1898	385
World War I	1917–1918	53,513
World War II	1941–1945	292,131
Korean War	1950–1953	33,651
Vietnam War	1961–1977	47,369
Lebanon	1982–1984	262
Grenada	1983	18
Panama	1989–1990	23
Persian Gulf War	1991	148
TOTAL		**650,858**

TABLE 2. GUN DEATHS FROM 1979–1997[5]

YEAR	Deaths[6]
1979	32,689
1980	33,477
1981	33,778
1982	32,682

YEAR	Deaths
1983	30,842
1984	31,078
1985	31,324
1986	33,126
1987	32,638
1988	33,757
1989	34,471
1990	36,866
1991	38,077
1992	37,474
1993	39,358
1994	38,187
1995	35,957
1996	33,750
1997	32,166
TOTAL	**651,697**

Notes

1. The 1994 World Almanac's table for casualties in "principal wars of the U.S." The Source is The Department of Defense and the United States Statistical Abstract.

2. The dates assigned to the wars are the years for which the deaths are counted.

3. "Battle deaths" figures indicate service personnel killed in action. This does not include non-hostile deaths and wounded.

4. Authoritative statistics for Confederate forces are not available.

5. The National Center for Health Statistics has an annual count for gun deaths for the years 1979–1997. In addition the NCHS (and its predecessor agencies from 1988 and earlier) and the National Safety Council have an annual count for gun homicides and gun suicides for the years 1933–1978. They also have gun accidents (unintentional) for select years from 1933–1978.

6. The gun death tolls are for homicide, suicide, unintentional, and intent unknown.